CW00541939

The Passion of
Dennis Potter

The Passion of Dennis Potter

International Collected Essays

Edited by

Vernon W. Gras and John R. Cook

MACMILLAN

© Vernon W. Gras and John R. Cook 2000

All rights reserved. No reproduction, copy or transmission of
this publication may be made without written permission.

No paragraph of this publication may be reproduced, copied or
transmitted save with written permission or in accordance with
the provisions of the Copyright, Designs and Patents Act 1988,
or under the terms of any licence permitting limited copying
issued by the Copyright Licensing Agency, 90 Tottenham Court
Road, London W1P 9HE.

Any person who does any unauthorised act in relation to this
publication may be liable to criminal prosecution and civil
claims for damages.

First published 2000 by
MACMILLAN PRESS LTD
Houndmills, Basingstoke, Hampshire RG21 6XS
and London
Companies and representatives
throughout the world

ISBN 0-333-80028-1

A catalogue record for this book is available
from the British Library.

10   9   8   7   6   5   4   3   2   1
09   08   07   06   05   04   03   02   01   00
.

Printed in the United States of America by
Haddon Craftsmen
Bloomsburg, PA

CONTENTS

ACKNOWLEDGEMENTS

John Cook: I would like to thank the British Cinema and Television Research Group at De Montfort University, Leicester, as well as my friends and colleagues within the Media Department for their help, encouragement and support during the gestation of this book, particularly in terms of the allowance of some research leave that enabled me to complete it. Also, to the British Academy Arts and Humanities Research Board, for providing a small grant to aid in aspects of Potter research. Thanks must also go to Professor Nick Zurbrugg of De Montfort for authorizing the initial travel costs that allowed me to travel to Washington D.C. in spring 1996 in order to give a paper at a Potter symposium out of which the idea for this book sprang. In terms of Washington, I must also acknowledge both the ideas and extremely good company of Peter Stead and Eckart Voigts-Virchow, two of my fellow contributors (conspirators?) to this volume. Other thanks are due to my friends and family for putting up with my interest in Potter over the years and to all those, too numerous to mention, who have met and helped me along in the same period with my work on the writer. Of these, some very special thanks must go to the following: Ken Trodd, whose personal generosity as well as support and interest in my work down the years, has been absolutely invaluable on so many occasions; to the late Dennis Potter himself, whose cooperation, in terms of granting an interview that really had nothing in it for him, I still find an amazingly kind act, nearly a decade on; and finally, to Vernon, my coeditor on this volume and his wife Marguerite, not only for their great hospitality in Washington but their friendship and support; their persistence in moving this idea along and in terms of Potter—oh how appropriately for this volume—their "passion."

Vernon Gras: I would like to thank Universitaetsverlag Carl Winter for permission to use "Dennis Potter's *The Singing Detective*: An Exemplum of Dialogical Ethics," which first appeared in *Why Literature Matters* (eds.) Ruediger Ahrens and Laurence Volkmann, 1995. Thanks also to Wayne Froman and John Foster, who encouraged my sponsoring a Dennis Potter session at the 1996 International Association of Philosophy and Literature, from which this book took its beginnings. The enthusiasm and reception of Potter's work by both my graduate and undergraduate students gave impetus to bring out this needed book. I would especially like to thank Gwen Connelly for volunteering to track down the early Potter TV reviews at the Library of Congress, enabling us to end-run Murdoch's financial barriers (access to information has to be paid for, particularly when he owns it). But this initiative by an English professor could not have succeeded without the knowledge and media expertise of John Cook, who undoubtedly knows more about Dennis Potter's works than any living mortal. Our collaboration has been broadening and invigorating for me. I would also like to thank all those who provided me with copies of personal tapes of Potter's TV work, especially Kenith Trodd and Sam Marinov. Without those tapes, a course on Potter isn't possible. We need more public/commercial access to this buried treasure still moldering in BBC vaults. Lastly, I wish to thank my wife, Marguerite, for listening and suggesting but most of all for bringing order to this project.

DENNIS POTTER

A CHRONOLOGY

1935: Born 17 May, Joyford Hill, off Berry Hill, deep in the Forest of Dean, West England, to Walter Potter, coal miner and Margaret Wale, a Londoner. His sister June, born June 1936.

1940: May: begins formal education, enrolling at Christchurch School, Berry Hill.

1945: Trauma ("that fateful age of ten": *Moonlight on the Highway* [1969]). Due to accommodation problems in the Forest, his mother takes Potter and his sister to Hammersmith, London to stay with her relatives. There, he is sexually abused (by his "Uncle Ernie" Wale)—an ordeal he is to keep secret for many years. He begs his mother to return him to the Forest beside his father and she eventually lets him go.

1946: Passes the 11-plus selection examination and enrolls at Bell's Grammar School, Coleford, Forest of Dean.

1949: Returns to Hammersmith, London with his parents, where he enrolls at St. Clement Dane's Grammar School, which he attends until 1953. He thrives there.

1953: March: sits the entrance exam and wins a state scholarship to attend New College, Oxford University to study PPE (Politics, Philosophy and Economics). But first, like nearly all the males of his generation at this time, he has to do two years' compulsory National Service in the British Army.

1953–55: Initially, he does "basic training" at Aldershot, then is transferred to the "Intelligence Corps" at Maresfield, Sussex, to enroll in the Russian language course. There, he meets Kenith Trodd, who will later produce many of his most famous TV dramas for the BBC. Both he and Trodd are jointly posted to the War Office, Whitehall, London, where they work for low-grade military intelligence (MI3) tracing Russian troop movements etc. during the height of the Cold War: an experience Potter will draw upon later for his dramas, *Lay Down Your Arms* (1970) and *Lipstick on Your Collar* (1993).

1956:   October: arrives New College, Oxford, to take up his state scholarship. He soon flourishes there as one of the new breed of "scholarship boys," rising to become a "celebrity" student politician, debater and actor.

1957:   Becomes editor of the Oxford Labour Club magazine *Clarion*. At home, in the Forest of Dean, he meets local girl Margaret Morgan at a dance. They will eventually marry.

1958:   March: becomes editor of the prominent Oxford magazine *Isis*. That same month, his first ever nationally published article appears in the *New Statesman* journal: "Base Ingratitude?," a personal perspective on social class. This leads to an invitation to appear on TV as a student discussing the effect of class in his life. The program, part of a series called *Does Class Matter?,* is transmitted 25 August 1958. It is his first ever TV appearance.

1959:   In January, he marries Margaret Morgan at Christchurch, Berry Hill. The couple will have three children: Jane (b.1960), Sarah (b. 1961) and Robert (b.1965). In July, having successfully applied, he begins a two-year general traineeship with the BBC that involves attachments to various TV current affairs programs.

1960:   At the BBC, he makes his own TV documentary about his native Forest of Dean, *Between Two Rivers,* which is transmitted in June. In February, his first book is published: a political polemic on the "condition of England" called *The Glittering Coffin*. Potter contributes scripts for a book program (*Bookstand*) from the summer and resigns his BBC traineeship in September, after only one year, in order that he can pursue freelance work.

1961:   Continues to work for *Bookstand* and writes articles for the left-wing newspaper, the *Daily Herald*. He joins the paper as a feature writer in August of that year.

1962:   He is later to claim "I was drowning at the *Daily Herald*." In March, the first symptoms of acute psoriatic arthropathy appear (a painful combination of psoriasis and arthritis): a "classic stress" illness that will dog him for the rest of his life. He is moved over to become the paper's TV critic—a job he can do from home. His second nonfiction book, *The Changing Forest* (an examination of postwar changes to his native Forest of Dean) is published.

1963:   In freelance partnership with *Herald* theater critic David Nathan, he contributes sketches to the new late-night BBC satire show, *That Was The Week That Was* (*TW3*). Continues as TV critic for the *Daily Herald*. Campaigns in East Hertfordshire, where he was selected (in 1962) to be a Labour Party candidate standing for Parliament at the next British General Election.

1964: February: Roger Smith, a best friend from Oxford days, becomes story editor of a new BBC TV anthology play series, *The Wednesday Play*, and persuades Potter to write his very first TV play, *The Confidence Course*, which the latter delivers in June. September: the *Daily Herald* relaunches as *The Sun* and makes Potter its leader-writer. October: the British General Election is held and Potter fights the safe Conservative seat of East Herts. for Labour. He loses and disillusioned with party campaigning, never returns to active politics again. He resigns from *The Sun* to concentrate instead on his new job of writing TV plays.

1965: His first TV play, *The Confidence Course*, is transmitted in February and in the very same year, three more Potter play scripts are produced for the celebrated *Wednesday Play* slot: *Alice*, as well as the famous semi-autobiographical, linked pair of *Nigel Barton Plays* (*Stand Up, Nigel Barton* and *Vote, Vote, Vote for Nigel Barton*) that will make his name, winning him Society of Film and Television and Screenwriters' Guild Awards in 1966.

1966: *Emergency—Ward 9* is transmitted "live" for the half hour BBC play slot, *Thirty Minute Theatre* in April; *Where the Buffalo Roam* for *The Wednesday Play* in November. A Potter *Wednesday Play* script for Christmas, *Almost Cinderella*, is refused production by the BBC because it "tinkered with the fairy story" of *Cinderella*. Potter leaks the row and it creates controversy in the British press.

1967: *Message for Posterity* is transmitted by the BBC *Wednesday Play*. Potter writes TV reviews for the *New Statesman* and in this year begins writing book reviews for the *Times* newspaper. The scripts of Potter's *Nigel Barton Plays* are published by Penguin, complete with an introduction by the playwright.

1968: In May, Potter's first play for commercial television (ITV), *The Bonegrinder*, is transmitted; another, *Shaggy Dog*, will follow in November—the same month as *A Beast with Two Backs* is transmitted by the BBC. From January, Potter writes TV reviews for *The Sun* newspaper and then from March through October, a special "Dennis Potter" column on more general matters. *Vote, Vote, Vote for Nigel Barton* is produced for the stage in late 1968 (by the Old Vic Company, Theater Royal, Bristol).

1969: *Moonlight on the Highway*, Potter's first play to be produced by Kenith Trodd and to give a leading role to the popular songs of the thirties, is transmitted by ITV (LWT). That same month, *Son of Man*—Potter's celebrated and controversial retelling of the

Gospels—is transmitted by the BBC and becomes a "news event." It is adapted for the stage later that same year.

1970:   *Lay Down Your Arms,* Potter's play about his and Trodd's National Service experiences, is produced by the latter for LWT and transmitted in May. In October, *The Wednesday Play* slot gains a new time slot and title and Potter's first contribution to the new slot (also, his first play to be shot in color), *Angels Are So Few,* is transmitted in November. The text of Potter's stage version of *Son of Man* is published.

1971:   *Paper Roses,* based on Potter's experience of the newspaper world, is produced by Trodd for Granada TV and transmitted in June. In October, the BBC transmits Potter's spy play, *Traitor* and in November and December, his first six-part serial, *Casanova*—a controversially explicit costume drama based on the memoirs of the famous eighteenth-century lover.

1972:   Potter experiences his worst ever period of illness, which permanently twists and damages his hands. His famously innovative TV play, *Follow the Yellow Brick Road,* is transmitted that summer by the BBC while he is still in hospital. From September to December, he writes TV criticism for the *New Statesman.*

1973:   Potter's first completed novel, *Hide and Seek,* is published by Andre Deutsch. His adaptation of Thomas Hardy's short story, *A Tragedy of Two Ambitions,* is transmitted in the BBC anthology series, *Wessex Tales.* His TV script of *Follow the Yellow Brick Road* is published in an edited anthology of TV drama.

1974:   Two completed plays—*Joe's Ark* about cancer and *Schmoedipus* about the relationship between a mother and a son—are transmitted by the BBC's *Play for Today. Casanova* is repeated in a revised, re-edited version authorized by Potter. Potter resumes TV reviewing for the *New Statesman.*

1975:   Potter's TV adaptation of Angus Wilson's novel, *Late Call,* is transmitted by the BBC as a four-part serial. In November, Potter's father dies suddenly of a heart attack.

1976:   In April, Potter has three TV plays lined up for BBC transmission, all within the space of a month—*Double Dare, Where Adam Stood* and *Brimstone and Treacle*—but the last is famously banned by BBC Director of Programmes, Alasdair Milne, on account of its depiction of "the Devil" raping a mentally handicapped girl. There is a huge public row. In October, Potter becomes TV critic of the *Sunday Times* newspaper.

1977:   In February, Potter tries a new drug, Razoxane, which for a time, seems to offer an apparent "miracle cure" for his illness. In a burst of creative energy, he writes his famous six-part TV serial, *Pennies from Heaven.* In August, he delivers a paper on his writing style at the Edinburgh Television Festival (where *Brimstone and Treacle* is screened in closed session) and in September, he visits the United States for the first time (his first ever trip abroad). The banned *Brimstone and Treacle* is first staged as a theater play in October (Crucible Theater, Sheffield, U.K.).

1978:   Potter's seven-part adaptation of Thomas Hardy's *The Mayor of Casterbridge* is transmitted by the BBC between January and March, quickly followed by the first TV screening of *Pennies from Heaven,* from March to April. *Pennies'* critical and popular success makes Potter a household name and wins him awards. On the strength of its success, he and *Pennies'* producer, Kenith Trodd, form their own independent production company, Pennies from Heaven Limited, with the aim of shaking up film and TV production in the U.K. The stage script of *Brimstone and Treacle* is published. Potter very publicly resigns as TV critic of the *Sunday Times,* in disgust at the management's lock-out of its workers.

1979:   *Blue Remembered Hills,* Potter's famous play about children, is transmitted by the BBC in January. In May, after a row with the Corporation over creative freedom, Potter and Trodd publicly leave the BBC, having struck a deal for their new production company to make plays for ITV (LWT). Potter meets American director Herbert Ross in England and enters into discussions about making *Pennies from Heaven* as a Hollywood movie.

1980:   Potter concludes a deal for the movie version of *Pennies* with MGM and begins to write script drafts for Hollywood. In July, the PFH/LWT deal ends in acrimony over production costs. The three completed ITV plays (out of an earlier six-play deal) are transmitted on commercial television in October, the same month that Potter is honored with a retrospective season at the National Film Theater, London.

1981:   *Pennies from Heaven* is filmed as a 20-million-dollar movie in Hollywood, starring Steve Martin as Arthur Parker. Released in the United States just before Christmas, it gains mixed reviews and proves a huge commercial disaster at the box office. Potter writes his own novelization of the movie, which is published. Despite the disaster of the MGM *Pennies,* Potter will continue to write a variety of (largely unproduced) screenplay drafts and script treatments for the movies throughout the rest of his career.

1982:   A feature film version of the still-banned-for-TV *Brimstone and Treacle* is produced by Kenith Trodd for the cinema and released in September. Potter's daughter, Sarah, pens the novelization.

1983:   A Potter feature film script—an adaptation of the popular novel,
            Gorky Park—is released as a Hollywood film, starring William
            Hurt and Lee Marvin; but production on another, *Track 29* (based
            on his 1974 TV play, *Schmoedipus*) dramatically collapses, just
            days before its original director, Joseph Losey, was due to start
            shooting. Potter's first original theater play, *Sufficient Carbohy-
            drate,* is staged at the Hampstead Theater, London in December,
            before going on to a run in London's West End commercial theater
            the following spring. Treatment of Potter's once "miracle drug,"
            Razoxane, has to be withdrawn after side-effects develop.

1984:   The scripts of three old TV plays—*Joe's Ark, Cream in My Coffee*
            and *Blue Remembered Hills*—are published by Faber and Faber
            under the title *Waiting for the Boat,* complete with introduction by
            Potter. Production on *Dreamchild,* a feature film script based on
            the "real" Alice of *Alice in Wonderland* (and Potter's own 1965
            TV play, *Alice*) begins at Thorn/EMI U.K. under director Gavin
            Millar.

1985:   Spring: as he reaches his half century, Potter writes the first drafts
            of what will prove to be his landmark BBC TV serial, *The Singing
            Detective.* In between drafts, he also writes a novel: *Ticket to Ride.*
            A TV adaptation of F. Scott Fitzgerald's *Tender is the Night* is
            transmitted by the BBC between September and October. *Dream-
            child* is first released (in the United States) in October, to excellent
            reviews but poor cinematic distribution. In December, Potter com-
            pletes the final revisions of *The Singing Detective,* ready for a New
            Year shoot.

1986:   *The Singing Detective* is filmed by the BBC between January and
            July, under director Jon Amiel. In September, Potter's novel, *Ticket
            to Ride,* is published in the U.K. to good reviews. In November
            and December, *The Singing Detective* is screened in the U.K. by
            BBC TV to enormous critical acclaim. The scripts are published by
            Faber and Faber (as will all Potter's subsequent British TV serials
            now be).

1987:   Partly to escape from under the shadow of *The Singing Detective,*
            Potter writes a novel, *Blackeyes,* which is published in September.
            Visitors, a TV film based on *Sufficient Carbohydrate,* is screened
            by the BBC in February. In June, BBC TV honors Potter with a
            post-*Singing Detective* retrospective of his past works, which fi-
            nally includes the "unbanning" of the TV *Brimstone and Treacle.*

1988:   *The Singing Detective* is shown on New York PBS, which leads to
            ecstatic reviews in the *New York Times,* sellout cinema screenings
            in Manhattan as well as public awards in the United States. The

previously aborted *Track 29* is finally shot as a movie by director Nicolas Roeg and released in August. A four-part TV serial, *Christabel* (based on the real life war-time experiences in Germany of Englishwoman Christabel Bielenberg) is transmitted by the BBC between November and December.

1989:   In January, Kenith Trodd resigns from Potter's next production, a four-part BBC TV version of *Blackeyes,* after a huge row revolving around sharing production credits with American producer, Rick McCallum. *Blackeyes* begins shooting in February and after several established directors turn it down, Potter decides to direct it himself. In November and December, when it is finally screened in the U.K., after enormous pre-publicity, Potter experiences a critical bloodbath centering around accusations over the very issues of misogyny and sexploitation he had declared he was trying to critique in the drama.

1990:   Following the split from Trodd, Potter sets up a new independent production company, Whistling Gypsy Productions and begins to gather around him a regular team of collaborators: the first announced project is a planned feature film version of his novel, *Ticket to Ride,* called *Secret Friends.* He also begins writing his next planned TV serial (for Channel Four, U.K.)—*Lipstick on Your Collar,* set in the fifties. In October, Potter completes a feature film screenplay version of *The Singing Detective* but this is never produced.

1991:   Potter directs the movie version of *Secret Friends* himself for Channel Four's *Film on Four* strand but the film has trouble finding a U.K. cinema distributor. Pre-production begins on *Lipstick on Your Collar* but in November, Potter is asked by its backers, Channel Four, to consider making way for another director.

1992:   In January, Potter flies to New York to appear with Kenith Trodd at a major international retrospective of his past TV work, held at The Museum of Television and Radio. From February, the *Lipstick on Your Collar* TV serial begins shooting under new director Renny Rye and with Potter acting as creative producer. In September, the *Secret Friends* film finally gets a limited U.K. cinema release, to poor reviews. In late 1992, Potter's wife is diagnosed with breast cancer.

1993:   *Lipstick on Your Collar* is screened by Channel Four TV in Britain between February and March 1993, mainly to critical indifference. A book of interviews with the writer, *Potter on Potter,* is published by Faber and Faber. Potter and his now regular director, Renny Rye, shoot a largely self-financed film, *Midnight Movie,* for the

BBC in the summer. In August, Potter delivers his now famous James MacTaggart Memorial Lecture at the Edinburgh International Television Festival, in which he denounces the commercialization of television in general and the BBC in particular. Production on an old feature film script, *Mesmer* (based on the life of Anton Mesmer), begins in Vienna in the autumn.

1994: On 14 February, Potter is diagnosed with terminal cancers of the liver and pancreas and is given three months to live. In March, he records a final TV interview for Channel Four, in which he discusses his feelings about death and announces that he is writing two final four-part serials, *Karaoke* and *Cold Lazarus*, which he wants to be jointly produced by the BBC and Channel Four. The final TV interview is transmitted in the U.K. in April, to much critical acclaim. Potter completes his two last TV works on time, before finally dying on 7 June, nine days after his wife Margaret's death, also from cancer.

1996: *Karaoke* and *Cold Lazarus* are screened posthumously in the U.K. by both the BBC and Channel Four, as Potter wished.

INTRODUCTION

Have you noticed that the world is full of reflecting surfaces? Everywhere. And not just mirrors. You can see what we do from a million angles. And we can see what we've done from a million more.

> —Mandy Mason (played by Louise Germaine) in
> *Midnight Movie* (1993), written by Dennis Potter.

THE PASSION OF DENNIS POTTER IS A BOOK THAT CONCERNS itself with one of the most vivid and remarkable writers to emerge from contemporary, postwar Britain: one who deliberately chose to make his career out of a world of reflecting surfaces and whose work, as this collection will show, can be viewed from a "million different angles," yet each serving to reflect and illuminate all the others.

By any standards, the career of the late Dennis Potter (1935–1994) was remarkable. Born into a working class coal mining background in the Forest of Dean in the West of England, he made the difficult and treacherous journey across the minefields of the British class system to end up, at the close of his life, a wealthy and feted literary celebrity. But he never forgot where he came from, nor the people he had left behind, back there in the Forest of long ago. His prodigious talents ensured he could have gone on to become a major English novelist, or a doyen of the London stage, or, as he once dreamed of being in his university days, a great campaigning left-wing politician. But through a combination of deliberate choice and accidental circumstance, he decided, in the mid-1960s, to devote the bulk of his life and energies to that most intellectually despised of all public media: television.

To American readers, such a decision may seem incomprehensible, but as Peter Stead also points out in the first essay of this volume, it has to be understood within the context of the peculiar reach and fascination that television had, and to an extent still exerts, within the small island of Great Britain. With only two main networks when Potter began writing for the medium in the midsixties, television offered him not only an unrivaled national platform, but the only means he could see of communicating his "passions," both to those in middle class intellectual circles *and* the ordinary working people he had left behind in the Forest. Bridging the gap between "dons and coalminers"[1] was his own shorthand way of expressing what he was trying to do—the creation of a "common culture" that would short-circuit all the hierarchies and snobberies of an English class system and establish, instead, a new, more democratic landscape, which by means of television would be much more open and accessible, socially and culturally. The grand dream had to be much revised and qualified in later life, as Potter angrily watched the gradual encroachment of commercial forces into his beloved medium. Nevertheless, this vocational passion compelled him to go into TV in the mid-sixties and, with only a few minor diversions over the years, kept him there right up until his death from cancer in 1994.

Crucial to his ideals was the existence of the one institution that seemed to offer a buttress against the "undemocratic" threats of old class hierarchy, on the one hand, and creeping new commercial power on the other: the British Broadcasting Corporation. The BBC was authorized by statute to be a public broadcaster, producing programs not for commercial profit but for the public good; in theory, for *all* the public. It was a stipulation that Potter, in particular, took to heart. On occasion, he did work for commercial television (and indeed, later in life, for Hollywood), but he always returned to the BBC, to which he gave his best work.

It is the original drama that Potter then began to write for British television over the next 30 years that makes him stand out and that, in a paradoxical way, eventually allowed his name and reputation to spread beyond the shores of his native island. Certainly, it is unusual to have a collection of essays (particularly, an international one such as this) devoted to a British writer of television, yet the size and astonishing range, as well as consistency of his writing—coupled with the sheer chutzpah of having (in defiance of cultural categories) done it for television—makes him both a remarkable and a worthy subject for international consideration. From early plays like *Son of Man* (1969), which reimagined Jesus as a very doubting, very human Messiah, racked by guilt, through to his first big popular success, *Pennies from Heaven* (1978: later remade as an MGM movie in 1981), and on to his much celebrated masterpiece, *The Singing Detective* (1986), Potter constructed a personal oeuvre of such remarkable character and consistency that it may never be equaled, anywhere, in the history of the television medium. Toward the end of his life, he came to be seriously recognized and honored internationally. Practitioners as well-known and diverse as Steven Bochco, Martin Scorsese, David Lynch and Alain Resnais all have acknowledged and paid tribute to his immense contribution and influence.[2] Most admired by others were his "nonnaturalistic" devices—flashback and fantasy sequences; direct-to-camera address by characters; the use of adult actors to play children; and, perhaps most famously of all as first seen in *Pennies from Heaven,* his much-analyzed "lip-synch" technique. Characters step out of dramatic action to burst into song, not in their own voices but miming, instead, to the original recordings of old popular songs.[3] Through this avowed use of a "non-naturalistic" style, Potter became one of the first TV writers to open up the screen to the landscape of the mind, and thereby helped raise television to the status of an art form. All of this was achieved under and perhaps even caused by conditions of extreme illness and suffering due to psoriatic arthropathy—a painful combination of psoriasis affecting the skin and arthritis crippling the joints—that Potter developed in 1962, while still a young man, and from which he was to suffer throughout the rest of his life.

The work and character of Dennis Potter—at times, the two seem almost indivisible—make for a particularly rich brew, and the reader of this volume looking for all the "grand themes" will not be disappointed. His work covers them all: betrayal; guilt; religion; class; sex; popular culture; memory; childhood; politics, and many others. He was like one of his own literary heroes, Samuel Coleridge, "myriad-minded,"[4] and yet at the same time, one can also see a remarkable consistency of style and approach in his work. Some themes and even some of the same scenes from old dramas will return again and again almost obsessively, even 20 or 30 years from when they were first broached. Clearly, Potter was writing out of his own "passion"—a desire to communicate his deepest and darkest fears, fantasies, wishes, and desires to a wider audience. Furthermore, he was determined that every inch of this "Potter's field"[5] should be scrupulously combed by himself, so that no nugget of gold, no ounce of personal insight and self-realization, would be left undiscovered or unexamined. Undoubtedly, this tension between the public figure, the mass communicator, and the private, at times somewhat agonized soul-searcher, makes "Potterland"[6] a particularly fascinating landscape for the rest of us to wander through and explore.

In February 1994, Potter's long history of defying illness finally caught up with him. He was diagnosed with terminal cancers of the pancreas and liver and given three months to live. His response was characteristic: he went on British television; first, to give a final interview as public farewell to the viewing audience he had nourished for nearly 30 years, and second, to announce he would spend his last days writing two linked TV serials, *Karaoke* and *Cold Lazarus,* which he hoped the public BBC and the commercial Channel Four would jointly produce and screen as a kind of "fitting memorial."[7] Nothing could have more convincingly illustrated or crowned his life's ambition of creating a "common culture" through television, nor demonstrated his consistent willingness to try the impossible to achieve it. To a large extent, that is exactly what he *did* do: the BBC and Channel Four *did* come together in an unprecedented way, putting their differences aside to make sure his final works were realized according to his wishes. In Britain, these last two works were transmitted by both networks between April and June 1996. Meanwhile, as his old friend and the producer of those last dramas, Kenith Trodd, points out in this volume, Potter himself achieved the impossible: he defied his own death in order to complete two complex, intricately linked, four hour serials in a space of approximately six weeks, in what must count as one of the most astonishing feats of physical and mental stamina of any writer—ever. Potter finally died on 7 June 1994, just nine days after his devoted wife, Margaret, who, in another one of those amazing twists of fate haunting this particular writer, had also succumbed to cancer.

Dennis Potter was a great dreamer and a great idealist, and in modern Britain, that made him enemies. Throughout his life, his work had always been subject to rows and controversy, usually about the depiction of sexual scenes and always, right-wing tabloid newspapers would delight in whipping up scandals about his work (which controversy Potter learned to milk in order to maximize audiences for his dramas). Yet as John Cook suggests in his essay in this volume, such a predictable and manageable climate of reception began to change for Potter in the last decade before his death, as the British press and also British TV came under increasing sway of the international media empire owned and controlled by Rupert Murdoch. By the early 1990s, Murdoch owned many of the most popular British newspapers (as well as the more "high-brow" London *Times*), and crucially, he had also begun to realize his long-term ambitions of challenging what he saw as the elite "public service" monopoly of British television (particularly the BBC) by launching his own competing satellite, and later digital, television services. It was a commercialization, and in Potter's terms, a "pollution" of British culture by outside forces that the writer publicly bemoaned, not least in his final TV interview in 1994 that was watched by millions.[8]

Whether such public criticism of Murdoch had a direct or indirect effect on the reception in Britain of *Karaoke* and *Cold Lazarus* when these were transmitted in 1996, is, of course, impossible to prove. But what certainly seemed the case was that large sections of the British media (including but not exclusively those outlets directly controlled by Murdoch) no longer seemed as keen as they once were to welcome Potter. It was as if, following the critical derision that had greeted Potter's controversial 1989 TV serial *Blackeyes*, the writer was no longer to be taken as seriously as he once had been. Modern Britain is a questioning and sceptical place, whose people are suspicious of the "grand gesture" such as that which the writer had tried to pull off with the production of his final works. British public and cultural life had clearly changed: now, in both character and attitude, it was much more commercially oriented, such that instead of trying to listen out when something different came along, for many it was much easier to mock. Alas, it *was* true: Potter had indeed tried to achieve the impossible.

In a way, therefore, "the passion of Dennis Potter" also signifies the media crucifixion that the writer has undergone in Britain during the last ten years:

one that reached its nadir in 1998, with the publication of a controversial posthumous biography, claiming to have unearthed details about Potter's sex life, which set off a whole new wave of muckraking headlines in the British press (see essays by Cook and Gwen Connolly in this volume for further discussion). But as every child of Sunday school knows (and Potter was certainly one), with every "passion" comes resurrection.

Interestingly, while Potter was being consigned to history in Britain, international attention to his work was growing. His remarkable final TV interview, shown all around the world and also released on video, had stimulated the curiosity of many to find out more about this unusual writer. Internet sites and newsgroups were gradually proliferating, and Potter was even being taught in university and college courses.[9] Particularly for one of the editors of this volume (John Cook), all of this came as a source of some amazement and bemusement. When he began researching the writer in Britain in 1989 (his thesis was first published in 1995 as *Dennis Potter: A Life on Screen*), it seemed to him that he must be the only scholar in the world at all interested in Dennis Potter! No longer is this the case. In May 1996, an international Potter symposium held at George Mason University, Virginia, USA and organized by Cook's coeditor, Vernon Gras, revealed a considerable amount of international academic interest and scholarly activity relating to Potter.[10]

Out of that symposium this edited collection has come. Its aim is to present a snapshot of the current critical knowledge and writing on Potter, in order to put the writer on the map of wider cultural debate. The international contributors assembled here in this pioneering volume (not all of whom were participants in the original symposium) probably number amongst the leading critical experts on Dennis Potter in the world today. Here are authors of several existing book-length studies on the writer, as well as those who have written/are writing doctoral theses on the author, not to mention other essays and papers. Crucially, and in the spirit of Potter's desire that his own work must always speak to more than university "dons," the essay collection embraces contributions of nonacademics who either knew or worked with the writer, or whose particular expertise might shed fresh light on the work. Thus, we have original contributions from the man who not only knew Potter professionally as a TV critic, but reviewed many of his plays for the British press when they first aired (Philip Purser); an American psychiatrist whose background and training may shed some light on the deeper psychological roots of Potter's art (Irving Harrison); and perhaps most especially of all, Potter's long-standing friend who also produced much of his most celebrated work for TV, Kenith Trodd. Finally, the collection ends with the words of the man himself: extracts from an extended interview Dennis Potter gave to John Cook in 1990, and that is published here, in book form, verbatim, for the first time. The result, we hope, is an eclectic and lively collection that, as suggested by the quote from

Potter's *Midnight Movie,* approaches the writer from a range of different "angles" but rather, like the proverbial mirror, serves to reflect a wider whole.

In putting this collection together, both editors noticed not only myriad different angles and perspectives, but also some distinct patterns of convergence. It is for this reason that we have decided to subdivide the book into three major sections (Class; Religion and Dialogism; Changing Cultural Values), each of which seem to us accurately to reflect the various journeys that Potter himself necessarily had to make during his career, both in terms of his private concerns as a writer and in terms of the wider culture.

In each section there are five essays, each section prefaced with a short introduction, followed by a fourth section with extracts from Cook's 1990 interview with Potter. Across these various pieces, the reader will find diverse arguments and points of view, some of which markedly contrast, on the significance of particular Potter works. That is as it should be, and makes for a lively collection. At the same time, the particular sections into which we have grouped these essays should not blind the reader to other correspondences and interrelationships of pieces *across* sections. Perusing widely with frequent cross-referencing, the reader should derive much coherence, satisfaction, and insight from this volume.

In terms of the assembled contributors and their backgrounds, it seems three main "centers" of Potter study have emerged in the years since his death: Britain, the United States and Germany. In Britain—the principal audience Potter wanted to reach—there is still a sense that his own culture does not quite know what to make of him. Because he defied so many established categories, constantly crossing the lines of cultural and social hierarchy, some British critics do not quite know where to place him, or whether, in the end, he is actually a subject for polite discussion at all. As a result, the critical tone is still often quizzical, sceptical, and spiky. One can find a few echoes of this in some of the pieces included here from British contributors. In the United States and Germany, by contrast, Potter is seen much more as a challenging, even exotic voice from outside their respective cultures, who deserves to be taken very seriously.[11] In academic terms, much of this scholarly interest arises from interpreting him as a challenging, "postmodern" writer.

Here, the two editors of this volume—one American; one British—must register their own debate around the applicability of this term to Potter, for clearly, it relates to their own particular cultural perspectives on the writer. Cook, in common with a number of other British academic critics,[12] regards Potter as the epitome of the modernist writer whose beliefs in the possibility of a "common culture" as well as of deeper spiritual "truths" seem to make him antithetical to the postmodern concern with surfaces. Gras, along with some of the other international contributors to this volume, regards Potter as a highly significant "postmodern" writer, precisely because in facing the loss of all centers of belief characteristic of the postmodern world, his work answers the problem via an alternative set of values and ethics structured around a dialogical self.

At first sight, this division of opinion along international lines might seem intractable—until, that is, one looks at the different essays in this volume. What becomes clear is that while the particular terminology and analytical perspectives may differ, the essays of Gras, Cook et al. in the second section of the book all point to the same process of a writer gradually discovering that he is the "author" of his own reality, and through this, finding a renewed sense of personal freedom. In other words, whether one sees Potter as a modernist writer fundamentally standing outside of postmodernism, or one who has found his own ethical path out of some of the most intractable postmodern questions, it is essentially the same issue—what Potter himself often called the discovery of the "sovereign self"—that is being addressed.

While many of the contributors to this anthology view Potter as a great postmodern writer, the difficulty with this ascription is twofold: first, the fuzziness in how postmodernism is often used; and, second, Potter's own attack on postmodernism in his "Some Sort of Preface" in *Waiting for the Boat* (1984), as well as in the novel, *Blackeyes* (1987). But any investigation of Potter's work will reveal that the focus of his psychodramas (and virtually all his work is psychodrama) has to do with the need to renovate the mental habitations of his protagonists and those of his viewers/readers. When Potter attacked postmodernism because "too many of those who should be or seem to be guerrillas against this . . . 'occupying power'" (the growing bureaucratization and commodification of culture—eds.) are actually helping "in the destruction of humanism," he was attacking the subversion of human agency by all those postmodernists who embrace the "death of the subject."[13] Potter had little sympathy with those Marxists and Structuralists who transform the human subject into the mere place or locus where discourses meet. He clearly saw that dissolving human agency into the passive product of hegemonic discourses with their interpellative forces, death of the author, dissolved subject, etc. was both a contradiction and a betrayal. But the humanism that Potter set up in opposition to the megaconstructs of government bureaucracy, global commodification, and poststructural critical ideologies is a dialogical process that begins with self-awareness. Potter accepts in part that human identity is a social construct. His humanism is based on the self-liberating, dialogical movement of each individual to endure the suffering ("passion") we find inescapable as historical beings. In this acceptance that we are both made and making, Potter can be taken as quintessentially postmodern (see especially in this volume the essays by Gras, Antor, and Connelly). At the same time, his self-proclaimed Christianity, lacking any specifically held belief or dogma, provides him with a hope that the conflictual process of exploration and investigation into his past beliefs will end in wider horizons and deeper insights (see the personal interview in appendix). In this he resembles that other believer in dialogism, Mikhail Bakhtin, whose faith in the open ended polyphony of human existence has similar theological affinities.[14]

A survey of Potter's works reveals that in this recurring agon of the split self, his early protagonists go down to defeat, while in his later works they emerge victorious. His early protagonists are usually overcome, bewildered, or co-opted by their preexisting milieu. Willie Turner in *Where the Buffalo Roam,* George in *The Bonegrinder,* Rufus in the *Beast with Two Backs,* David Peters in *Moonlight on the Highway,* Jesus in *Son of Man,* Clarence in *Paper Roses,* and Harris in *Traitor,* all undergo a "passion" or suffering just trying to survive or escape the entanglements of their milieu. They all fail. There seems no escape for these heroes to the exposure and acceptance of nihilism, other than clothing themselves with a new delusionary wardrobe, as Jack Black does in *Follow the Yellow Brick Road.*

In arguably his greatest work—*The Singing Detective, Pennies from Heaven, Blackeyes* (the novel) and his last two dramas that are really one, *Karaoke/Cold Lazarus*—Potter embodies in dramatic form the ethical plight of the inescapable split-self that human existence becomes under the cultural aegis of postmodernism. What is remarkable about Potter's work is that the terms of this split-self, though variable, reflect the actual suffering and breakthrough of their author. His journey from a childhood working class milieu, with its religious fundamentalism, folk culture, moral simplicities, and sexual repressions, finds its fictional equivalence in his TV plays. The dialogical ethics embraced by the protagonists of his mature works is not a sudden achievement, a gift received from an unexpected revelation. The freedom of the sovereign self finds illustration in various guises and situations in his later work, but it is reached only through much suffering and conflict.

What is at stake, always, for Potter's protagonists is ultimately to realize their condition as self-creating and interpretive beings. The movement from being controlled by an external authority inscribed within the hero at a young age, to the insight and understanding that such authority is socially constructed and subject to the will of the hero, is repeated in most of Potter's later works. Their combined and repeated message to the TV viewer is "don't remain scripted"—don't allow the social unconscious to rob you of your innate imaginative ability to shape your future, to make your own life, free of bogus religious inhibitions or seductive consumer placebos. Potter knew his enemies very well because he, personally, lived through their formidable entanglements. Though his education gave him the intellectual clarity and self-awareness to critique the shortcomings of his childhood horizons, nonetheless the emotional ties to home, family, and region were not so easy to displace. What makes Potter significant, then, is that he dramatizes the journey that most of us, his contemporaries, have had to travel while facing the same options for evasion and self-deception. Most of us won't face this conflict head on; we compromise. Potter's legacy to us says don't remain scripted, say no to the "occupying power," and become an active creative agent for the future. Don't be victimized by entanglements from the fundamentalist past, and guard against present and future commodification of the imagination. Don't be usurped in your sovereignty, but author your own life.

Thus, though some of the terms may differ, what all the contributors to this book *do* finally display in common is their own particular "passion" for Dennis Potter, and a united recognition that while he may now be dead, he is far too important to be forgotten. All agree he must not "remain scripted" as a distant relic of the past. Ironically in this respect, Potter's cause has not been helped by the fact that he chose to embrace the popular TV medium and become a very public personality. As Ken Trodd points out in his essay, the problem arising after Potter's death is due to so much of his best work having been done for British television; very little of it is now publicly available, and the little that has been released from the British TV archives (such as video edit versions, published scripts, and so on) is often less than accurate or complete. Evidenced by the amount of Potter E-mail traffic on the World Wide Web, as well as in academic books, college courses, not to mention the appearance of this volume itself, an international demand for access to Potter material is growing. But one of the big problems in recent years for the student of Potter has been negotiating the late writer's estate. Administered by Potter's daughter Sarah and his former literary agent, Judy Daish, the estate, very sadly, still appears to be in a state of paralysis, as a result of their tremendous grief and loss following the writer's death in 1994. All of this is highly understandable. The shock to the Potter children of the double blow of losing both their parents at the same time must have been enormous. Their subsequent commissioning of a posthumous "official" biography that went so badly wrong in the portrayal of their father has simply made matters worse in terms of an already existing tendency to pull the shutters down to outsiders (see John Cook's essay for further discussion of the posthumous biography).

As editors, however, with our own "passion" for Potter, we would like to end by making a strong appeal to the estate that it is only through a concerted effort to make his TV plays available to the general public (for example, on video) that a truer, more rounded picture of the writer will emerge, and his reputation be secured for posterity. Without greater public access to his material, the current wave of interest in him will surely fade away and then, Potter really will die and be forgotten. As all the essays in this volume hopefully attest, such an outcome would be an artistic tragedy of the first order. If, to paraphrase Potter's character in *Midnight Movie*, the appearance of this volume can do anything to change things in this respect, helping in its own small way to shed "a million" different points of light on this fascinating writer, then, truly, it will have done its job.

John R. Cook
Vernon W. Gras

NOTES

1. See, for example, Potter's description of writing his early TV play, *Stand Up, Nigel Barton* (1965): "But with television, I knew that, in small family group-ings, both coalminers and Oxford dons would probably see this play" (Dennis Potter, "Cue Telecine—Put on the Kettle," *New Society*, 22 September 1966, p.457. Also reproduced in Potter's introduction to *The Nigel Barton Plays* [pub-lished scripts] (Harmondsworth: Penguin, 1967).

2. Steven Bochco, writer and creator of such hit U.S. TV shows as *Hill Street Blues* (1980–1987) and *NYPD Blue* (1992-), acknowledged Potter's influence when, on 15 January 1992, he appeared at a seminar with him at the Museum of Tele-vision and Radio in New York in honor of Potter's contribution to television. Meanwhile, in 1998, Alain Resnais, esteemed European director of such art house classics as *Hiroshima Mon Amour* (1959) and *L'Annee Derniere a Marienbad* (1961), directed *On Connait la Chanson*—a feature film that pays tribute to Potter by using his same "lip-synch" technique of characters miming to recordings of popular songs. Martin Scorsese and David Lynch both sought Potter out during his life to write scripts for them, though sadly, neither project ever got off the ground; similarly, *The Way to Somewhere* (which was very sim-ilar to *Blackeyes*) and *The White Hotel* (an adaptation of the D. M. Thomas novel that Yugoslavian director Emir Kusterica is now slated to direct).

3. The "lip-synch" technique has indeed been much copied: for example, by ad-vertisers (in Britain, a series of 1990s TV commercials for the insurance com-pany Allied Dunbar); by Steven Bochco who employed it in his ill-fated TV police series *Cop Rock* (1990), which Potter despised; and (as indicated in note 2) by Alain Resnais in *On Connait la Chanson*.

4. "Coleridge said that Shakespeare was 'myriad-minded' but the term can also be applied to its gifted originator too." (Dennis Potter, *Hide and Seek* [his first pub-lished novel], London: Andre Deutsch, 1973; repr. London: Faber and Faber, 1990).

5. "I think any writer has a small field to keep ploughing and eventually you turn up the coins you want." (Dennis Potter, quoted by Graham Fuller, introduction *Potter on Potter*, ed. Graham Fuller (London: Faber and Faber, 1993), p.xv.

6. "Potterland" is a useful and memorable term, first coined by Paul Delaney for the title of an article on Potter that appeared in *Dalhousie Review* 68, part 4 (1988): 511–521. It was one Potter read and liked.

7. "If they [BBC and Channel Four] could do that . . . I could go out with a fitting memorial" (Dennis Potter, final TV interview by Melvyn Bragg, first tx. Chan-

nel Four, 5 April 1994; text published in Dennis Potter, *Seeing the Blossom: Two Interviews and a Lecture* (London: Faber and Faber, 1994), p.28.

8. Potter, *Seeing the Blossom*, p.14.

9. For example, Dave Evans, a contributor to this volume, runs the world's currently most detailed and comprehensive Web site on Potter and in 1998, had over 14,000 "hits" and queries from Web users: see http://www.ucrysj.ac.uk/potter/index.htm. Evans, Cook and Gras have all taught university and college courses on Potter. Many other courses in universities all around the world incorporate Potter as part of wider television and television drama courses.

10. The precise details of the Potter symposium were as follows: "The Passion of Dennis Potter," Session OS18, International Association of Philosophy and Literature, 20th Anniversary Conference, George Mason University, Fairfax, Virginia, U.S.A., 10 May 1996. Amongst the participants who were invited and gave papers were contributors to this volume: Heinz Antor, Gwen Connolly, Peter Stead, Eckart-Voigts-Virchow, as well as coeditor John Cook.

11. Certainly, Potter's view was always that critics abroad were much more "open" to his work than those at home in Britain. See Cook's essay, note 5, for further discussion of this, based on his interview with Potter.

12. For example, British academic contributor to this volume, Glen Creeber, is of the same opinion as Cook that Potter's was an "essentially 'modernist' vision of broadcasting" (see Glen Creeber, " 'Reality or Nothing'? Dennis Potter's *Cold Lazarus* (1996)" in *Dissident Voices,* ed. Mike Wayne (London: Laurence and Wishart, 1998), p.19.

13. Dennis Potter, *Waiting for the Boat: On Television* (London: Faber and Faber, 1984), p.26. On dissolving the subject, see Michel Foucault, "What Is an Author?" in *Language, Countermemory, Practice,* ed. Donald Bouchard (Ithaca: Cornell University Press, 1977).

14. See especially Michael Holquist, *Dialogism: Bakhtin and His World* (London: Routledge, 1990), and Alexandar Mihailovic, *Corporeal Words: Mikhail Bakhtin's Theology of Discourse* (Evanston: Northwestern University Press, 1997).

PART I

Class and Culture

ONE OF THE MOST PREVALENT WAYS IN WHICH POTTER'S prolific body of work has come to be examined and made sense of by academic critics is from the perspective of what might broadly be termed "cultural studies." This influential approach, having its origins in the work of British critics such as Stuart Hall, Raymond Williams and the Centre for Contemporary Cultural Studies, Birmingham, England, posits that a cultural artifact can only be properly understood when placed in explicit relation to the context in which it was produced—the wider society, politics and history within which it was formed and through which it circulates. To borrow Raymond Williams's famous title, *Culture and Society* are indivisible.[1] "Art" is not pure and it does not stand alone: rather, it is inextricably bound up with the social, political and class relations of its time and it has to be understood on those terms.

For the study of Dennis Potter, such an attempt to place his work within a wider cultural perspective clearly confers certain advantages. It allows the critic, for example, to avoid having to make constant recourse back to the dramatist's own personal biography in order to account for the work, enabling it instead to be explained in terms of the wider political, social and cultural forces that may have been acting upon it and that an over-preoccupation with the personal and the biographical can all too easily serve to obscure. And certainly, as a number of the following essays make clear, there is ample critical scope for tracing the wider influences that acted upon and helped form the views of the young Dennis Potter: the self-same influences, interestingly, that also helped shape the emerging discipline of "cultural studies" itself.

Thus Richard Hoggart, who went on to form the Birmingham Centre for Cultural Studies, also had a profound effect upon the early Potter; it seems clear that Potter avidly read and absorbed Hoggart's seminal study of the decline of working class culture, *The Uses of Literacy* (1957), while still a student at Oxford. It seems he found in it innumerable points of identification with his own experience, as well as, suddenly, a ready-made language in which to express his own personal feelings and anxieties about the social class divide in Britain. Likewise, Raymond Williams's work: in Potter's first ever published book—a nonfiction student polemic entitled *The Glittering Coffin* (1960) that railed against the condition of England—he explicitly placed it on a pedestal with that of Hoggart.[2]

In this way, one can see why many "cultural studies" critics would wish to claim Potter for their own. At the same time, such an attempt to explain the writer in terms of his influences raises as many questions as it answers. For example, how far are we justified in applying the "Left culturalist" arguments that clearly shaped the ideas of the young Potter, to the entire following three decades of his creative writing? Is there a danger of being over-deterministic? And anyway, to what extent should "art" and the artist be regarded simply as a function of wider social factors? Was Potter a product of his time and place or, as his work progressed, did he change and begin to find his own voice, such that far from conforming to the tenor of his times, he actually came to write against them? What precisely *is* the relationship between the artist as individual agent and his or her social and cultural context?

In their own individual ways, the following five essays attempt to wrestle with these important questions. The section kicks off with Peter Stead's analysis of precisely this question of the relationship between "the public and the private" in Dennis Potter. Stead takes the entire sweep of Potter's career in television and with admirable concision and clarity, attempts to illuminate some of the wider social, cultural and industrial contexts that informed it. He suggests that from the very outset, the writer really has to be understood in relation to the basic fact that Britain is "a small country with a highly centralized national television service." Particularly for international readers who may be unfamiliar with these contexts, Stead's essay provides a useful introduction to some of the broader cultural contexts, as well as to the whole subject of Dennis Potter himself and the question of whether he was a product of his time or, in fact, writing "against the grain" of it. Stead's tone—slightly sceptical; slightly barbed—also reflects wider prevailing critical attitudes to Potter in Britain.

From this broad introduction, Glen Creeber's essay then goes on to consider more specific influences on Potter's work. Very much in line with the school of British "cultural studies," he focuses on the relationship between Dennis Potter's work and that of Richard Hoggart, author of *The Uses of Literacy*. Creeber demonstrates how much of Hoggart found its way into Potter's early work and also how Hoggart's denouncements of the encroachment of Americanized mass culture into Britain in the 1950s, may have profoundly shaped Potter's own, always ambivalent, attitudes to popular culture in his subsequent dramas.

Rick Wallach's essay shares many critical assumptions in common with Creeber, though in his, he provides the reader with an opportunity to explore in depth a single Potter work, *Lipstick on Your Collar* (1993), which he argues is a "socialist allegory." In contrast with Potter's other "serials with music," *Pennies from Heaven* (1978) and *The Singing Detective* (1986), *Lipstick* tends to be critically overlooked. But in a lively analysis, Wallach suggests that it is a much more directly "political" work than those other two: its abundant references to fecal and sexual imagery making it a kind of socialist satire on the "excesses" of materialism and consumerism—a reading that may in part justify Potter's own claim for *Lipstick* at the time of production that it is "a deceptive piece. There was more in the script than seems to be the case."[3]

From *Lipstick,* Dave Evans takes us back to Potter's first big "musical success," *Pennies from Heaven*. In a comprehensive analysis, he looks at the role of popular music in the drama; what he labels "the mythic structures" of *Pennies;* and finally, the drama's relationship to its period setting: England of the 1930s. Significantly, however, he parts company with overly "cultural" readings of Potter that see the attitudes to popular music expressed in the drama as profoundly determined by the Hoggartian influences that the writer absorbed in the 1950s. For Evans, this fails to "grasp the constellation" of ways in which, by the 1970s, Potter's attitudes to mass popular culture had begun to shift and to resolve themselves in a much more personal, slightly less judgmental fashion.

In the aptly titled "Cornucopias of Tinsel," Eckart Voigts-Virchow confronts Potter's complex relationship to mass culture head on, by looking at the attitudes expressed throughout the writer's plays to that ultimate ideological tool of consumer capitalism: advertising. Voigts-Virchow examines how Potter's various critiques of advertising relate to wider cultural paradigms and he also puts forward his own views of why he thinks those critiques may well be outdated. Nevertheless, in a conclusion that seems appropriately to round off this section, as well as encapsulate its overall themes and approaches, he ends by recognizing how much Potter, throughout his work, is almost always moving deep within our own wider "cultural heartland."

NOTES

1. Raymond Williams, *Culture and Society: 1780–1950* (Harmondsworth: Penguin, 1958), which became a key text foundational to the development of "cultural studies."
2. Dennis Potter, *The Glittering Coffin* (London: Victor Gollancz, 1960), p.8.
3. Dennis Potter, interview by Graham Fuller, *Potter on Potter,* ed. Graham Fuller (London: Faber and Faber, 1993), p.104.

CHAPTER 1

THE PUBLIC AND THE PRIVATE IN DENNIS POTTER

Peter Stead

NOBODY IN THE BRITAIN OF 1996 COULD HAVE BEEN unaware of the imminence of *Karaoke* and *Cold Lazarus*. Clearly, they were to constitute what the British have now come to identify as a "major media event." The build-up ran along well-established and predictable lines. Newspapers were stuffed full of previews and every personality who had known the author was asked to write immediately on why the nation should watch and what the nation should expect. Radio shows rushed to join in the crescendo of hype; the British Film Institute held sell-out previews and a television promotional campaign set out to maximize the audience by stressing that an important drama—classy, glossy, star-studded and unmissable—was about to begin. For a while in April 1996, the subject of Dennis Potter was as much on the nation's lips as Northern Ireland and the Middle East. Once again, the British were debating one of their favorite topics; one deemed central to the culture.

Britain is a small country with a highly centralized national television service and a national press characterized by a comparatively small number of London-produced titles. It is a culture in which television looms large and in which readily identifiable and sizable segments of the population follow very similar and predictable patterns of viewing. Given this combination of circumstances, it is comparatively easy for the television companies, in alliance with a press that relies on broadcasting for an increasing amount of its raw material, to launch "a media event." But by any standards, the hype for the two Potter plays was remarkable. The explanation, of course, is fairly straight-forward. Potter had established a long-standing reputation as a challenging and controversial television playwright. For years, his every TV play had tended to become an event. Then came the spectacularly dramatic circumstances of his short final illness, his remarkable exploration on television of how his final plays were to be produced and then his death. No writer in history has so carefully ensured that not only would there be extensive initial obituaries but that within two years, the nation would again have a specific opportunity to consider the degree of its loss.

Given the hype, it was inevitable that there would be something of a reaction. The disappointing quality of Potter's work after *The Singing Detective* (1986) had already prompted some critics to suggest that he was overrated and was being overindulged. Many of the offensive excesses of *Blackeyes* (1989) were attributed to his own direction[1] and *Lipstick On Your Collar* (1993) was generally thought to be made up of familiar and yet underwritten and overstretched material. A backlash to the high praise for *The Singing Detective* was bound to come, but what gave it added impetus and edge was a distaste for the way that Potter seemed to be exploiting the sense he had of being a national institution. To an astonishing and unprecedented degree, an author was putting his private self as much in the public eye as his work. There was remarkable publicity for his 1993 Edinburgh onslaught on media tycoons and for his collaboration in 1994 with the very sympathetic Melvyn Bragg (both events now available on video and in published form[2]) in which he set up his death and final works. One sensed that he had gone too far; a little later, in what were to be her final months, the Princess of Wales made the same mistake. British television lives off and loves the notion that it is an integral part of every household; its stock-in-trade is the employment of real, and the creation of fictional, characters whom we are invited to take into our own families. High quality production and presentation usually sustain the bond between programs and audiences, but every now and then there comes a moment of excess, a faux pas that necessitates television having to be reminded that it is but one strand in a more complex and pluralistic culture. Potter had perhaps claimed too much; both he and television needed to be put in their place. The nation was fascinated by his performance; it was clearly a great event but what did it really mean? In 1993, Paul Johnson reminded us that "after all, he is only a television dramatist, not a proper one."[3] Perhaps not surprisingly, it was the London *Times* (owned, of course, by Rupert Murdoch, the tycoon Potter most loved to hate and after whom he named his cancer[4]) that carried an article by Mark Steyn headed "The Dramatist Who Made An Art Form Out of Plagiarism"—a reference to Potter's heavy dependence on the words of songwriters.[5] On the day of *Karaoke*'s first transmission, Murdoch's *Sunday Times* carried a piece by A. A. Gill declaring that Potter had been "overindulged to the bitter end." Gill thought the play "dreadful" and in particular considered "the harking back to images and issues of the 1940s and 1950s" to be "the rantings of a saloon-bar bore."[6]

These three gifted journalists make some substantial critical points, but essentially their argument with Potter was political. What gave their pieces edge was their shared view that Potter had been sponsored, promoted and institutionalized by a small elite of administrators and producers responsible for the output of Britain's terrestrial television services. For Johnson, "Potter's brew is the tipple of the chattering classes";[7] Steyn thought of him as "mainly writing for that smug metropolitan coterie he affected to despise,"[8] and Gill suggested to his readers that *Karaoke* and *Cold Lazarus* were made for a reason "that has very little to do with me and you, and an awful lot to do with television." For Gill, the plays constituted "an in-house eulogy." What is more, he concluded, "it won't happen again."[9] Here, the critic is reiterating a point made in an earlier and surprisingly appreciative *Times* obituary that had reflected on the fact that "the changing structures and priorities of British broadcasting" were making it likely that "Potter's oeuvre may well stand alone for ever."[10] To an extent, Potter's reputation inevitably will have to stand or fall alongside that of the highly structured and controlled system of British terrestrial television. In the minds of those right-wing critics campaigning against broadcasting elites and advocating more competition and choice in broadcasting, Potter not only represented many of the faults of the whole system but was a product of them. Referring directly to a generation of television executives, Gill dubbed Potter "their creation, their standard-bearer."[11]

Gill and other like-minded critics were justified in this close identification of Potter with his masters, collaborators and sponsors. The hype of 1996 was the culmination of a process whereby television bosses asked us to believe that Potter was the doyen of their writers and a central reference point in the culture. To study Potter, one has to look at his work in the context of the public debate on it and that means starting with the question of why he became a standard-bearer. He did so, in large part, because he himself took television very seriously, more seriously perhaps than anyone else. As with almost every subject and especially manifestations and expressions of popular culture, his views were ambivalent: respect and enthusiasm mixing with contempt and disgust. At first, he hated television's ubiquitous, unrelenting yet bland obtrusiveness but from his university days on, he sensed both its power and its potential significance for his own career. It was a chance combination of circumstances that led him first to work in television and then to review it just at that moment when it was becoming a national craze. Similarly, it was the misfortune of his illness that made him dependent on it for his income.[12] Initially, it was his left-wing democratic socialism that allowed him to feel comfortable working within the context of a highly regulated British broadcasting system that for him, offered the possibility of a genuinely common culture; then later, he released his full fury at the capture of television by money-grabbing tycoons who commercialized every aspect of it. Nevertheless, when his illness was under control, he loved to use both radio and television as an interview platform to introduce and develop the themes of his dramatic work. That personal experience, taken with the demand for his scripts, proved that he had found his natural element; all his experience of other media—the novel, the theater and Hollywood—confirmed that television was the only vehicle that allowed him to be himself. As he justified his chosen but traditionally underrated profession of TV writer, he helped give a whole industry a new sense of dignity. His success as a television writer led him to identify himself with the whole notion of quality, independent, culturally concerned television and his employers were all too willing to confirm him in that role. Television critics and profile writers by the score rushed to join the campaign to boost Potter as the symbol and guarantee of television's place within the culture. Rarely, do we find writers setting themselves up in this way and then being accepted as cultural bastions on their own terms. The British stage playwright John Osborne had willingly colluded with favorable critics to sustain the notion that he was an important personality and that what he did was done in the national interest. In its time, British television has spawned literally scores of serious writers, most of whom settled for such an anonymous professionalism that they would have been surprised if any member of their audiences had identified their faces or their voices. It was not Potter's way. As a young man, his first experiences of journalism and television occasioned controversy and required subsequent personal explanation.[13] That became a pattern he willingly settled into and, like the American writers Norman Mailer and Gore Vidal, he took it for granted that both his work and his auxiliary comments were the heart of the national matter.

Undoubtedly, Potter's political and personal commitment to television was seized on by executives as a legitimizing testimonial, but what was crucial were the elements that constituted his work. The writer was a member of a specific generation—as it happens, the generation that was to reshape British popular culture, especially television, in the 1960s. Potter was immediately and forever thereafter identified as a leading representative of people whose parents' lives had been dominated, first, by the Depression of the 1930s, and then by World War II; whose own values and codes of behavior were learned first in Sunday school and then in the cinema; whose sense of national identity and love of popular music was established by the radio programs of the BBC; and who received an excellent academic education in grammar schools, before going on to encounter the realities of a class system at university and in the armed forces. Potter was a quintessential product of this mid-century generation that grew up in a post-war, Cold War world—a world characterized, on the one hand, by a Welfare State that offered a range of public services, including broadcasting, and on the other, a middle-class dominated culture that eschewed social analysis and artistic innovation. Far more than any other literary work of the "Age of Anger," it was Potter's two *Nigel Barton* plays—*Stand Up, Nigel Barton* and *Vote, Vote, Vote for Nigel Barton* (both 1965)—that announced the arrival of new energies and possibilities. Potter's claims both for and on television were part of a process that saw the arts and education as a whole pass into the hands of his generation. Not surprisingly, his concerns were to be their concerns; and very largely, they related to class, sex and popular culture.

These issues were important for a whole generation and they provided the basic themes of television soaps, serials and genre writing. Potter was different in that he was fashioning highly unusual, individual plays or series relating the public preoccupations of his generation to intense, sensational and controversial crises in the personal lives of vividly created characters. Each script called for bold, innovative techniques in casting, presentation and editing; each had satisfying elements that appealed to producers; juicy parts for good actors to develop; shocking moments that would constitute television firsts; and finally, an overall seriousness of purpose that invited audiences to consider important issues relating to personal crises. From play to play, the quality of the writing and plotting varied enormously and all too often, one was aware of crude stereotypes, especially in the depiction of aristocrats, those in authority, women and (as Mark Steyn has pointed out) Americans. Part of the problem was that Potter, as the London *Times* obituary noticed and *Cold Lazarus* was to indicate, was no satirist and was always at his weakest attempting to mock authority or those in opposition to his values. Nevertheless, each production identified a problem of particular intensity that was usually resolved by revisiting and reliving the occasion of the crisis. What enabled Potter to generate such intensity was his inclination to relate experience of class and sexual dilemma to moments of betrayal. Disgust and guilt were the qualities that guaranteed the power of the plays.

In each work, there were great issues to be discussed by critics and viewers in a rational and dispassionate way. But they rarely were; rather, rows developed over productions that were explicit and controversial. Once again, middle-class taste had been offended and the strict code of television censorship breached. Each play became a matter of national debate. Producers loved that and one came to suspect that the mischievous and opportunistic Dennis Potter loved it too.

As Potter's reputation developed, so did a highly formulaic routine. Claiming to represent the best interests of the public, crusading watchdog associations, religious leaders and the popular press would denounce the outrageous permissiveness that had sanctioned the plays, while producers and serious critics would strenuously defend television's right to deal with sexual, social and religious issues in such an artistic way. In many respects, this "traditional debate" on Potter was unsatisfactory, for it was always conducted as if the issue was the very existence of controversial matter, rather than its meaning in the context of the play. One often sensed that Potter's producers and supporters alike were merely grateful for controversy and that they did not examine the full implications of the crisis that had been depicted. What seemed to matter was that they had been given powerful plays that were always establishing television's right to enter new territory. The playwright was welcomed as a pioneer and an emancipator but little was said about the precise nature of the crises undergone by his characters. It was an age preoccupied by sex, but not one prepared to admit that it was necessarily a personal problem—rather the reverse. In fact, Potter was saying things that were not at all in keeping with the spirit of his age, but that was something that only his fiercest critics in the popular press would point out. Producers must always have suspected that they were dealing with an author who had his own private preoccupations—preoccupations not only personal but to some degree, aberrant. But the issue was not presented in that way. This was a disservice to all concerned, not least because it prevented both the puritanical opponents of his work and his liberal champions to recognize that abuse, sex-related violence and guilt were far more common in actuality than anyone suspected or admitted at that time. An emphasis on the particular points of crisis in each play would have allowed that point to be made, even as it was more generally admitted that sex need not necessarily be associated with guilt and that most people who graduated from the working-class into the middle-class did so without any sense that they had betrayed someone. The public had its own notion of Dennis Potter and, by and large, refused to discuss what was private in his work—private, that is, for either the characters or the author.

I have always felt that there was a good deal of hypocrisy in the ways Potter was promoted by television companies and by certain critics and indeed, in how he was greeted by middle-class audiences. He was always judged in terms of a wider cultural debate, rather than through a precise assessment of what had happened to his central characters. This failure to tackle Potter on his own ground is best illustrated in response to his uses of the past and of various kinds of music. Television producers, whether of drama, comedy or commercials, soon discovered that technically any period could be evoked utterly convincingly and audiences would lap up all the period detail. The British are particularly susceptible to nostalgia. Potter denounced it as an easy and meaningless exercise, even as he gained a personal following for his re-creation of former decades that, for all their problems, seemed satisfyingly familiar. This paradox became particularly apparent with his increasingly frequent references to popular culture and above all, in his use of popular music, especially that of the 1930s and 40s. Most notoriously, we have the example of *Pennies from Heaven* (1978), where Potter intended the extensive, crucial and carefully selected songs to illustrate the weaknesses of his central protagonist, Arthur Parker—his hopeless romanticism and his preoccupations with sex, pointing the way to the inevitability of his demise. And yet all of this mattered little to an audience that was grateful to hear tunes and words they loved and that, furthermore, they happily associated with an Arthur brought to life in a very charming, affectionate and humorous way in the original TV version by Bob Hoskins.[14] The writer offered us a weak and foolish man seduced by cheap, meretricious music; we, the audience, saw a man in love with life whom the authorities in the drama and indeed the playwright himself, unjustly did down.

On several occasions, Potter explained that he tended to associate the popular music of his childhood and adolescence—music he heard constantly courtesy of the radio—with the hymns he would sing every week in chapel. Potter spoke of the hymns of Sankey and Moody, which had been so loved in his gospel hall and of their power to mislead and disappoint; the words and tunes offered a solace and a balm that could never be fulfilled. As was the case with the secular offerings of the radio, tunes and words had the power of lodging in the mind and their constant and often surprising recall were forever a reminder of how life had fallen short. Again, this is a common phenomenon to which Potter added his own spin and his own edge. Popular songs, of course, can be very different from hymns, but can be alike in offering pleasant melodies and pleasant thoughts—and most people are happy to recall them on that basis. There are some brilliant songs, many that "best express what oft was thought" and those written in the 1930s and 40s constitute a genuine popular poetry. Surely, very few of us feel betrayed or misled by either hymns or songs. Perhaps in Potter's case, his feelings of resentment can be explained in terms of his very physical, indeed sensual, response to the words. He often used the word "sweet" with regard to hymns and songs, almost as if he were actually tasting the succor that was on offer. His susceptibility may have been special and extreme. If so, he may have experienced real disappointment. What is certainly true is that his personal sense of deprivation allowed a huge public to appreciate genuinely, either with nostalgia or with newly found pleasure, a whole delightful repertoire.

Dennis Potter was a showman: a professional television writer who fully appreciated that his story and his characters, however good, needed to be presented ingeniously, in ways that were striking, shocking, challenging and attention-grabbing. There is no doubt in my mind that this "showman" element in his work more often than not distracted audience attention away from the heart of the matter. As his critics have argued, to a far greater extent than with other leading television writers, his scripts were to depend for their impact on great acting, haunting tunes and beautiful women, as well as innovative directing and technical work. The eye and the ear were always being seduced, even as the mind and the conscience were diverted. This meant that there was every temptation to ignore the religious element in his work. Here, we have the biggest irony of all, for the liberal generation that so revered Potter as an emancipator, prided itself on having shaken off religious constraint, puritanical guilt and above all, the concept of sin. Only very belatedly was it accepted that not only was Potter the product of a gospel hall, but in effect he had never left it. Both before and after the worst days of his illness, Potter operated very much as a metropolitan, bohemian intellectual, loving good long lunches in a London of which he was far more a product than anyone ever realized. All the while, however, his work was rooted in a theology that fully accepted the reality of sin and evil; that was all too aware of the suffering of those who sinned and were sinned against; and which firmly believed that redemption, if it were possible at all, could only come by reliving the moment of transgression—by passing back through it in some private, internal process of therapy.

Potter's generation was probably, for all its cultural brio, far more stricken by guilt than it ever admitted, but that guilt was nearly always a question of class and new-found wealth. For the most part, it had become a secular age, one in which the arts were debated in terms of political and social considerations rather than personal salvation. Potter's own personal position was always very different—indeed, in terms of the popular culture, unique. Undoubtedly, it was his sense of guilt that gave his work its power, although this point was rarely made until comparatively late in his career. There was nothing general about his guilt: it was specific and direct. As elusive, ambivalent and misleading as he was always to be, all the evidence of his plays, commentaries and interviews leave us in no doubt that he was writing out of personal experience, all the while working toward a reconciliation of personal matters. Sins are committed and undergone; nothing in life prepares one for that and there is very little in life that subsequently allows one to come to terms with the consequences. These sins are manifestations of evil, an evil that works through and on people and against which there is little protection. The sense of shame in having directly experienced sin becomes an integral part of one's personality, as well as an intensive aspect in one's closest relationships with other people. One is unclean, unwholesome, truly wounded; and forgiveness of oneself, by others and for others, is a tortuous process of revelation and reconstruction.

This intensely personal sense of sin, with its accompanying feelings of guilt and flawed inadequacy, grew out of a Christianity in which Jesus and His love had been as real, as close and as physical as any family relationship. Many of Potter's broadcasts had all the power and immediacy of religious testimony. He was miles removed from Catholicism and its tradition of confession to intermediaries. His was an upbringing in which one had been taught to talk to a friend Whose balm was as palpable and real as the language in which it was expressed. The sweetness of religious language came from "Sweet Jesus" Himself. In *Karaoke*, Christ is referred to as that "sweet, silly bugger."[15] Of course, it was that "sweet, silly bugger" who, in Potter's Gospel play, *Son of Man* (1969), had spoken to God in precisely the same terms as so many evangelical believers had adopted themselves: "Dada, you are—

near—NEAR. Nearnearnearnearnear—Here!"[16] At the time of its TV transmission, that wonderful play was spoken of as having offered a Jesus who was essentially human, but of course, Potter was also revealing that Christ's experience could be shared by any person. As a successful, middle-class intellectual, Potter was to travel far from his gospel hall and his chats with Jesus, but he took with him not only a sense of evil but also a language that was always used when the need arose for a spiritual balm as real as it was personal.

In all his commentaries, Potter was at pains to stress that "a play is a play is a play," and he despised anyone who wanted to discuss his work as autobiography. He was to concede that his plays took up themes in his own life, but nonetheless he was always dramatizing those themes so they ceased to be in any way autobiographical. Of course, the mischievous Potter loved playing this game and over the years, he delighted in releasing titbits of autobiography in a way guaranteed to tease his followers. Information about his life would be released first in interviews and then similar events would be dealt with in the plays themselves. Whatever the degree of fictionalization, one was left in no doubt that like the character of Mrs. Haynes in *Karaoke*, the playwright was more frequently placing pieces in the great jigsaw puzzle that was his work.[17] Clearly, he was reworking themes that at the very least, were suggested by his own early experiences. Perhaps the most fascinating aspect of being a Potter follower was the process of living with him through his exploitation of certain situations over 30 years. With each piece in the puzzle, one learns a little more and sees things a little differently. By his own admission, he was drawn to drama rather than to the novel as it allowed him to avoid some of the confusion of narrative conventions. With plays, audiences do not have to ask "Who is saying this?"; they merely accept that they are being allowed direct access to a slice of life as slice of history. In other words, there is every opportunity for the writer of screenplays to operate, or indeed to hide either inside or outside, his characters and to apportion his dramatized autobiography to whatever characters are at hand. He argued that the novel was dead; was bourgeois and was flawed by its need for a storyteller, either of the named or assumed kind.[18] All of this seems a remarkably dismissive response to the most versatile and challenging of literary forms and in any case, does less than justice to his own contributions to the form, which he always regarded as being, in part, exercises.

I like and admire Potter's novels and find them more satisfying than many of his plays. The format allows him to play all his games about levels of reality and yet ideas can be developed at length; experiences can be followed through without one being distracted, confused or prejudiced by acting, music, physical attraction and slick editing. Of course, his first published novel, *Hide and Seek* (1973), seems, at times, like a collection of extracts from various articles, lectures or interviews, but it was no more an exercise than *Karaoke* and *Cold Lazarus* were; and I suspect that at the time of its publication, a smaller percentage of its

readers assumed it to be pure autobiography than was the case when television
audiences first saw *The Singing Detective*. *Hide and Seek* is still the most intriguing of all handbooks for those interested in the career and works of Dennis
Potter: take the name off the cover and it remains a fascinating postmodernist
analysis of a novelist's relationship with his material. It is bleaker than *The
Singing Detective* but just as challenging and perhaps more logical; it is, of
course, in a different class from *Karaoke*. It was clearly meant as Potter's own
farewell to the novel form; perhaps it was meant as the last novel to be written
by anyone. I think of it as an intriguing and highly promising first novel by a
man who could have been one of England's greatest novelists—one who had it
in him to revive the form and to place it once again at the center of British culture. Perhaps too much went into *Hide and Seek*. In screenplays, basic material
and situations can be constantly reworked and reallocated among different characters. This is harder in novels. Potter opted for dramatic intensity rather than
considered reflection, and of course, he wanted to speak to a mass public within
a common culture and not to an intellectual elite.

As it happened, Potter was not done with the novel in 1973, for he actually went on to write two more. I exclude here his novelization of the *Pennies
from Heaven* MGM movie (1981), which one critic unfairly used to illustrate
how weak a writer Potter was without his music and his actors, forgetting that
he had a separate existence as a sophisticated novelist. *Ticket to Ride* (1986) is
indeed the "masterpiece" that *Punch* magazine thought it to be and far superior to the feature film version, *Secret Friends* (1992), that developed out of it.[19]
It is a psychological thriller, far more tense than any Potter play other than
Brimstone and Treacle (1976). It is a great English "roman noir," brilliant on
the tension between a corrupt city and rural domesticity, and an extended study
of sexual guilt and disgust. *Blackeyes* (1987) is a more flawed novel but it is a
fascinating investigation of the difficulty male authors have in creating female
characters, just as men as a whole have trouble perceiving actual women as individuals in their own right. It was a tremendously convincing depiction of extreme chauvinism, spoiled by a multilayered structure that was too clever by
half and by excessive relish that left in the mind a memory of a larger-than-life
English novelist stumbling from lunch to lunch: the women who needed some
life of their own remained cyphers. Potter himself directed the television version
in 1989, which offered us an Uncle Maurice (played by Michael Gough) as
splendid as we imagined him, but then lapsed into a masturbatory fantasy.[20] As
the whole nation realized that it was now being invited to share what was obviously the whole venture's preoccupation with and celebration of the beauty of
the actress Gina Bellman who played Blackeyes, any appreciation of his work
as a dramatist collapsed as we all envied him his freedom to indulge himself.

By the time of the televised *Blackeyes* in 1989, one fully sensed that Potter was having great fun. With him more than with any other screenwriter, one

had felt that he must have derived tremendous satisfaction from the way in which the camera and actors brought his words and stories alive. Now, he knew every trick, and could precisely prescribe every effect he wanted to create, whether it be in terms of actors, props or sets. He was in love now with all these things for their own sakes and that indeed amounted to an indulgence. Television was his toy and he was in total control of it. Amazingly, there were those who were prepared to play his game with him, almost without questioning the dependence on stereotype, the depiction of women, the growing number of in-jokes and personal references, the use of music or the length and format of the story. The show had to go on.

Dennis Potter was a very able man whom some of his Oxford contemporaries thought would go on to be Prime Minister or a great journalist. He was partly by accident and partly by political choice thrown into a relationship with television and for that medium, so central to English culture, he wrote some masterpieces. He was identified by an intellectual generation as a pioneer and as a champion of liberal causes. Much of the enthusiasm was based on a misreading of his work. In many ways, he was writing against the cultural grain of his era, certainly against the grain of people who produced television. What has been termed "Left Culturalism" was still the order of the day for the Arts Establishment, whereas Potter was talking openly, but with some sense of surprise, of Tory attitudes that he was discovering in himself.[21] Meanwhile, it remained the case that there was less interest in what his plays were saying than in the ways in which they were produced. Thus it had always been. It was a public Potter that many different groups seemed to want and he was prepared to play that game.

As he became an institution, so he sensed the extent to which the medium was his to do with it what he liked, and he pretty much did. In interview after interview, in many articles and in his plays, he settled old scores and gave full vent to all his prejudices. As those of us who met him found, he was a charming but also difficult and arrogant man, something of a bully, and very much a hypocrite.[22] He was a man and a writer who needed to be seriously and judiciously assessed. He was not: in his life, he was both demonized and mythologized. He condemned out of hand what was happening to a television culture that in reality, employed many other very talented writers. As Jonathan Coe has argued, Britain has a culture that in recent years has been adorned less by its serious writers and far more by its highly professional crime and comedy writers.[23] Popular culture, original popular culture, is what Britain does best. But Potter demanded, and was given, special treatment. He deserved some of it; he had written some great television, but he also had gone along with those who wanted to build him up into something more. For me, he was a brilliant but wicked, tricky and thoroughly opportunistic "old bugger."

NOTES

1. In 1989, Potter himself decided to direct the television version of his 1987 novel, *Blackeyes*, after several other directors turned it down. See Kenith Trodd's essay in this volume for more details and also John R. Cook for extended analysis of British media reaction to the TV *Blackeyes*.

2. Potter's "1993 Edinburgh onslaught" was his 1993 James MacTaggart Memorial Lecture, "Occupying Powers," delivered at the Edinburgh International Television Festival, 27 August 1993; his "collaboration" with Melvyn Bragg was his famous final TV interview with Bragg, first transmitted on Channel Four, 5 April 1994. Transcripts of both of these are published in full in Dennis Potter, *Seeing the Blossom: Two Interviews and a Lecture* (London: Faber and Faber, 1994), pp.33–56 and pp.3–29 respectively.

3. Paul Johnson, "The Potter Calls the Digger Black," *The Spectator,* 3 April 1993.

4. " . . . my cancer, the main one, the pancreas one, I call it Rupert, so I can get close to it, because the man Murdoch is the one who, if I had the time— . . . I would shoot the bugger if I could." Dennis Potter, final TV interview, quoted in Potter, *Seeing the Blossom,* p.14.

5. Mark Steyn, "The Dramatist Who Made An Art Form Out of Plagiarism," *The Times,* 9 November 1995.

6. A. A. Gill, "Over-indulged to the Bitter End," *The Sunday Times: The Culture,* 28 April 1996, p12.

7. Johnson, "The Potter . . ."

8. Steyn, "The Dramatist . . ."

9. Gill, "Over-indulged . . ."

10. "Obituary," *The Times,* 8 June 1994.

11. Gill, "Over-indulged . . ."

12. In 1962, while still a young journalist, Potter developed psoriatic arthropathy— a particularly severe and painful combination of psoriasis affecting the skin and arthritis crippling the joints—that despite periods of remission, would dog him for the rest of his life. In terms of his immediate career, it necessitated his switching roles from reporter to TV critic (a job he could do from home) and later, of course, to that of TV screenwriter.

13. In 1958, Potter's first appearance on TV, as a student being interviewed on the subject of "class in personal life," generated tabloid headlines such as "Miner's Son Ashamed of Home. The Boy Who Kept His Father Secret." In 1960, as a young television trainee, a BBC TV documentary he made about his native Forest of Dean, *Between Two Rivers,* led to ill feeling among his local, native community and a sense in him that he may have betrayed his roots. In many ways, Potter's early TV play, *Stand Up, Nigel Barton* (1965), in which a miner's son realizes he has betrayed his own father in a TV documentary, is just such an attempt to offer "a subsequent personal explanation" of both incidents through the less politically sensitive medium of drama. See Glen Creeber's essay in this volume for further discussion of both these early forays into the world of TV journalism.

14. A subsequent, less critically and commercially successful Hollywood feature film version of *Pennies from Heaven* was produced by MGM in 1981, starring Steve Martin in the role of Arthur Parker.

15. This is how Potter's alter ego Daniel Feeld (played by Albert Finney), the central screenwriter protagonist of *Karaoke* (1996, posthumous) describes Christ at one point. See Dennis Potter, *Karaoke and Cold Lazarus* (published scripts), (London: Faber and Faber, 1996), p.100.

16. Dennis Potter, *Son of Man: A Play* (stage script), (London: Samuel French, 1970), p.39. In fact, only in Potter's subsequent revised script, designed for theater staging, do these lines appear. They do not feature in the original BBC TV production of *Son of Man,* transmitted on 16 April 1969.

17. Mrs. Haynes (played by Alison Steadman, who also played the central protagonist, Philip Marlow's mother in *The Singing Detective*) is the physically and emotionally scarred mother of Sandra Sollars (Saffron Burrows), the female lead in *Karaoke*. Because of her condition, Mrs. Haynes spends all her days at home, carefully putting the pieces of a giant jigsaw puzzle together. The jigsaw shows a photographic image of Hammersmith Bridge in West London: an image motif that runs through many of Potter's later works; for example, *The Singing Detective.*

18. For example, see Dennis Potter, interview by Graham Fuller, *Potter on Potter,* ed. Graham Fuller (London: Faber and Faber, 1993), p.127.

19. A "grey, forbidding masterpiece of suspense and horror . . . Potter has written a spellbinder" was how *Punch* magazine described *Ticket to Ride.* Quoted on the dust jacket of Dennis Potter, *Ticket to Ride* (London: Faber and Faber, 1986), paperback edition.

20. Maurice James Kingsley is the "larger-than-life English novelist" in *Blackeyes* who steals his niece Jessica's past life experiences as a glamor model and to her extreme anger and consternation, embroiders them into a sexy, soft-core bestseller. See Gwen Connolly's essay in this volume for further discussion (and alternative analysis) of *Blackeyes* the novel.

21. " . . . there is that element in the Conservative Party which I quite respect—that Old Tory, Dr. Johnson element, if you like, as opposed to the canting humbug of the Left. Obviously, I could never bring myself to vote Conservative and I suppose it would be accurate to say that I am on the left, but many of my feelings are what would commonly and crudely be called right-wing. Emotionally, I believe the greatest danger to the human race is lack of order. That doesn't necessarily imply a sanctioning of hierarchies, but it does imply a belief in law. It's complicated." Dennis Potter, interview by Graham Fuller, *Potter on Potter,* p.21.

22. In May 1993, Peter Stead interviewed Potter at a special public event at the Hay-on-Wye literary festival. As Stead puts it, it was "perhaps the best England-Wales contest for several seasons" (Peter Stead, *Dennis Potter* (Bridgend: Seren Books, 1993), p.8.

23. Jonathan Coe has made this point in his journalism but also substantiates it in his excellent novel, *What a Carve Up!* (London: Viking, 1994), in which the memory of a 1961 British movie becomes the basis of a savage denunciation of Mrs. Thatcher's England.

CHAPTER 2

"THE ANXIOUS AND THE UPROOTED"

Dennis Potter and Richard Hoggart, Scholarship Boys

Glen Creeber

He both wants to go back and yet thinks he has gone beyond his class, feels himself weighted with knowledge of his own and their situation, which hereafter forbids him the simpler pleasures of his father and mother. And this is only one of his temptations to self-dramatization.[1]

IN DENNIS POTTER'S *STAND UP, NIGEL BARTON* (1965), its protagonist is racked with guilt for the way he blatantly uses his own family and friends selfishly to promote himself and his career. "I was acting it up a bit, over-dramatizing," he confesses to his girlfriend about his role in a TV documentary on social class. "You're like a performing animal," she replies. "It all comes out too smoothly. You could have read it in some paperback."[2]

If there is one "paperback" that Nigel may have read in his pursuit for self-advancement, it is surely Richard Hoggart's *The Uses of Literacy* (1957). Published while Potter was still at Oxford, the book's arrival on the cultural scene marked a growing interest in social class; an interest that Potter (like his fictional alter ego) seemed only too keen to exploit. Like Potter, Hoggart was originally from a working class background, his book articulating the growing "schizophrenia" of the new "scholarship boy"—those working class children who (through postwar legislation) had now been given the chance to win a scholarship to study at university.[3] Indeed, both Potter and Hoggart came out of a similar cultural moment: products of the postwar reconstruction that brought about the British 1945 Labour Government.[4] However, with the gradual disillusionment of this "New Jerusalem," they came to symbolize a generation who felt that their highest principles and ideals had been betrayed. While both writers were at great pains to dissociate themselves from England's Imperial past, they shared a deep-rooted sense of regret for an England that, like the scholarship boy himself, was forever torn between two worlds.

Educated at Leeds University, Richard Hoggart joined the Workers' Education Association as a teacher after active service in World War II. The W.E.A. also attracted the likes of Raymond Williams who, along with Hoggart, is now widely regarded as one of the founding fathers of British "cultural studies."[5] Both from humble backgrounds and both prominent figures in the British New Left, they must have seemed exciting and exemplary figures to the ambitious undergraduate. They were certainly instrumental in the formation of the British Culturalist movement, which can be seen as part of a remoralization campaign centered upon the study of English literature appropriated by F. R. Leavis, whose ideals and aims, at least, partly informed their work.[6] As with E. P. Thompson's *The Making of the English Working Class*, culturalism attempted to conceive traditional working class "folk culture" as a site of political and cultural resistance. While Raymond Williams's *Culture and Society* clearly inspired Potter's growing fascination for the possibility of a "common culture," Hoggart's work gave him both a personal and cultural context within which he could frame his own views and opinions about working class life.[7]

In a tradition already set out by writers like George Orwell, *The Uses of Literacy* attempted to portray and critique contemporary working class culture. Originally conceived as a novel, its mixture of observation and autobiography certainly offered an eclectic and unique account of postwar British life.[8] The book begins with a heartfelt evocation of traditional working class culture taken from the memories of the author's childhood during the 1920s and '30s. With unmistakable fondness (if not a little detachment), he describes the working men's clubs, coach trips to the seaside and the close-knit communities of his boyhood, which he describes as "The Full Rich Life." This is followed by a critical and polemical attack on 1950s popular culture: the glossy and hedonistic "Candy-Floss World" offered by "The Newer Mass Arts." Hoggart's argument is that this new commercialized "pop culture" (spreading in primarily from the United States) was in danger of destroying the older, more traditional way of life. Nowhere is this more clearly demonstrated than in the "juke-box boys," with their appreciation of the new café bar, pulp fiction and rock 'n' roll. Finally, there is Hoggart's description of the "Anxious and Uprooted": the postwar "scholarship boy" who is painfully torn between his working class roots and his middle class aspirations. "For such a boy," Hoggart wrote, "is between two worlds of school and home; and they meet at few points. Once at grammar school, he quickly learns to make use of a pair of different accents, perhaps even two different characters and differing standards of value."[9]

Not surprisingly, the book must have struck a chord with the young Potter, who not only identified with Hoggart's description of the upwardly mobile, but longed to be able to articulate his own ambiguous feelings toward working class life. Its influence can certainly be detected in the two works of nonfiction he would write before turning his attention to drama in the mid-1960s. Like *The Uses of Literacy*, both *The Glittering Coffin* (1960) and *The Changing Forest: Life in the Forest of Dean Today* (1962) combined an unusual mixture of sociology, politics and autobiography in an attempt to reassess British life as it, too, stood between two worlds: its working class organic past and its commercialized and increasingly Americanized future.[10] Certainly, Hoggart's evocative portrayal of working class culture and his damning denouncement of American mass culture must have appealed to Potter's own complex mixture of puritanical British socialism. While *The Glittering Coffin* set out a personal and political manifesto for postwar Britain, *The Changing Forest* used his own working class background as a case study to decry the changes taking place in postwar British culture:

> I feel the decline of the distinctive Forest culture, not so much in the healthy and necessary senses, but in the almost neurotic turning aside from the label 'working class' and from the older loyalties. Part of this may be inevitable in any situation of rapid change, but more of it, I regret, is due to the meaningless nature of "choice" between the older values and the newer, brighter, corroding uniformity of the new so-called post-capitalism.[11]

Like *The Uses of Literacy*, both books also deal with the dilemma of the scholarship boy, seen through the eyes of their author. Indeed, Potter gained his first ever television appearance because of his willingness to speak openly and frankly about his predicament. In Christopher Mayhew's BBC TV series *Does Class Matter?* (1958) (which also included an interview with Hoggart), he spoke animatedly about the gulf that education had opened up between him, his roots and his family. "My father is forced to communicate with me almost, as it were, with a kind of contempt," he declared in his newly acquired Oxford accent.[12] Not surprisingly, the tabloid reaction to such a confession was less than sympathetic: "Oxford Student Ashamed of Home," the *Reynold's News* announced. "The Boy Who Kept His Father Secret."[13] Yet for much of Potter's early career, he appeared happy to present himself as the living embodiment of Hoggart's unhappy individual. "At home, my parents grew away as I grew up," he wrote in *The New Statesman*. "The atmosphere and cohesion disintegrates only gradually, but inevitably."[14] Most famously,

Nigel Barton became the dramatic portrayal of the anxious scholarship boy, torn in two by conflicting class loyalties: "I don't feel at home in either place," he complains. "It's a tightrope between two different worlds and I'm walking it."[15]

But it was *Between Two Rivers* (1960), Potter's first and only TV documentary, where Hoggart's influence was most pronounced. Indeed, the program employed a surprisingly similar structure to *The Uses of Literacy*. First, there are Potter's nostalgic memories of his *own* working class childhood during the 1930s and '40s. With "mum" playing the club piano and "dad" a member of the village brass band, he constructs a warm and evocative portrayal of traditional village life. This old world is shattered, however, with the arrival of the education system. As before, the description of the displaced scholarship boy is both vivid and personal: "Even at home with my parents," he confesses, "I felt a shame-faced irritation with the tempo of a pickle-jar style of living . . ." However, on returning from university, he finds that he actually learns fully to appreciate the culture of his past and the final part of the program is concerned with defending it from its rapid corruption by modern mass culture. The tone of the narration has distinct echoes of Hoggart, even launching a vicious attack on the "juke-box boys" and their idolization of Elvis and American pop culture. "We want our daughter to know something of the land between the two rivers," he concludes. "To see it before it's beaten down by the world of pop . . . seventeen inch screens and *Double Your Money*."[16]

Potter's attraction to popular culture was always tinged with a certain ambiguity. Indeed, his early TV plays openly criticized the ever increasing influence of "mass culture" on traditional British life. Obsessed with the Hollywood western, the young protagonist of *Where the Buffalo Roam* (1966) actually ends up shooting his mother and grandfather because he dangerously confuses the glossy images of American mass culture with his real life in Swansea. Certainly, Potter's anti-American feelings were evident in a play such as *The Bonegrinder* (1968), which has the home of the respectable George King (or King George) invaded by (Uncle) Sam Adams, a coarse and loud-mouthed American sailor. Indeed, the protagonist of Potter's stage play, *Sufficient Carbohydrate* (1983), is only one of many of his characters to display distinct anti-American feelings. "This tiny island has no Coca Cola signs," Jack Barker proclaims on holiday in Greece, "no muzak, no hamburgers, not a sniff of cocaine or a single sud of a sodding soap opera . . . It's as though America lived in vain. Everywhere else I've been—especially ye olde England—is a pocket-sized imitation of the Land of the Free."[17]

As his early documentary revealed, Potter shared Hoggart's belief in a cultural 'Fall' from a healthy working class culture to a debased modern mass culture—and it is the growing "scholarship boy" who inevitably experiences this "Fall" most intensely. The rural heartland of the Forest of Dean and its industrial, coal mining community certainly represents an organic "Eden"; a world that existed before England's own fall from grace during the Americanized 1950s.[18] As with Hoggart, that older way of life (though also shown to be restrictive and intolerant) seems to encapsulate an English tradition now so ruthlessly torn apart by modern mass culture. In *Pennies from Heaven* (1978), set in the 1930s, this "Garden of Eden" (epitomized by the virginal Eileen, the village schoolmistress) is destroyed by the arrival of Arthur, an unfaithful and dishonest salesman from London. As the initials of their Christian names suggest (their story echoes that of Adam and Eve), the result is her expulsion from "paradise."[19] Similarly, *The Singing Detective* (1986) has London and the Forest of Dean caught up in a complex Oedipal narrative that suggests an inevitable Fall from grace for both child and community. In dreaming of his father's singing in the working men's club of his boyhood, Marlow suddenly finds himself alone inside the club as it stands in the present—empty, abandoned and in despair. While in *Blue Remembered Hills* (1979), the organic kinship of seven working class children during the Second World War is shattered (and a "Fall" clearly takes place) when they realize that they are responsible for the "murder" of their innocent and abused friend.

Even Potter's treatment of popular music clearly has links with this view of British culture. Both Hoggart and Potter certainly share an obsession with the music of their childhoods. Despite the commercial origins of many of the songs they cite, they both tend to conceive the music as part of a more traditional working class culture of the past. "They are vulgar, it is true," Hoggart insists, "but not usually tinselly . . . they still touch hands with an older, more handsome culture."[20] As I have written elsewhere,[21] Potter's treatment of the songs (particularly the lip-synch technique first employed in *Pennies from Heaven*) constructs them within an older "folk" tradition by giving an *amateur* and essentially *British* context to commercially produced American music. A similar technique is employed by Hoggart, who is at great pains to play down the American mass produced origins of the popular music enjoyed by the working class audiences of his childhood. While Potter has the songs clumsily lip-synched by his characters, Hoggart emphasizes the ability of the working class to transform the commercialized popular music for their own purposes. This is suggested in his description of a song that Potter himself would later employ in *The Singing Detective*:

> I first heard "Paper Doll" sung in the "red hot" fashion by an American crooner and it seemed quite unsuitable for transplantation to northern England; but two or three years later, a local amateur sang it whilst I was in a Hull pub and it had been beautifully translated. "I'd rather have a paper doll to call my own/ Than just a good-for-nothing real life gal" was delivered in the American version with immense speed and attack and the final "gal" was a

powerful sock of a drawl. In Yorkshire, the whole thing was taken at half
speed, the rhythms pulled out to the usual up-and-down pattern and the "gal"
transmuted into the standard Northern English moan—ending on "er."[22]

Surprisingly, perhaps, Potter's view of television fits into a similar tradition. Despite his enthusiastic promotion of the "democratic medium," he
did not eagerly support any other system of broadcasting other than that offered by the state-funded BBC. Here again, Potter and Hoggart seemed to
be in complete agreement. Indeed, Hoggart went on to form part of the Pilkington Committee, which advised the government on the future of broadcasting in the early 1960s, condemning commercial television, which he
clearly saw as a corrupt symptom of "the newer mass arts." According to
the Committee, "many mass appeal programmes" were "vapid and puerile;
often derivative, repetitive and lacking in real substance."[23] Despite later
working for commercial television, Potter's conception of British public service broadcasting remained akin to Hoggart's. As late as his 1993 James
MacTaggart Memorial Lecture, he was still attacking the increased commercialization of the medium.[24] Although many of Potter's sentiments were
often commendable, his conception of broadcasting was actually rooted in
a rather nostalgic vision of the past. Arguably, British television became
what it is today because of the increased competition offered by the new
commercial channels. One cannot imagine the BBC's *Wednesday Play* slot
(where Potter learned his trade as a television dramatist), if ABC (an early
commercial TV company) had not produced the groundbreaking *Armchair
Theatre*.[25] But for both Potter and Hoggart, the memories of a "Reithian"
public service broadcasting era[26] are tied up with their own experiences of
a working class childhood punctuated by the paternal BBC: bringing
glimpses of another world and offering the lofty delights of high culture to
a grateful working class audience.

What is remarkable is that these very issues were still clearly evident up
until Potter's last piece of work for television. Written just before his death,
Cold Lazarus (1996, posthumous) offers a conclusion to themes and issues
that had driven his entire career. Set in the year 2368, public service broadcasting has been entirely replaced by a commercialized, profit-minded global
industry. The President of U.T.E. (Universal Total Entertainment) is David
Siltz, a vacuous, hard-boiled American who cares nothing for quality programming and everything for profit. In contrast is the story of Daniel Feeld,
whose head has been cryogenically frozen 400 years earlier. It transpires that
Daniel was a British scholarship boy whose past life is now able to be viewed
via new technology. As the scientists delve into his memories, they discover a
world now scarcely imaginable, where people could still "mingle and touch
and hope."[27] The Forest of Nead (Dean spelled backward), with its chapel,

dance halls and dense woodland, portrays, as the script puts it, "another land";[28] one infinitely more "natural" and "organic" than their sanitized and commercialized future.

Formed by the cultural landscape of the 1950s and by writers and critics who had experienced a similar cultural journey, Potter and Hoggart were clearly products of their time. Their work attempts to articulate England's cultural "Fall"; an organic (if inward-looking and intolerant) community is replaced by a commercial and inherently corrupt way of life. Within this simple framework is an ambiguous mixture of anger and regret, a longing for an Eden that never was and a neurotic sense of guilt for originally abandoning that mythical world. In particular, both Hoggart and Potter's feelings of guilt were originally transferred onto the "evils" of mass culture, which they blamed for destroying traditional working class culture—thereby relinquishing them of their *own* deep-rooted sense of betrayal. For the archetypal scholarship boy is forever torn between two worlds, claiming to miss the very culture he once despised and from which he once desperately longed to escape. It is Potter, however, who literally dramatizes the "schizophrenia" of the scholarship boy's situation: a condition reflected in England's own cultural journey from benevolent socialism to the economic individualism of Thatcherism. Hoggart may have been engaged with similar themes and obsessions, but his "sociological" distancing from his subject lacks the tension of a novel or the "intersubjectivity" of drama. The brilliance of Potter's television drama lies in its ability to dramatize both the psychological *and* the cultural landscape of British society since the war. Anxious and uprooted, his protagonists share an inescapable sense of loss; a belief that they (like England itself) have forsaken an invaluable part of their authentic identity.

NOTES

The author wishes to thank Susan Burnett for her patient editorial review of this essay.

1. Richard Hoggart, *The Uses of Literacy* (Manchester: Manchester University Press, 1957; repr. Harmondsworth: Penguin, 1990), p.301.
2. Dennis Potter, *The Nigel Barton Plays* (published scripts), (Harmondsworth: Penguin, 1967), pp.70–71.
3. Potter was, like thousands of other postwar British working class children, a beneficiary of R. A. Butler's 1944 Education Act. Actually passed by a coalition Government, it introduced the "tri-partite" system of schooling, which attempted to divide children at the age of eleven into "grammar," "technical" or "modern" schools, depending on their measured ability. The term "scholarship boy" clearly reflects the bias in attention given towards the male student; a bias also reflected in Hoggart's book.

4. The British 1945 Labour Government created the whole notion of the "Welfare State" which aimed to care for every British citizen "from the cradle to the grave." The National Health Service, national insurance and the nationalization of the transport, coal and steel industries were part of major legislation. "One of the great governments of British history," Potter told Melvyn Bragg in his final TV interview, published in Dennis Potter, *Seeing the Blossom: Two Interviews and a Lecture* (London: Faber and Faber, 1994), p.9.

5. Hoggart actually went on to found the Birmingham Centre for Contemporary Cultural Studies. This center would have a profound effect on the study of popular culture and the mass media in Britain as a whole.

6. For a full and lucid discussion of the British Culturalist movement, see chapter 2 of Graeme Turner's *British Cultural Studies: An Introduction* (London and New York: Routledge, 1990). For Potter's views on E. P. Thompson and Raymond Williams, see Dennis Potter, "The Long Non-Revolution of Dennis Potter," interview by John Wyver, *Time Out*, 17–23 October 1980, pp.18–19.

7. E. P. Thompson, *The Making of the English Working Class* (Harmondsworth: Penguin, 1963); Raymond Williams, *Culture and Society 1780–1950* (Harmondsworth: Penguin, 1958).

8. For an interesting discussion of the book and its place in British cultural history, see Robert Hewison, "The Uses of Culture" in *Culture and Consensus: England, Art and Politics since 1940* (London: Methuen, 1995).

9. Hoggart, p.296.

10. Dennis Potter, *The Glittering Coffin* (London: Victor Gollancz, 1960); Dennis Potter, *The Changing Forest: Life in the Forest of Dean Today* (London: Secker and Warburg, 1962; repr. London: Minerva, 1996).

11. Potter, *The Changing Forest*, pp.131–132.

12. Quoted from the transcript of "Class in Private Life," Programme Two of the *Does Class Matter?* series, tx. BBC TV, 25 August 1958 (BBC Written Archives Centre, Caversham: TEL1/C/1273/11372).

13. Potter actually writes about this incident in *The Glittering Coffin*, p.71.

14. Dennis Potter, "Base Ingratitude?" *New Statesman*, 3 May 1958, p.262.

15. Potter, *The Nigel Barton Plays* (published scripts), p.73.

16. Dennis Potter, voice-over narration (soundtrack), *Between Two Rivers*, tx. BBC TV, 3 June 1960. National Film Archive Viewing Print. *Double Your Money* was one of Britain's first game shows to arrive on commercial television (ITV). It was criticized at the time for being both too commercial and too American in its appeal.

17. Dennis Potter, *Sufficient Carbohydrate* (published stage script) (London: Faber and Faber, 1983), p.14.

18. 1956 seems to have been the very year in which this cultural decline set in, not least because of the Suez Crisis and the arrival of the "teenager" in the form of Elvis and rock 'n' roll. Not surprisingly, Potter chose to set *Lay Down Your Arms* (1970) and *Lipstick on Your Collar* (1993) in this pivotal year.

19. Eileen actually becomes a prostitute in London and goes under the name of Lulu, a clear indication that her previous life and persona have been completely destroyed.

20. Hoggart, p.163.
21. See Glen Creeber, "Banality with a Beat: Dennis Potter and the Paradox of Popular Music," *Media, Culture and Society* 18, (1996): 504.
22. Hoggart, pp.160–161.
23. The Pilkington Committee, *The Future of Sound Radio and Television: A Short Version of the Pilkington Committee* (London: Her Majesty's Stationery Office, 1962), p.10.
24. Dennis Potter, "Occupying Powers," 1993 James MacTaggart Memorial Lecture, delivered at the 1993 Edinburgh International Television Festival, 27 August 1993. Published in Potter, *Seeing the Blossom,* pp.33–56.
25. Detecting the need for original, contemporary television aimed at mass (working class) audiences, ABC brought over producer Sydney Newman from Canada in the late 1950s to produce *Armchair Theatre.* After the phenomenal success of the play series, the BBC simply "poached" Newman in 1963 to become Head of TV Drama, and eventually he developed (with producer James MacTaggart) a similar series of plays under a different title. The BBC's *Wednesday Play* slot ran from 1965 to 1970, when its title was changed to *Play for Today.*
26. "Reithian public service broadcasting": the phrase refers to John (Lord) Reith (1889–1970), first Director-General of the BBC (British Broadcasting Corporation), who laid out the foundations and ideals of public service broadcasting that the Corporation has subsequently, with varying degrees, tried to adhere and live up to throughout its history.
27. Dennis Potter, *Karaoke and Cold Lazarus* (published scripts) (London: Faber and Faber, 1996), p.307.
28. Potter, *Karaoke and Cold Lazarus* (published scripts), p.247.

CHAPTER 3

SOCIALIST ALLEGORY IN DENNIS POTTER'S *LIPSTICK ON YOUR COLLAR*

Rick Wallach

CRITICS USUALLY TREAT *LIPSTICK ON YOUR COLLAR* as a stepchild to Dennis Potter's preceding musical serials, *Pennies from Heaven* and *The Singing Detective*. W. Stephen Gilbert's dismissal of the series is characteristic: "The outcry over *Blackeyes* and the box-office failure of *Secret Friends* had a deplorable effect on Potter as a writer. He ran for cover and safety and tried to appeal to an old audience with familiar material and techniques."[1] Pop psychologizing like this, when substituted for critical analysis, is a concomitant of the biographical format that afflicts so much Potter criticism. According to the biographical view, his dramas and fiction merely reconfigure his physically tortured, politically frustrated life. Potter himself may be held accountable for the limitations of his exegetes, because his volubility and often self-indulgent cooperation with the cottage enterprise of biographical readings, even when grudging or cantankerous, has spoiled his critics and made them lazy in matters of interpretation. Complexity and ambiguity, qualities that challenge critics of other authors, appear to repel his. In the first book-length study to buck this trend, Glen Creeber contends—and I enthusiastically agree with him—that "in their desperate desire for consistency and progression, critics have unanimously failed to appreciate the profoundly dialectical nature of [Potter's] work as a whole."[2] Clearly, we need to invest as much attention in Potter's work, on its own terms, as we have expended on the details of his life.

Lipstick on Your Collar, upon closer examination, demonstrates considerably less safety and familiarity in its structure, material, and technique than reviewers like Gilbert would have us believe. *Pennies from Heaven* and *The Singing Detective* are deeply landed, localized in geography and spirit. Arthur Parker is rarely more than a few hours' drive from home, and Marlow doesn't move far beyond his hospital bed; their reveries and memories evolve within tightly circumscribed English ambits. If a world beyond their experience exists, it is not especially material to them. *Lipstick,* on the other hand, invokes a global sensibility, while utilizing fundamentally different dramatic and comic strategies. Unlike its predecessors, it broadly engages the politics of imperialism, organically connecting British colonialism with the same issues of class exploitation that passionately concerned Potter in his earliest pronouncements as a student journalist at Oxford and persisted until *Cold Lazarus.* From the first episode's newsreel footage of a nuclear air raid drill in New York, with its collages of Wall Street and the stock exchange, to the bombardments depicted by the newsreel that closes Episode 6, *Lipstick* unfolds against a background of international capitalism and superpower confrontation. This symmetrical gambit emphasizes that tides of history, breaking upon a farther shore, impact the lives of *Lipstick*'s characters.

Furthermore, *Lipstick* is rarely preoccupied with expressions of authorial and textual reflexivity, a thematic essential of its predecessors. Much of the visual text of both *The Singing Detective* and *Blackeyes* reenvisioned graphic texts authored by their protagonists, but *Lipstick* eschews this most signatory of Potter's conceits. Its merely residual self-consciousness derives from the image of the flickering projector lens that directly meets the gaze of the viewer to open the first episode and close the last. We might justifiably interpret this image as an oblique parody of Vertov's *Man with a Movie Camera* (1929), which, Stam reminds us, had as its primary subject "the laying bare of the mechanisms of film within the social context of a continuum of productive forces."[3] The same theme, I will argue, underlies *Lipstick on Your Collar.* Emphasizing the sense of globalization that broadens the purview of *Lipstick* beyond Potter's previous serials, the opening frame shifts from the recursive image of the lens to an aerial view of Wall Street, heart of the capitalistic "continuum of productive forces." Early on, this series declares its concurrent structural as well as thematic reorientation.

The formal reflexivity of the opening scene of the projector lens parodies itself because, of course, the medium of this series is not cinema, but television. *Lipstick*'s key media metaphors include the cinema and the phonograph record, and to a lesser extent, the wireless. Raymond Williams recounts that in Britain "the full investment in [television] transmission and reception facilities did not occur until the late 1940s and early 1950s, but the growth was thereafter very rapid."[4] He continues, "The enclosed room of the naturalist drama—the world of the private family or group—was exposed, by new techniques, to the public pressures that were seen as determining it. . . . By the mid-1950s, that is to say, by the period in which television drama became the majority form . . . in some ways television was now replacing the cinema as the major dramatic institution."[5] *Lipstick* depicts an historical juncture wherein the emergence of television was a significant development, not least as a mechanism the withering imperial regime utilized to arouse public outrage and mold public opinion during a national crisis. Yet television is so absent in the dystopia of Potter's 1956, one has the impression that it hasn't even been invented. In fact, to the extent that *Lipstick* exhibits any other consciousness of itself as a phenomenon of the gazing or voyeuristic lens, it is only during the "I See the Moon" production number, wherein the gaze of the lens is deflected by a well-aimed squirt of camel shit.

The anti-reflexive bias of *Lipstick on your Collar* resonates with a determination to shape an original neo-socialist aesthetic. The series is not realistic in the colloquial sense but in the Marxist tradition, deploying "that method and that intention which went below this surface to the essential historical movements, to the dynamic reality."[6] More outward-turned and countersubjective in its insistent subversion of its own most subjective scenes, especially the musical ones, *Lipstick* demarcates a significant shift in Potter's technique, contrary to the assumptions of many of his critics that the series merely retreads his traditional concerns. It also displays a renewed urgency in his political voice.

The comparative unselfconsciousness of *Lipstick*'s narrative, given its deferral to such faux-reflexive metaphors as the projector lens, may be linked paradoxically to Potter's belief that television, even at an early stage of its dissemination and development, constituted the electronic collective *un*conscious of the society. Television "expressed English condescensions and the English class system, and was timid and smug at the same time."[7] Hence, for Potter, the phenomenon of television was from its institutional inception a function of the class structure of English society.

In order to equate the principal thematic and visualizing movements of the series, I have arrogated the poetic license to dub its framework of eroticized allusions to the phallus, rectum, sodomy, and excretion as "socialist allegory." Potter choreographed this amalgam of grossly sexual and scatological images into a very funny critique of the last days of British Imperial capitalism. Now, "socialist allegory" is a term I must distinguish from "allegory of socialism," since, as Potter was fond of complaining, there was so little socialism left in Britain to allegorize. The socialist programs of postwar England had been undertaken, he felt, by "a brave and steadfast people" who had shared "an aim, a condition, a political aspiration." He suffered acutely with the deterioration of English socialism under the conservative regimes of the 1980s and early 1990s, declaring that "those five, six years of creating what is now being so brutally and wantonly and callously dismantled was actually a period to be proud of, and I'm proud of it."[8]

But perhaps even more acerbically, Potter's scatological allegories target the American-inspired cultural dead-endedness, and regression into conservatism, that followed Imperial decline. His disdain for mass culture locates

Potter firmly within the socialist critical tradition of Richard Hoggart and Raymond Williams. As Creeber has noted, his work "longs to remember England before its 'Cultural Fall,' a time before it had been soiled and corrupted by an American mass society which had destroyed Britain's own organic and vibrant folk communities. . . . From *Between Two Rivers* (1960) to the posthumous *Cold Lazarus*, his work attempted to dramatise and articulate this paradigm, never straying far from the agenda of the early New Left from which he, Hoggart and Williams had all emerged."[9]

Among the capitalistic conceits exposed by Potter's socialist allegory is the masquerade of imperialism as a genuine collective cultural identity, the subverting of national aspiration by the dead weight of nostalgia, and the vitiation of self-awareness and emotional vitality by rampant commodification. The hierarchy of military authority implicit in the War Room set emphasizes how, as Jameson puts it, "the quality of the various forms of human activity, their unique and distinct 'ends' or values, have effectively been bracketed by the market system, leaving all these activities free to be ruthlessly reorganized in efficiency terms, as sheer means or instrumentality."[10] The young clerks are mere premechanical commodities. The system in which they work reifies and strips their talent of its "immanent intrinsic satisfactions as activity,"[11] and reduces them to means to an end, as vividly illustrated when Major Church derides Francis' translation of Pushkin: "Caterpillar tracks, Francis. Artillery ranges. Calibrations. . . . Those are the words you need in this office. Military words. Not mush."[12] Moreover, Jameson argues, "the reproduction of 'copies' which have no original characterizes the commodity production of consumer capitalism and marks our object world with an unreality and a free-floating absence of 'the referent' (e.g., the place hitherto taken by nature, by raw materials and primary production, or by the 'originals' of artisanal production or handicraft)."[13]

In lieu of this observation Private Francis Francis Francis, with his echolaliac name, is a walking contradiction. A country bumpkin thrust into a megalopolitan nightmare in which he immediately gets lost, Francis incarnates the vestiges of a declining rural proletarian world resistant to mass reification. Unfortunately, his resistance, such as it is, assumes the form of an all but decadent romantic idealism. He does not finally stand the test of his own instrumentalization by his superiors, nor of his urge to possess, re-form and manipulate Sylvia to his own romantic satisfaction. Nonetheless, he is inefficient to the point of pain, as well as late, clumsy, and absentminded. He visibly but impotently resents Major Church's sardonic attempt to package him in distinctly reified terms: "Graceful movements. Superb brain. An economical name."[14] Yet while his problematic constitution recalls Raymond Williams' observation that "the contrast of the country and the city is one of the major forms in which we become conscious of a central part of our experience and

of the crises of our society,"[15] his bookishness imparts a heterodox and dis-
connected urbanity to his rural demeanor. Although Potter has agreed to the
assertion that "all characters, because of their social backgrounds, their aspirations, are perforce political," he also cautions that "if you don't set out to
make them representatives or mouthpieces for this or that ideology or political stance, you retain the possibility of surprising yourself about how complicated they are."[16] And Francis is complicated indeed. His odd, psychically
fragmented combination of rural naivete, romantic idealism and erotic appetite baffles the tough, sexually savvy yet emotionally frustrated Sylvia. The
idealism he has constructed out of his literary interests is so profoundly displaced by his erotic awakening that he resists Corporal Berry's attempt to hu-
manize himself when he apologizes for pushing Francis's head into a toilet. In
Episode 3, while sitting with Berry at the local pub during one of the junior officer's few moments of vulnerability, Berry struggles to express his dissatisfaction with his marriage, but Francis is only capable of "making conversation"[17]
that discloses the whereabouts of Berry's wife, Sylvia, whom he desires. Francis thus reveals that he, no less than those around him, is capable of using his
peers—in this case, manipulating his less intelligent and visibly pathetic colleague toward his own gratification.

As Raymond Williams notes, the modern bourgeois home in the late
1800s "might appear self-sufficient but could be maintained only by regular
funding and supply from external sources, and these . . . had a decisive and
often a disrupting influence on what was nevertheless seen as a separable 'family' project. . . . Already in the drama of the 1880s and 1890s (Ibsen, Chekhov)
this structure had appeared: the centre of dramatic interest was now for the
first time the family home, but men and women stared from its windows, or
waited anxiously for messages, to learn about forces, 'out there,' which would
determine the condition of their lives."[18] Not only does Berry's and Francis's
pub conversation disintegrate during a discussion of family life, but Hopper's
infatuation with Lisa, a beautiful but self-absorbed American bookworm,
founders on his inability to appreciate Chekhov's domestic drama, *The Seagull.* In contrast to both *Pennies from Heaven* and *The Singing Detective,* the
musical numbers in *Lipstick* comment as much if not more on the diegetic
movement of history as they do upon the unconscious desires and anxieties of
the protagonists. Sitting in the theater with Lisa, Hopper distractedly transforms Trigorin's description of the murder of the seagull by an interloper from
"out there" into Fats Domino's "I'm in Love Again."

Several of the series' musical scenes are shared or decentered among the
characters, in a manner that leaves the identity of the generating consciousness
ambiguous. An excellent example is the "Blueberry Hill" number in Episode
2, wherein Hopper and Francis sing alternate verses and both may be equally
implicated in its lyrical themes. Although John Cook bemoans the sacrifice of

the simplicity of *Lipstick*'s precursor, *Lay Down Your Arms,* in the division of its original protagonist into two characters whose attributes complexly "mingle and blur,"[19] this ambiguity is a heuristic project in its own right. As Fredric Jameson reminds us, the kitsch mentality of the bestseller "has tended to produce a quasi-material 'feeling tone' which floats about the narrative but is only intermittently realized by it: the sense of destiny in family novels, for instance, or the 'epic' rhythms of the earth or of great movements of 'history' in these various sagas can be seen as so many commodities towards whose consumption the narratives are little more than means, their essential materiality then being confirmed or embodied in the movie music that accompanies their screen versions."[20] Jameson's subjects read like a catalogue of *Lipstick*'s concerns.

The series' concentric plots and romances, mixing historical and political criticism with cross-class and implied transgendered desires, progressively emphasize the refusal of the bourgeoisie to relinquish either the erotic or the idealized dimension of its insular universe. *Lipstick* represents this anal obstinacy in comically objectified terms, amplified to represent the anxious condition of British society on the eve of the Suez crisis. In the sustaining allegory of the entire work, the rectum displaces the lens as both subject *and* object of the gaze. Bracketed by the opening and concluding images of the flickering projector, the concatenated iconography of ordure and rectum dominates the series from beginning to end. The classical narrative conventions conjured up by "once-upon-a-time," ostensibly the provenance of that magic lens, are preempted by Major Hedges as he pronounces the first line of dialogue of the series: "Bum holes." Gazing into space with an expression at once enraptured and voyeuristic, he continues: "I conjure up for your delectation the image of row upon row of bare arses. A whole choir stall of them."[21] Shortly thereafter, we observe a slender, oily-haired young man in the theater audience in Episode 1 distracted from the screen to gaze at Sylvia's undulating buttocks—a view upon which the camera lingers lasciviously. Similarly, the first comments Francis hears Sylvia utter in response to Aunt Vicki's warning not to slam the door as she enters the foyer of their flat are "And up yours too" and "Kiss mine."[22] Turning to follow her as she ascends the staircase, tight skirt accentuating her buttocks as they again command the center of the frame, his enraptured gaze replicates in posture as well as expression Major Hedges's countenance when he envisioned his choir stall of bums. In turn Aunt Vicki, whose vivacity has been beaten down by her sanctimonious husband Fred, misconstrues "Ah, soul" as "asshole" when he mutters the lyrics of a hymn.[23]

If the human posterior is ubiquitous, its inevitable concomitant, fecal imagery, appears just as frequently. Even Gilbert, in a rare flash of acuity, notes "the constant awareness of bodily function in Potter's writing."[24] Essentially a love story, *Lipstick* has indeed pitched its mansion in the place of excrement; that paradox becomes an essential current of its political satire. Ever the avatar of narrative movement, Hedges is the first to enunciate this motif with his exasperated sigh, "Christ in shitty napkins, what a life."[25] In Episode 2, when Francis recoils from Hopper's disclosure that British agents steal from Soviet army waste buckets old correspondence the Russian troops have used as ersatz bog roll, Hopper responds that their translating job is "all bullshit."[26] This conversation segues nicely into the "Blueberry Hill" set piece, wherein the office is buried under piles of soiled toilet paper and the officers are envisioned relieving themselves behind their desks. In Episode 4, during the "I See The Moon" extravaganza, the young clerks gleefully splatter their officers with handfuls of dung. Shortly thereafter the camel, wheeling its rectum to face the lens, discharges its own commentary on the proceedings. Like the splayed beams of the cinema projector that initiates Episode 1 and closes Episode 6, this stream of camel ordure meets the viewer's gaze head-on, establishing thereby a direct correlation between shit and the projected image itself.

Lipstick's narrative weaves this excretory symbolism intricately among its other motifs. The persistent references to derrieres are erotically bipolar, exploiting not only the paradoxical metonymies of buttocks with heterosexual stimulation and feces, but also, sodomite associations with the rectum. The "Little Bitty Pretty One" set piece confirms our earlier suspicion that Hedges's enraptured vision of bums is at the very least homosocial, a product of barrack showers and military prep school. As the officers salaciously ogle and grope Hopper, and pass him back and forth amongst each other, we are afforded a musical window into Hopper's psyche and his not too deeply repressed anxieties about being sodomized by his superiors. And his officers soon demonstrate that Hopper's fantasies may not be unfounded. Major Church leeringly interpolates himself into Francis's translation of Pushkin's line, "You stood before me like a momentary vision" by responding, with mock salaciousness, "Did I?"[27] Responding to the homoerotic implications of their banter, Hopper imagines Church leaping to his feet to dislodge a fig leaf from his groin and offer it to Francis, as their superiors once again cavort lewdly around the office in the "Garden of Eden" musical number.

This sequence underscores how *Lipstick* transforms into social criticism what had been mainly infrapsychological dramatic materials in previous Potter works. Whereas he had always treated the theme of sexual abuse with acute seriousness, as in *Moonlight on the Highway* or *Hide and Seek,* these musical numbers treat the threat as farce whose real subject is the young clerks' experience of how Imperialist social hierarchies distribute and husband power. In "Garden of Eden," the officers turn kitsch lyrics about love's mystery into a lesson in military obedience through their accusatory gestures and expressions. Their "lecture," as it were, concludes when Hopper's "dream girl" presents Francis with a penis-headed serpent that celebrates the conservation of phallocentric desire by Army discipline.

Having symbolically expelled Francis from innocence, *Lipstick* resurrects the threat of sodomization with augmented intensity during Episode 2, when Brigadier Sanders enters the office. Described in the screenplay as "an elegant, probably even slightly perfumed man with a bad limp and a walking stick,"[28] Sanders negotiates around the legs and prominently protruding buttocks of Francis, who is down on his hands and knees gathering dropped papers from under Church's desk. Sanders suggestively extends his cane toward Francis, forcing the clerk to retreat into a submissive cringe. This action, and Sanders's salacious remarks about "well-scrubbed" young men, inspires a lewd comment from Hedges, which clearly insinuates that Hedges knows something about the general's sexual predilection: "Too well scrubbed, surely." Nevertheless the clerks' horror of buggery is less specifically erotic than a logical extension of their awareness that they are mere objects of utility to the clannish Spartans they serve. As the screenplay describes the aftermath of Sanders's and Hedges's salacious repartee, "Francis sits at his desk . . . too obviously seething with resentment at the impersonal way he is being discussed."[29] Corporal Berry, who occupies a middle ground between the imperious officers and their nervous subalterns, also conflates sexuality with violence when he threatens to stick his "dingaling" into Francis's ear and "shag some sense" into him,[30] a threat he repeats to Hopper a few days later.[31]

Hopper, in contrast to Francis, is the urban quintessence of eroticized efficiency. He incorporates what Jameson describes as "the other-directedness of contemporary conspicuous consumption and of the sexualization of our objects and activities . . . and we consume less the thing itself, than its abstract idea, open to all the libidinal investments ingeniously arrayed for us by advertising."[32] It is no accident, then, that his muse presents the naïve Francis with the snake to conclude "Garden of Eden." Utterly in thrall to the kitsch gratification of rock 'n' roll, he has developed an efficient new form of percussion notation using nothing but dots and U's. But Hopper's system of musical notation, "bum-tit-tit, bum-tit-tit,"[33] also summarizes the oscillation of focus between the young clerks' heterosexual fantasies and their paranoia about their officers' sodomite arrogation. If we remember, though, that each of the musical fantasies in which Hopper envisions himself as a rock 'n' roll star emphasizes his own dreams of sexual predation, it should be no surprise that the process of reification his notational system exemplifies should confabulate sexual and excretory imagery.

In Episode 2, Sylvia also composes her Welsh shepherd fantasy with images of commodity valuation, eroticized utility, and confused sexual identity. Her strange idyll exemplifies the urban imposition of stereotyping on rural lives that Williams argues to be the domestic precursor of foreign imperialism, but it also anticipates—and parodies—her dark twin Lisa's far more intellectualized self-insinuation into the Chekovian fantasy she has built out of *The*

Seagull. Recoiling from her disgusted recollection of the "rub" she transacted with Atterbow for a few quid, Sylvia envisions an idyllic gingerbread cottage from whose lintel she breaks an unmistakably penis-and-scrotum shaped chunk that she promptly bites in half. This scene is suddenly displaced by a shot of Major Hedges, whose façade of jovial cynicism is finally corroded by the pressures of his work. Flinging down his own phallic pen he explodes with frustration, crying "Rectal orifices!" and "Bum holes!" Emotionally spent, he apologizes and resumes his work of preserving the imperial order, whereupon the scenes rapidly shift through Francis's memory of Sylvia being beaten by Corporal Berry back to Sylvia's own ennui-inspired daydream of their storybook cottage, set to the tune of "At the End of my Prayer." Her fantasy vividly recalls Hoggart's observation that, with the subsumption of working class communality into mass culture, "for those whose sense of life is essentially personal, love may perhaps be inflated to fill the gap, may be not merely linked with religion (as in the older songs) but made a substitute for religion."[34] Intellectually prone before the movies and newsreels she must repeatedly watch as an usherette, Sylvia envisions bucolic life with sentimentalized grandeur. Replete with painted backdrops and watercolor sunset, her vision neatly tracks Hoggart's conclusion that such reveries consist in "no more than a vague sense of uplift-going-on, of dawns perennially rising, of great chords sounding some sort of affirmative gesture towards the universe—as in the classic ending on a close-up clinch of the romantic films. . . ."[35]

But Sylvia is not yet finished modeling the hidden machinations of consumer capitalism and grounding her malaise in her economic situation. She explodes her own idyll by expressing disappointment that Francis has fallen just shy of a million pounds return on the sale of his flock. Here, Sylvia purposefully overwrites an erotic utility with a financial one; left unremarked amid her fantasies is the gutter cliché about the Welsh shepherd's erotic attraction to his sheep.

The narrative mingling of economic, erotic, and scatological imagery climaxes, as it were, when in response to Lisa's disclosure that her "philistine" daddy owns Texas oil fields,[36] Francis envisions an oil gusher. The black viscous liquid mixes fecal and semen-al imagery, while at the same time it consummates the threads of socialist critique woven through the drama. No less decisively than Sylvia's subversion of her pastoral idyll, his sudden desire for financial wealth explodes the Platonic standards of romance that Francis has struggled to sustain. Surely, this scene also resonates with England's last meaningful Imperial gasp by gesturing toward the oil fields of the Middle East. The gusher segues into images of British troop ships loading for the futile voyage to Egypt, invoking the cold war paranoia of the newsreel that opened Episode 1. At the same time, the scene anticipates Britain's transition from the colonial model of capitalism that dominates its past, to the American model of financial imperialism, represented by Lisa's family, which will define its immediate future.

With vicious irony, these inferences of the obsession of a dying empire with foreign petroleum usurp the image of the native colliery with which Potter began his earliest documentary. *Between Two Rivers,* given its contrast of puddles and slag heaps with the glittery world of the jukebox, of the proletarian colliery universe with the dead eyed after-hours of mass consumerism, is a truer progenitor of *Lipstick*'s collision between fecal imagery and the tinselly productions of mass culture than either of the two prior musical series most often compared with it. Moreover, the oil gantry erupting from the material earth within Francis's imagination, when he discovers that his would-be beloved is an heiress, underlines the reification of the texts upon which Francis and Lisa base their romantic ideals. Francis concludes the exchange by exclaiming, "Oh, it's so good to have a *real* conversation,"[37] a humorous moment that is both poignant and pathetic. The violent gusher that swamps his imagination upon Lisa's revelation of her family wealth both disrupts and emphasizes the paradox of their exchange of quotations from Hemingway and Nietzsche, two celebrants of predatory masculine eroticism. Ostensibly an attempt to fathom the difference between love and infatuation, their commerce in textual fragments deflects the couple's affections into disjunct bits of unrelated texts just as Francis's dream of wealth reifies his affection and redirects it, atavistically, toward the acquisition of a potential dowry. In terms of human damage, it is the end product of reification, wherein lovers can only struggle to convey emotions by trafficking in shards of their toppled icons. This *reductio* of intimacy consummates Potter's socialist allegory.

Copyright © 1998 by Rick Wallach

NOTES

1. W. Stephen Gilbert, *Fight & Kick & Bite: The Life and Work of Dennis Potter* (London: Hodder and Stoughton, 1995), p.285.
2. Glen Creeber, *Dennis Potter: Between Two Worlds* (London: Macmillan, 1998), p.5.
3. Robert Stam, *Reflexivity in Film and Literature* (New York: Columbia University Press, 1992), p.80.
4. Raymond Williams, *Television: Technology and Cultural Form* (New York: Schocken, 1975), p.29.
5. Williams, *Television*, p.57.
6. RaymondWilliams, "A Lecture on Realism," *Screen* 18:1 (1977): 65.
7. Dennis Potter, *Potter on Potter*, ed. Graham Fuller (London: Faber and Faber, 1993), p.24.
8. Dennis Potter, *Seeing the Blossom: Two Interviews, and a Lecture* (London: Faber and Faber, 1994), p.9.
9. Creeber, p.196.

10. Fredric Jameson, *Signatures of the Visible* (New York: Routledge, 1992), p.10.
11. Jameson, p.11.
12. Dennis Potter, *Lipstick on Your Collar* (London: Faber and Faber, 1993), p.20.
13. Jameson, p.17.
14. Potter, *Lipstick,* p.19.
15. Raymond Williams, *The Country and the City* (New York: Oxford University Press, 1973), p.289.
16. Potter, *Potter on Potter,* p.21.
17. Potter, *Lipstick,* pp.92–3.
18. Williams, *Country,* p.27.
19. John R. Cook, *Dennis Potter: A Life on Screen* (Manchester: Manchester University Press, 1995), pp.295–6.
20. Jameson, p.13.
21. Potter, *Lipstick,* p.2.
22. Potter, *Lipstick,* p.23.
23. Potter, *Lipstick,* p.37.
24. Gilbert, p.30.
25. Potter, *Lipstick,* p.6.
26. Potter, *Lipstick,* p.43.
27. Potter, *Lipstick,* pp.19–20.
28. Potter, *Lipstick,* p.59.
29. Potter, *Lipstick,* p.60.
30. Potter, *Lipstick,* p.15.
31. Potter, Lipstick, p.72.
32. Jameson, p.12.
33. Potter, *Lipstick,* pp.3–4.
34. Richard Hoggart, *The Uses of Literacy* (London: Penguin, 1992), p.229.
35. Hoggart, pp.229–30.
36. Potter, *Lipstick,* p.201.
37. Potter, *Lipstick,* p.200.

CHAPTER 4

"GRASPING THE CONSTELLATION"[1]

Dennis Potter and the Mythologies of Popular Culture

Dave Evans

EILEEN: (*gently*) Nobody ever, ever stops—yearning, Mr. Warner.
HEADMASTER: (*Recovering*) Then they jolly well better had, Miss Everson.
EILEEN: No. I don't think so.[2]

THERE IS A BROAD CONSENSUS AMONG POTTER commentators[3] that *Pennies from Heaven*[4] represents a significant turning point in the styles and techniques and in the popular fortunes of Dennis Potter. This six-part television serial was first transmitted on British TV by BBC1 from 7 March 1978 and attracted 12 million viewers to its first episode. It was repeated within six months and won two British Academy awards. It was, in Cook's words, an "instant classic," and in retrospect "is celebrated as a significant event in British television history."[5]

Following a resumé of the narrative of the serial, I shall review a variety of critical readings of *Pennies* in a synthesis that will attempt to link the piece with some critical moments in Potter's life and work. Such an analysis will, I argue, ascribe to *Pennies* perhaps more significance than has been acknowledged traditionally and will locate it not so much as a turning point in an otherwise linear development of work but rather as an important vantage point from which some of the depths and complexities of Potter the playwright's motivations—political, professional and existential—can be viewed with greater critical clarity.

Two of the initial focal points of the analysis will be, unsurprisingly, Arthur Parker himself and what some might see as the characteristic feature of *Pennies*: the songs with which the serial is replete. More widely, though, an attempt will be made to consider in greater depth, some 20 years on, the "power of the mythologies"[6] with which Potter was dealing. But I turn first to the narrative context in which these mythologies are embedded.

"LOVE IS GOOD FOR ANYTHING THAT AILS YOU . . ."

The year is 1935, the Jubilee year of George V's reign, and England is still emerging from a global economic depression, initiated by the Wall Street crash of 1929. Arthur Parker is a commercial traveler who attempts to make his living traveling the A40 between his suburban London home and Gloucestershire in the West of England, selling sheet music to reluctant shopkeepers. But business is slack and times are hard for Arthur. His wife, Joan, has money (her father's) but she won't part with it easily. And money is not the only thing that Joan won't part with easily. Her sexual distaste and reticence leave Arthur unsatisfied, exasperated and "empty." This is Arthur's "real life"—but not his only life. For the thing about Arthur is that he believes in the songs. . . .

He travels to Gloucester to peddle the sheet music of a new American song, "Roll Along, Prairie Moon" and, en route, picks up a hitchhiker who plays the accordion, busking "wherever two or three . . . busy streets intersect."[7] The hiker tells Arthur that he plays hymns: "That's all I can play, you see. I don't know any other tunes, sir."[8]

In a music shop in Gloucester, Arthur sees a young woman customer who immediately entrances him and, romantic and dreamer that he is, he falls in love with her. He eventually seeks her out on a later trip to Gloucester and inveigles his way into her home. Eileen Everson is an attractive but rather prim, homely and hesitant elementary school teacher who lives in the nearby Forest of Dean with her father and brothers. Eileen is soon taken in by Arthur's charms, attentions and lies, and is ultimately seduced by his tangled web of deceit. Out of pity, she surrenders her virginal body to him on the floor of the Forest cottage.

After his long absence, Arthur reluctantly returns home, where he discovers that Joan has made special efforts to win him back, having been persuaded by one of her friends that Arthur has been playing fast and loose and that she is in danger of losing him. The couple discuss the possibility of setting Arthur up in a gramophone record shop with some of Joan's money and they make love: "A bit of capital and a bit of affection. I told you it was all I needed,"

Arthur reassures her.[9] On his return to Gloucester, he meets a blind girl walking in a field where he has taken a break from his journey.

Eileen, unsurprisingly, finds that she is pregnant, and when this news is shared with Arthur, the true account of his marital status and of his deceit is revealed. But her newly awakened desires allow her to overlook his double-dealing. She is a new woman, released by sexual energy from her former primness.

Her pregnancy, however, leads to her dismissal from the school and ineluctably, to Arthur's disappearance from the scene, leaving Eileen with only a false address. On his journey back to London, Arthur is detained by the police for questioning in connection with the murder of the blind girl whose body has been found in a field off the A40.

Meanwhile, Eileen has left her father and brothers and traveled to London where she finds herself a small room in a cheap hotel. While Joan is reluctantly setting Arthur up in his new shop, Eileen is gradually falling into the clutches of a pimp, Tom, who arranges an abortion for her and sets her up on the game under her professional name of Lulu, in close proximity to Arthur's new gramophone record shop. Before long and of necessity, Arthur and "Lulu" meet and rekindle their sexual relationship back at his shop. Before they leave, they symbolically say their goodbyes to Arthur's entrepreneurial ambitions and begin to smash the gramophone records.

While Lulu's "professional" career provides the couple with shelter, food and an improving lifestyle, Joan has notified the police of Arthur's disappearance and the clues that emerge begin to point toward Arthur's involvement in the blind girl's murder. The accordion-playing hitchhiker who has appeared intermittently throughout the narrative eventually drowns in the Thames, from Hammersmith Bridge, his confessions to the blind girl's murder having been ignored.

Arthur is now a wanted man and he and Eileen steal a car and go on the run. They are caught red-handed by a farmer while making love in his barn, but Eileen manages to shoot and kill the farmer. On the road back to London, Arthur thinks he sees the accordion player hitching a lift and stops the car. A passing police car picks them up, as Arthur prematurely runs away to avoid arrest. Ironically, it is the combination of Arthur's deceitful past and the truths he tells in court that ultimately secure his conviction. He is sentenced to death by hanging. The sentence is duly carried out, but in the closing scenes, Arthur is resurrected and reunited with Eileen on Hammersmith Bridge, just as she contemplates following the Accordion Man's suicidal leap into the Thames.

From what we have come to expect of Potter, this appears at first sight to be an uncharacteristically linear and naturalistic narrative. But then there are the songs . . .

"THEY TELL THE TRUTH, SONGS DO . . ."

The songs play a complex and central role in *Pennies*. In Kenith Trodd's words: "The essence of Dennis's way with the songs was to dislocate us firmly from the entrenched naturalism of television drama."[10] Among other roles, the songs break down the otherwise naturalistic feel of the story line—in Potter's words, "puncturing reality."[11] Even when Potter utilizes other devices—flashbacks and dreamlike sequences—these are typically accompanied, prompted even, by the songs. And of course, the thirties songs are not sung by the actors; they are lip-synched with the original voices from the recordings, irrespective of gender match.

As well as fulfilling this antinaturalistic and alienating function, the songs play an even more significant role for Potter, which will be considered in greater depth toward the end of this essay. In comparing the songs in *Pennies* to the psalms, Potter points out to Fuller that popular songs "are saying the world is other than it is. . . . It's the idea of the world shimmering with another reality. . . . As soon as we start to sing, dance, remember, things are not as they are."[12]

As Peter Ansorge rightly claims, the use of popular music in *Pennies* "inevitably brought a sense of past and present to every scene [and] Potter found a way of dramatizing memory on television that had eluded the majority of his contemporaries."[13] In this way, Potter succeeds in "grasping the constellation" that he has formed between his own era and the thirties and, at the same time, centrally incorporates popular music and popular culture more widely, as valuable and legitimate media for examining basic human yearnings.

Cook argues that it is in the songs of *Pennies* that we can find the optimism of the piece, in opposition to what he regards the pessimism and "repression" of the central narrative[14]—and *Pennies* is seen commonly as one of Potter's most optimistic works. What, then, gives rise to such optimism?

One factor would seem to have been the personal circumstances of Potter's own life:

> 1977 was for Dennis a virtual cocoon of personal satisfaction, comfort and happiness which I doubt he enjoyed before or since in his entire life. . . . From a slightly embittered and reclusive cripple frequently having to endure lengthy periods living under a Cellophane eiderdown, he became for a blissful while a running, jumping and loving adorable human being. In that euphoria he wrote *Pennies*.[15]

For 16 years, Potter had suffered unceasingly from the ravages of psoriatic arthropathy, but in 1977 he went into Guy's Hospital and was treated with what was then seen to be a miracle drug: Razoxane. For a short period, this gave him release from the arthritic pain and psoriatic indignity and suffering that had characterized his existence for so long. In an interview with Cook, Potter recognized 1977 as a turning point: "'77, as they were administering Razoxane and I was at Guy's, I started *Pennies.* I see that as the change."[16]

This change in Potter's health is reflected, too, in attitudinal change reported by him in an interview, prior to the transmission of *Pennies:*

> "No matter what happens, life is all right." But there is some sense in which you can actually assume the ultimate optimism, no matter the degradation, the miseries the world inflicts on you. The final claim is not that it doesn't matter—it matters in your ligaments, your emotions, your betrayals—but that there is some sense of order, a rationality that is sheer optimism.[17]

These words resonate with the experience and responses to them of Arthur Parker and may go some way to explain the apparent optimism that overcame the bleakness and unproductive nature of his life. For Arthur, the rationality that is sheer optimism and the sense of order are to be found in the fantasy world that his songs conjured up for him.

THE IMAGE OF REDEMPTION[18]

Whatever the balance of optimism and pessimism one reads into the serial, the closing scenes, as Cook argues, confirm the piece as optimistic, indeed as redemptive.[19] As Gilbert has it: "like every Potter hero, Arthur is redeemed."[20] Arthur's redemption in the closing scene is far-fetched, unexplained and runs counter to the naturalistic tone of the narrative. But as Arthur explains with a smirk to Eileen: "Couldn't go all through that wivaht a bleed'n 'appy endin' now, could we?"[21]

In his redemption, though, it is sometimes difficult to see *from what* he has been redeemed. In spite of the court's verdict, Arthur knows (and we, the viewers, know with him) that his alibi was genuine and that at the moment the blind girl was being murdered, Arthur was "selling" his copies of "Roll Along, Prairie Moon" to the shopkeeper, Mr. Barrett, in return for Eileen's address. He didn't kill the blind girl, though he may indeed have been touched by her beauty and moved by her blindness. And he may well have really wanted to take off her knickers. But he was innocent of the charge of murdering her.

As Stead argues, "On the face of it, no man deserves to go to the gallows because he asks his wife to paint her nipples and to go without her knickers. Neither would there seem to be a moral case for capital punishment for a man who has an affair, even if he does subsequently abandon the girl."[22] The system finds Arthur guilty and the system, as far as this work of fiction is concerned, is Potter, its author. But it is also Potter who chooses to redeem Arthur from the system's conviction. For all the weakness of the character he

has created, Potter sees in Arthur something worth saving. Arthur may indeed be all the things Potter has accused him of: "an adulterer and a liar and
was weak and cowardly and dishonest"[23]; "simple . . . inauthentic . . . a cork
on the water."[24] But even for Potter, Arthur has some redeeming features:

> There was something that he was responding to, and although it was cheap
> and banal and all those things, he nevertheless had that part of himself which
> was responding to a myth of a kind, which was wanting the world to be other
> than or better than it was, and therefore wanting himself to be other than or
> better than he was.[25]

Arthur believed in the songs and although it may have been his innocent
and naive belief in them that led him into most of his difficulties, it was the
songs that ultimately redeemed him for Potter. Because of Potter's desire for us
to avoid reading television drama, *Pennies* included, in a naturalistic way, we
can suspend our rationality about the anomalous features of the tale. We don't
need to ask why Eileen's murder of the farmer goes unpunished or why
Arthur's execution is followed by his resurrection. Rationality is not enough to
explain these things: " . . . politics, like religion, like love, like almost any important activity I can think of, is not rational in that . . . if it's not rational altogether, then it has no validity, it has no claim upon you . . . but if it's only
rational, then it won't work."[26]

If Potter is right, and we can't afford to read *Pennies* solely from within a
rational discourse, we need to begin to unpack the nature of the myths to
which Arthur may have been responding, if we're to understand what Potter
was trying to get across to the viewer through Arthur's predicament. This
choice of analytical approach seems justified by virtue of Potter's claim that in
Pennies: "it was the power of mythologies, really, that I was dealing with."[27]

Several mythic structures are available for us to examine in *Pennies*. First,
there are the frequent allusions to a fairy tale structure. Second, there are the
readings that encourage us to see Arthur as some form of universal type representing mankind. Third, there are the mythic structures related to religious
and, specifically, Christian, perspectives. Fourth, there are the myths by which
cultural periods (in this instance, the thirties) are representable. And finally
there are those myths that feed Potter's understanding of and attitudes toward
popular culture and its legitimacy.

"FAIRY TALES CAN COME TRUE . . ."

Fairy tales, as Cook argues cogently, are "a powerful ingredient" in Potter's
work.[28] In *Pennies*, there are two such fairy tales that find explicit reference—
Rapunzel and *Snow White*. Each of them is recounted by Eileen to her class of

eagerly listening children and each of them has resonance with aspects of the story line in which they are set.

There are three "installments" of *Rapunzel*.[29] The first describes the Prince's romantic and optimistic rescue of Rapunzel from her incarceration in the tower. This coincides with Eileen's growing realization that the world she inhabits is full of aspects that cause her unhappiness and distress: cruel and overbearing headmasters who physically punish children who talk "out of turn" in assembly and terrorize their charges; boorish and ignorant brothers who take Eileen's domestic work for granted and devalue her professional status; not to mention the lack of a romantic or sexual outlet for her as yet undiscovered yearnings and impulses.

These aspects are part of a context from which she dreams of escaping. Her moments of quality (magical?) time are those spent with her class of children on nature walks in woodland clearings or in the haven of her own classroom, where she can indulge herself and the children in the fantasy and romanticism of fairy tales and express to them (and to us) her dreams of her own fairy tale prince: "It happens sometimes like that, you know. He looked at her and looked at her and decided that no one else in the whole kingdom . . . was sweet enough to be at his side. . . ."[30]

The second "installment" of *Rapunzel*—recounting the Prince's first meeting with the beautiful girl, trapped in her tower—coincides with Arthur's arrival at the forest cottage where Eileen lives with her father and brothers. The dreamlike, or, more accurately, fairy-tale-like mise-en-scène of the events of this key scene from Episode 2 makes quite explicit the links between Arthur's courting of Eileen and the Prince's introduction to Rapunzel. Arthur drives through the Forest of Dean toward Eileen's cottage, lip-synching Al Bowlly's "Dreaming a Dream," just in time to see Eileen rushing away from the cottage to escape a violent scene between her two brothers. As he follows Eileen and approaches her, her voice-over reads excerpts from the *Rapunzel* fairy tale and is accompanied by what the script directions call "classic-style pen and ink drawings of the Brothers' Grimm fairy tale, *Rapunzel,* showing prince watching girl at window of tower in the forest."[31] Arthur startles Eileen as he snaps a dry twig on his approach but begins to calm (and to mystify her) by his explanation of his presence there: "I've been looking for you. . . . I've been looking everywhere for you. Everywhere. . . . You've been in my head, Eileen. And in my heart. In my soul." His true motivation is given away in his opening remarks: "There's a song—like in a song . . . They tell the truth, songs do."[32] What Arthur has been looking for and, it turns out, has now found, is the romantic ideal encapsulated in the songs he loves so well and believes in so fervently.

The final reference to the *Rapunzel* tale comes later in *Pennies* and reflects the harsher realities of the situation in which Eileen now finds herself—her pregnancy that is about to be confirmed and her dawning awareness of Arthur's probable desertion of her. In this episode of the fairy tale, things have started to go wrong for the Prince and Rapunzel, as indeed they appear to have done for Arthur and Eileen. As the Prince climbs Rapunzel's long tresses to reach her at the top of the tower, it is, in fact, the witch he finds. He is told that Rapunzel is lost to him forever and that he will never see her again. He falls from the tower, is blinded, and wanders around in misery, until many years later, he comes across Rapunzel again, with the twins who have been born to her in the meantime. He regains his sight and, of course, they live "happily ever after." As Eileen completes her reading to the class of children, one of them mischievously asks how Rapunzel could have given birth to twins: "Her warn't married, was her, Miss?"[33] The home truth is too painful for Eileen and as the class's embarrassed laughter reaches its peak, she loses her usual classroom demeanor and screams at the children to be quiet.

The second fairy tale employed in *Pennies* is *Snow White and the Seven Dwarves*. This is less predominant than the *Rapunzel* motif but the ambience it helps to create is of a similar kind. There are three instantiations,[34] the first two of which are placed in close juxtaposition to each other in a sequence of scenes in which mirrors play a significant part in the televised version.[35] Halfway through the second episode, while Arthur is away playing Prince to Eileen's Rapunzel, Joan is becoming more agitated and concerned about his lengthy absence. She moves out into the hallway and stands next to a mirror as she rings her friend Irene, seeking company and reassurance. The script tells us that as she ends the phone call, "she puts down the phone, her face grim. Then she looks at herself in the hall mirror. Gingerly, she touches her cheek bones and then the contours of her face."[36] As she does this, Joan pleads that Arthur will not leave her and the camera picks up her distraught and helpless gaze, reflected in the mirror.

At this point, the scene changes to the Forest of Dean classroom where Eileen is teaching Standard One, "orchestrating the 7-times table" as they chant their responses. Satisfied with their performance, she moves on to read them a story: "Seven sevens are forty-nine. But what do seven dwarves make?" As she begins to tell them the tale, the script directions indicate a "sharp cut" to Joan looking at herself in the hall mirror. Again, "gingerly, she touches her cheek bones, and then the contours of her face." In fact, in the televised version, the sharp cut takes us instead to Arthur, shaving in the mirror of his lodging house room and singing (not lip-synching) some lines from "Couldn't be Cuter." Another sharp cut takes us back to Joan, sipping her morning tea in front of the three angled mirrors of her dressing table. As she sips, a voice-over asks: "Mirror, mirror, on the wall, who is the fairest one of all?" The published script tells us (though this is not immediately recognizable from the voice) that it is Eileen's voice that poses the question for Joan.[37] Again, the scene changes, this time revealing (as a reflection in yet another mirror) the breakfast table at Mrs. A.'s lodging house where five commercial travelers (including Arthur) discuss the sorry state of England.

The final reference to *Snow White* is on page 143 of the script. Here, it is used as an ironic term of abuse by one of the regular prostitutes who frequents the bar where Eileen makes contact with the pimp, Tom.

The use Potter makes of these fairy tale references draws upon his own belief that in such fairy tales are encapsulated a number of truths, similar perhaps to those truths that are equally well locked up in the songs. These kinds of truth may, it is true, fail to conform to our understandings of the real or the actual in the world around us, but though rooted in fantasy, romanticism and wishful thinking, they nevertheless resonate with what we intuitively sense to be the way the world might really be, at least on an existential or emotional level.

As a televisual device, the use of fairy tale, as with the use of lip-synched popular, romantic song, allows Potter at once to alienate the viewer from what may seem to be the naturalistic phenomenon of what emerges from the screen, whilst anchoring the same viewer in universal, almost archetypal, known territory where the iconography and the narrativity are familiar and the outcomes predictable.

At the same time, though, Potter (and by implication Piers Haggard, director of the TV *Pennies,* presumably responsible for those adjustments from the script) will not allow us to rest in these charted waters, and the use of the mirror in the scenes discussed above challenges us to consider whether what we are viewing is indeed realistic, or rather merely a constructed reflection seen through a lens or a frame. This is, of course, consonant with Potter's desire to use the grammars of television to arrest and alienate viewers from accepting a naturalistic perception of "reality." He made this clear in an interview with Fuller:

> They used to call [television] "the window on the world," as though you were looking out at reality. And the whole grammar of television is based upon that assumption, that you are just looking at things, and those things are real. But I think television lends itself . . . to a totally non-naturalistic treatment. . . . Non-naturalism and its use of the inside of your head is more likely to remind you about the shreds of your own sovereignty.[38]

Whereas most television shows us the picture in the frame, Potter is here explicitly pointing to "the frame in the picture."[39]

What we appear to have, then, in the combination of the songs and the fairy tales, is an attempt by Potter to do several things for the viewer simultaneously. He tries, first, to challenge the viewer's inclination of seeing the narrative as representative of "reality"—the use of the songs and the fairy tale motifs are too far-fetched to allow for that. As Ib Bondebjerg puts it: "The worlds of the songs and the fairy tales are used metaphorically to contrast and comment on the realistic world, and at the same time they function as a distanciation mechanism or a sort of meta-fictional device."[40] Second, perhaps, the intention is to draw on the cultural memories of at least that part of the audience for whom the songs themselves, and indeed the childhood memories of the fairy tales, may evoke identification and familiarity, so that they are anchored in some deeper cultural meanings. And finally, on an even broader level, the purpose may be to evoke a sense of timelessness in the narrative that attaches a more universal and mythological appeal. In the next sections, the power of two such mythologies will be examined: the timelessness and universal nature of the hero, Arthur and the "cheap form of Christian structure" that Potter claims to have utilized and explored.[41]

ARTHUR AS EVERYMAN:
THE PRESENT AS THE "TIME OF THE NOW"[42]

Arthur may be viewed as one of British television's timeless "heroes" and appropriately, as timeless hero, he appears to have no past—or what there emerges of it is vague and questionable. "If he had any past, he'd lie about it," Potter tells us.[43] Equally, Arthur appears to have no future—his aimlessness and hapless lack of good fortune (and good judgment) traces out for us no clear direction for him other than toward ultimate failure. And although Potter tells us that Arthur lived in the present tense, this "nowness" is virtual and based on fantasy, self-deception and wishful thinking. He refuses to face up honestly and authentically to the harsh economic and emotional realities that surround and impose themselves upon him. What is reality for Arthur are the songs.

Arthur is so completely taken up in his belief in the fantasy world of the songs that he appears to suffer no inner conflict or alienation worthy of Potter's attention:

> He was a cork on the water. You didn't need to see what was below the cork because the cork was always floating on top of it. . . . With other, more complicated characters, who are searching for something else, you need to know why they are searching, where they come from, what they are, what they think, what they believe. Because their beliefs have moral authenticity, even when they lose them or are in despair, they have some idea of what it is like to believe, trust or hope something, as opposed to Arthur, who could actually believe in something given by popular culture like "Roll Along, Prairie Moon." He was simple, and they aren't.[44]

Arthur's inauthenticity represents, for Cook at least, a significant shift away from Potter's previous concentration on what goes on inside people's heads; a blurring of the divide between "spirit" and "flesh" and a concentration instead on the externalized aspects of Arthur's life and existence.[45] Potter, too, makes a similar point in the interview with Graham Fuller, when he indicates that the viewer can't afford to believe the things Arthur says and that the only access to who Arthur really is through what he does and what happens to him.[46]

This timelessness, however, confers on him an almost mythological status resonant, perhaps, of his legendary name. He is Everyman; Adam; Bunyan's Christian even, a universal archetype with whom the viewer can perhaps identify. At the same time, he is not so much a well-drawn, classically heroic characterization, but rather a set of human attributes that, more typically of the modern human condition, involve failure, inadequacy, an anchorless search without success. Fraught with disappointment and frustration, he embodies a loss of direction and a yearning for a shape to one's life. All of these aspects characterize Arthur and allegorically, it may be argued, the existential plight of modern man.

In this sense, Arthur's timelessness locates him in the present "as the time of the now." His "adventure" appeals not just to those who are seeking an heroic tale from the undated, archetypal past, nor even a narrative drawn directly and nostalgically from its contemporary setting of the thirties. (Nor even, as we look back on it now, 20 years later, as a fictive tale that came to our screens in the late 1970s.) Arthur's dilemma still strikes us as contemporary in its relevance, perhaps because it is rooted in the same ordinary emotions, fantasies and yearnings as echo the banalities of our own lives.

"A CHEAP FORM OF CHRISTIAN STRUCTURE"

Graham Fuller, in his introduction to his 1993 edition of interviews with Potter, perceptively asserts that Potter was a "graduate of Sunday school as well as Oxford" and that the structures and metaphors—the mythologies, if you like—that Potter employs in much of his work are frequently taken from the chapel teachings he received as a child.[47] This religious heritage finds ample exemplification in the vocabulary, imagery, structure and mythologies that permeate *Pennies* and that add yet another layer of other-worldliness to that provided by the use of those mythologies we have already considered.

Potter himself admits to this in response to a claim by Fuller that *Pennies* lacks any kind of moral order, in that Arthur is hanged for a crime he did not commit: "No, but he had committed various crimes and it was like a lurid melodrama in that sense. But also, he comes back at the end. It was a cheap form of Christian structure."[48]

The structural dimension Potter has introduced here seems to be little more than the structure of a tale of redemption, as discussed above. Beyond this, close parallels with Christian mythology are not easy to find. To go as far as Gilbert does and see Arthur as a Christ figure (and the accordion-playing tramp as a John the Baptist figure) is perhaps to press the parallel too far.[49] But there are, admittedly, many features of *Pennies* that might be interpretable as deriving from a Christian allegorical intention.

Arthur Parker and Eileen Everson's names, for example, may suggest to some an initial reference to Adam and Eve (choice of names frequently seem to be significant to Potter, though it is not always easy to detect the nature of their significance). More than once, Potter seems to imply a resonance between the Forest of Dean and the Garden of Eden. There is explicit reference made to the Garden of Eden by Eileen's headmaster, Mr. Warner, when, in gently dismissing her from her teaching position because of her pregnancy, he propounds his own educational ideology. He pursues a harsh regime of schooling, he says, so that the children will "learn enough to keep a job down the pits. What do they want with visions, or trees shaped like diamonds? Or any memory of the Garden of Eden? Cheap music will do, cheap music. And beer. And skittles."[50] Life, he goes on to explain, is dreadful unless you obey the rules. And if you question the rules, as happened in the Garden of Eden, you have to pay the price.

Arthur, too, makes implicit references to the Garden of Eden, or more specifically to Paradise, when, in different contexts, he makes clear what the two main components of paradise are for him: sexual fulfilment and the promise of happiness offered by the songs. As the first episode closes, we find Arthur and Joan in bed, their unsatisfactory lovemaking over. Arthur tries to persuade Joan that "it" is not meant to be a duty (as presumably, Joan has convinced him by her performance that she thinks it is): "It—it's supposed—Joan. Joanie? Angel? It's paradise. It's supposed to—like in the songs and, and . . ."[51] Arthur yearns for a romantically and sexually satisfying, paradisiacal consummation. He fails to achieve this with Joan but sees the promise of fulfilment in his new relationship with Eileen, as he reveals to his fellow commercial travelers over breakfast in Episode 2.

Potter paints a starkly contrasting picture in this scene between the undiluted commercialism (appropriate to their trade) of the commercial travelers on the one hand and Arthur's newly instantiated romantic idealism on the other. It is their commercialism that prevents them from seeing the bigger truths conveyed by the songs. Or is it the songs and his belief in them and what they stand for that prevent Arthur from facing up to the commercial realities facing him? No. For Arthur, the truth is in the songs: the patch of blue sky, the gold of the dawn, the light in somebody's eyes—the Pennies from Heaven. And his colleagues (and the rest of the world) can't see them "clinking and clinking, all around, all over the place."[52] They cannot grasp the constellation of beautiful, paradisiacal, wonderful things that Arthur can envisage through the songs and yearns for.

In examining the mythologies we have considered here—the fairy tales; the character of Arthur as emblematic of a timeless Everyman, "waiting for the viewer to project onto him"[53] the cheap form of Christian structure—what Potter appears to have done is bring together a range of catalysts to evoke a pastiche of broad cultural memories that engage and yet, in combination, challenge the viewer in what otherwise could be seen as a fairly traditional and uncharacteristically linear narrative structure.

What Potter also succeeds in doing, not only in *Pennies* but also, later, in *The Singing Detective* (1986) and in *Lipstick on Your Collar* (1993), is to conjure up a nostalgic sense of particular periods of cultural "history" that coincide with the first decades of his own life. In his chapter entitled "Serials with Songs," Fuller describes these three works as forming "a trilogy about the mediating effects of popular culture in, respectively, thirties, forties and fifties England."[54] But Potter is not attempting to present us with historically accurate documentaries of these decades. Rather, he sets his serials in a "past that has been cannibalized and transformed into the workings of the head."[55]

MEDIATING THE THIRTIES
THROUGH POPULAR CULTURE

In their excellent analysis of *Pennies* that constitutes part of their "exploration of the relationship between history and fictional representation," John Baxendale and Christopher Pawling analyze the strategies that Potter employs in "revisiting the Thirties as a site of historical memory."[56] They do not share with Purser[57] the "stumbling block" of reading Potter's portrayal of 1935 England as insubstantial, but rather they see *Pennies* as much as an allegory as it is an attempt at realistic representation—an allegory that "sets out to explore the 'myths' of the period as much as the objective reality."[58] Purser admits as much himself but perhaps inadvertently: "Potter's objective England of 1935 is not really any more substantial than the dream world of the songs. It is drawn not from life but from superficial associations with which the Thirties are lumbered."[59]

Such lumber of superficial associations is the stuff of myths and the stuff with which Potter is dealing. He could hardly be expected, even if he had wanted to, to have drawn a portrayal of the thirties "from life," since by the time he was born, the thirties—at least as a decade of historical time, if not as a cultural construction—was halfway through. But the associations he deals in are seen by Baxendale and Pawling as "a set of representations which activate

the cultural memory of the viewer and the meaning of the drama is the outcome of a creative dialogue between text and audience."[60]

At the center of these associations are the songs. In *Pennies*, Potter uses the
songs as emblems of the past to draw out a range of emotions, memories and
yearnings that, while not attempting to represent the past historically, as they
might if they were merely nostalgic, nevertheless allow the audience to share
in the emotions, memories and yearnings they themselves may experience in
the present. As Potter put it to Alan Yentob in 1987: "I've used the immediate
past to intrude upon the present, so that it isn't a thing out there, the past,
which is done with, it is actually running along beside us now, and its misconceptions and its values and its correct conceptions can be seen just that degree
more clearly . . . just simply letting that time be in order to show what this time
is like."[61]

What is surprising (as Baxendale and Pawling and also Creeber point out)
is that Potter chose to employ "those sickly and sugared old tunes"[62] as the
significant mediating aspects of the mythologies he wanted to investigate in
Pennies. As Creeber argues, popular cultural forms held a profound fascination for Potter throughout his career and yet his attitude toward them was ambivalent.[63] Creeber charts eloquently not only the antipathy that Potter
repeatedly evidenced throughout his early career against the commercialization, Americanization and degradation of postwar English culture. He also
suggests the Leavisite, Orwellian and Hoggartian influences in Potter's political and intellectual development that presumably fueled this antipathy, quite
probably while he was immersed in the elitist context of the Oxford of the
fifties.

But by the time *Pennies* was written, I believe there is a case to argue
that this ambivalence had begun to resolve itself and that Potter had begun
to view popular culture in a clearer and less judgmental light, shifting his attentions and attacks rather toward the "occupying powers" against whom
he vituperated so acerbically in his James MacTaggart Memorial Lecture of
1993.

In the concluding part of this essay, I want to argue that *Pennies* represents
a particular kind of turning point in Potter's attitude and approach to popular
culture: a platform from which we can look back at his earlier work with more
clarity and also view what followed *Pennies* in a sharper analytical light.

THE WORLD IS OTHER THAN IT IS

In an interview with John Wyver in March 1978, Potter talked about the six
new plays that constituted *Pennies:* "I don't think these plays are like anything
that I've done before, on the surface, in their apparent structure and texture.

But I think the plays do explore some of the same territory, or try to. In particular, what actually goes on in your head when you perceive your desires through the filter of what is the general culture."[64]

This was not by any means the first time Potter had admitted to the power of "general" popular cultural forms in offering the human subject the possibility of making sense of the world or of finding meaning in it. As early as 1960, in *The Glittering Coffin,* Potter had, albeit begrudgingly, indicated his realization that popular culture had a significant role to play: "Somehow we are able to discern that a great deal of that which is true and valuable in traditional working-class culture is still reflected in the slicker, cheapened 'pop' culture, however obliquely, however much like a ray of light shining through a filthy window."[65]

His concern here was with "the central problem of our culture" as he perceived it to be in 1960: the gap and the lack of contact between the popular cultural forms that were gaining increasingly widespread influence in the postwar decades and the "other artificial brand" of culture (the more '"superior"' and elitist sort "relayed to minority audiences by the B.B.C.'s Third Programme").[66]

From the initial onset of psoriatic arthropathy in 1962 and Potter's almost simultaneous disillusionment with and rejection of a political career, it appears that his ambitions came to be related precisely to making the attempt to bridge this cultural gap. By utilizing the medium of television drama, he yearned for "a possibility at least of a common culture,"[67] making the art form he was engaged in accessible to the anonymous and classless television-viewing public. Throughout his early career, though, his ambivalence toward the popular forms remained.

By 1978, however, he was able to reveal to John Wyver his acceptance of the power and legitimacy—even the essentially politically subversive nature—of the ordinary, commonplace things of people's everyday lives; of the banal:

> And I think it's only when we play football, or act or sing or dance or make love that we actually disrupt their categories and we can start to get that sort of vague feeling . . . like Arthur says, "If life could only be like the songs." That is the remark of a stupid man, and yet I believe it is a fundamentally true yearning.[68]

This yearning is the desire that the world shall be a sweet or perfect or whole place. In *Pennies,* it is personified in Arthur Parker who was responding through the songs to a popular cultural myth that "although it was cheap and banal and all those things," it nevertheless was wanting "the world to be other than or better than it was."[69]

As Creeber puts it:

Potter's work paradoxically presents popular culture (despite its banal commercialism) as fulfilling an inherent need within the human subject to transcend the basic realities and inequalities of everyday life. Where once those utopian aspirations and dreams were channelled through an older working-class tradition or through religious or quasi-religious narratives and images, they are now firmly claimed by the commercial forces of contemporary culture.[70]

In *Pennies,* this shift in Potter's loyalties and concerns is well expressed in the competing (some would say complementary) characterizations of Arthur and the Accordion Man. But where Creeber sees this as portraying the "continual conflict between mass culture and folk art," it can also be interpreted as a conflict within Potter himself, which finds its resolution in *Pennies.*

In his James MacTaggart Lecture he describes how, in the early sixties, the onset of his illness gave him the opportunity of "making (himself) up all over again" and of giving him "what I have to call a sense of vocation."[71] It seems likely that his first, partial release from that illness in January 1977 gave him a new opportunity for re-assembly and that what emerged was a more optimistic, open-ended and all-embracing perspective.

Pennies is indicative of a renewal of Potter's vocation: a renewal that led on to fresh bursts of creativity, which gave rise to *Blue Remembered Hills* (1979), *The Singing Detective* and all that followed. This later Potter is marked by a greater readiness to give a central and positive role to the power of popular culture and to embrace more fully a range of forms including serialization and film: "grasping the constellation," as it were, of the full spectrum of cultural activity; of the pennies from heaven that clink all around us.

NOTES

1. This phrase is borrowed from the penultimate paragraph of Walter Benjamin's "Theses on the Philosophy of History" in Benjamin, *Illuminations* (London: Fontana, 1973), p.265. I am indebted to John Baxendale and Christopher Pawling's use of the phrase in their *Narrating the Thirties—A Decade in the Making: 1930 to the Present* (Basingstoke: Macmillan Press, 1996), p.8, which first drew my attention to Benjamin's ideas, and further provided me with much food for thought that I hope has been developmental in the analysis I put forward in this essay.

2. Dennis Potter, *Pennies from Heaven* (published scripts) (London: Faber and Faber, 1996), pp.118–119.

3. For example, John R. Cook, *Dennis Potter: A Life on Screen* (Manchester: Manchester University Press, 1995); W. Stephen Gilbert, *Fight and Kick and Bite: The Life and Work of Dennis Potter* (London: Hodder & Stoughton, 1995); Peter Stead, *Dennis Potter* (Bridgend: Seren, 1993).

4. This essay will concern itself only with the original, six-part television version of *Pennies from Heaven* that was first transmitted on British TV (BBC-1) between 7 March and 11 April 1978. The scripts were made available in published form by Faber and Faber in 1996. I shall not comment on the MGM/Hera film production that was released in 1981, accompanied by a Potter novelization of the movie script that was published by Quartet Books, also in 1981. For convenience, I shall adopt the normal convention of abbreviating the full title of the serial to *Pennies*.

5. Cook, p.171.

6. Dennis Potter, *Potter on Potter*, ed. Graham Fuller (London: Faber and Faber, 1993), p.88.

7. Potter, *Pennies from Heaven* (published scripts), p.11.

8. Potter, *Pennies from Heaven* (published scripts), p.14.

9. Potter, *Pennies from Heaven* (published scripts), p.97.

10. Kenith Trodd, introduction to *Pennies from Heaven* (published scripts) (London, Faber and Faber, 1996), p.xi.

11. Fuller (ed.), p.86.

12. Fuller (ed.), p.86.

13. Peter Ansorge, *From Liverpool to Los Angeles: On Writing for Theatre, Film and Television* (London: Faber and Faber, 1997), p.67.

14. Cook, p.181.

15. Trodd, p.xiii.

16. Cook, p.165.

17. Dennis Potter, interview with John Wyver, quoted in Gilbert, p.240.

18. "Our image of happiness is indissolubly bound up with the image of redemption" (Benjamin, p.265).

19. Cook, p.181.

20. Gilbert, p.240.

21. Potter, *Pennies from Heaven* (published scripts), p.247.

22. Stead, p.97.

23. Fuller (ed.), p.88.

24. Fuller (ed.), p.84.

25. Fuller, (ed.), p.88.

26. Dennis Potter, "Paradise, Perhaps," interview with John Wyver, *Time Out*, 3–9 March 1980, p.12.

27. Fuller (ed.), p.88.

28. Cook, p.137.

29. Dennis Potter, *Pennies From Heaven* (published scripts), pp.51–52, 59–60 and pp.97–99 respectively.

30. Potter, *Pennies from Heaven* (published scripts), p.52.

31. Potter, *Pennies from Heaven* (published scripts), p.59.

32. Potter, *Pennies from Heaven* (published scripts), p.60.

33. Potter, *Pennies from Heaven* (published scripts), p.98.

34. A fourth, perhaps minor, reference appears on p.78 of the published script where Joan recovers from the experience of receiving an obscene phone call.

35. The sequence of scenes differs from this in the published script.
36. Potter, *Pennies from Heaven* (published scripts), p.62.
37. Potter, *Pennies from Heaven* (published scripts), p.63.
38. Fuller (ed.), p.30.
39. Dennis Potter, "Realism and Non-naturalism 2." Paper presented at the 1977 Edinburgh International Television Festival, published in *The Official Programme of the Edinburgh International Television Festival 1977*, August 1977, p.37.
40. Ib Bondebjerg, "Intertextuality and Metafiction: Genre and Narration in the Television Fiction of Dennis Potter," in *Media Cultures: Re-appraising Transnational Media*, eds. M. Skormand and K. C. Schroder (London: Routledge, 1992), p.17.
41. Fuller (ed.), p.88.
42. Again, this phrase is from the penultimate paragraph of Benjamin, "Theses," p.265. It strikes me as highly reminiscent of Potter's delight in "the nowness of everything," a phrase he luxuriated in during his remarkable interview with Melvyn Bragg, first broadcast on Channel Four on 5 April 1994 and published in Dennis Potter, *Seeing the Blossom: Two Interviews and a Lecture* (London: Faber and Faber, 1994), p.5.
43. Fuller (ed.), p.82.
44. Fuller (ed.), p.84.
45. Cook, p.173.
46. Fuller (ed.), p.84.
47. Fuller (ed.), p.xiv.
48. Fuller (ed.), p.88.
49. Gilbert, p.240.
50. Potter, *Pennies from Heaven* (published scripts), p.116.
51. Potter, *Pennies from Heaven* (published scripts), p.40.
52. Potter, *Pennies from Heaven* (published scripts), p.69.
53. Gilbert, p.240.
54. Fuller (ed.), p.80.
55. Fuller (ed.), p.85.
56. Baxendale and Pawling, pp.171–172.
57. Philip Purser, "Dennis Potter," in *British Television Drama*, ed. George W. Brandt (Cambridge: Cambridge University Press, 1981), p.187.
58. Baxendale and Pawling, p.172.
59. Purser, p.187.
60. Baxendale and Pawling, p.173.
61. Dennis Potter, interview with Alan Yentob, first transmitted *Arena*, BBC-2, 30 January 1987. Published in Potter, *Seeing the Blossom*, p.67.
62. "Would someone with a hard face please protect me from those sickly and sugared old tunes?" was how Potter summed up his ambivalent attitude to the popular songs of the thirties during his James MacTaggart Memorial Lecture, "Occupying Powers," delivered at the Edinburgh International Television Festival, 27 August 1993. Published in Potter, *Seeing the Blossom*, p.43.
63. Glen Creeber, *Dennis Potter: Between Two Worlds: A Critical Reassessment* (Basingstoke: Macmillan, 1998), p.110.

64. Potter, "Paradise, Perhaps," p.12.
65. Dennis Potter, *The Glittering Coffin* (London: Gollancz, 1960), p.121.
66. Potter, *The Glittering Coffin*, p.122.
67. Potter, interview with Alan Yentob, *Seeing the Blossom*, p.65.
68. Potter, "Paradise, Perhaps," p.13.
69. Fuller (ed.), p.88.
70. Creeber, p.117.
71. Potter, "Occupying Powers," *Seeing the Blossom*, p.50.

CHAPTER 5

"CORNUCOPIA OF TINSEL"

Dennis Potter and the Culture of Advertising

Eckart Voigts-Virchow

MAPPING THE FIELD: CULTURE AND CONSUMERISM

IN 1977, WHEN DENNIS POTTER LEFT BRITAIN for the first time, he wrote about
New York:

> The presence of money and the lack of it are the two poles between which the
> city turns and preens and cowers. . . . the shop windows like great cool caves
> full of wonder, it was impossible not to feel that this was an alluring, earthly
> version of Paradise—a mock semblance of heaven. . . . You felt both exhila-
> rated and ashamed, free to be anything and yet trapped for ever in a cornu-
> copia of tinsel. A swanky, vulgar city of endless display and cruelty. . . . If New
> York is the most likely vision of the future we must learn to be more alone,
> more aggressive, more callous, more greedy and more vulgar than at any time
> since we were in the playpen.[1]

Despite self-confessed xenophobic tendencies, it is less anti-Americanism
than a British tradition of cultural skepticism that prompts Dennis Potter to
view New York as symptomatic of a society in which public relations have de-
teriorated to "PR." Time and again, Potter has attacked an Americanized,
mass-mediated trend toward a globalized and homogenized ubiquitous culture
of commercialism recently termed (with the flavor of Orwellian newspeak)
"Adcult" by James B. Twitchell.

In Potter's *Where the Buffalo Roam* (1966), it is the movie-induced
Western myth that causes the disorientated youngster Willy Turner to turn

schizophrenically into the revolver-toting Shane and into a triple murderer. In *The Bonegrinder* (1968), Potter gives the United States the ugly face of Sam Adams, who, "smelling the blood of an Englishman," allegorically challenges Britain, which is impersonated by George King. A similar constellation may be found in the 1983 stage play *Sufficient Carbohydrate*, in which the Englishman Jack Barker is confronted with the American Eddie Vosper, who threatens him with surrogate food, professional efficiency and sexual power. In *Blackeyes* (1989), Potter wages war on the advertising world, through which a towering Uncle Sam figure stalks around, while in *Cold Lazarus*, multinational corporations corrupting both science and England are personified in the California-based David Siltz and Martina Matilda Masdon. While the blandness of the lyrics in bygone decades of popular song is gilded by their connection with Potter's own youth, in his images of advertising one may see a crass indictment of a culture gone to the Murdochian dogs.

Potter's various declarations of war reiterate a paradigm that has metamorphosed from the Romantics' quest of individual expression in the nineteenth century. Reactions to the disintegration of a common culture were clearly delineated by class distinction in Matthew Arnold's *Culture and Anarchy*, and then through various modernist, socialist and Marxist guises, such as F. R. Leavis's and Denys Thompson's *Culture and Environment*, the English culturalists Richard Hoggart and Raymond Williams, and the Frankfurt School Marxists. I do not wish to erase the obvious differences in the remedies suggested for this cultural decline—from paternalism through nostalgic reversal to class war or other changes in education. At least in terms of analyzing a society in the grip of mass culture, however, the championing of modernism by the Frankfurt School is not very far from the paternalist culturalist, moralizing humanist or elitist modernist views of culture. The similarities are obvious in the deeply entrenched cultural skepticism and the binary approach to culture.

Potter's quest is to a large extent based on the humanist nineteenth-century struggle against materialism. He is Arnoldian in his skepticism of contemporary culture and in his diagnoses of the time as diseased, and the working classes as corrupted—not, however, by an anarchy resulting from a lack of culture (as Arnold has it), but by lethargy resulting from overexposure to the culture of advertising. Like Arnold, he maintains that we are to get "our friends and countrymen to seek culture, to let their consciousness play freely round their present operations and the stock notions on which they are founded";[2] in other words, to pursue a kind of "total perfection," not of individuals, but the society at large through cultural activity, to be arrived at by employing the (once) powerful medium of national broadcast television. Potter is Leavisite in his nostalgic view of a culture uncorrupted by commercial interest, in seeing cultural activity debased and standardized in the marketplace by machine media such as films, broadcasting and newspapers, and especially advertising.[3] As late as 1973, in *Discrimination and Popular Culture*, Denys Thompson reiterated the points that had been made for decades:

> Young people are issued with a culture package that exploits any elements of a genuinely popular music and poetry there be. Such a manipulation ought to be prevented. . . . For example the power of advertising especially should be curtailed, hostile as it is to the education of the young and far too influential in agenda-making for adults through its effects on films, television and the printed matter that carries it.[4]

Potter sees an "entropy of culture under an alien rule" and "a people only half conscious of their 'subjection'."[5] His cultural diagnosis is, of course, to a large extent that of Richard Hoggart's *The Uses of Literacy* in the mid-fifties. Hoggart equates a "poorer kind of classless" culture with a "faceless" one:

> Most mass entertainments are . . . full of a corrupt brightness, of improper appeals and moral evasions. . . . they tend towards a view of the world in which progress is conceived as a seeking of material possessions, equality as a moral levelling, and freedom as the ground for irresponsible pleasure. These productions belong to the vicarious spectators' world; they offer nothing which can really grip the brain or heart. They assist a gradual drying up of the more positive, the fuller, the more co-operative kinds of enjoyment. . . . [6]

Communities have been dissolved into a "flickering illusion of communality"[7] and collapsed into the category of the individual.

Potter reflects the critique of advertising from such diverse quarters as John Berger's *Ways of Seeing,* J.K. Galbraith's *The Affluent Society,* or Christopher Lasch's *The Culture of Narcissism,* but also very palpably the culture-conscious neo-Marxist Frankfurt School, most of all probably Leo Löwenthal and Herbert Marcuse. In Adorno or Marcuse, popular culture is the means that, in a climate of affluence and consumerism, incorporates the masses into the capitalist system. Again, true needs of creativity and autonomy are pitted against false needs, which are generated and vicariously satisfied by a consumerism crucial to capitalism's need to generate markets for its ever-increasing mass production. Potter also echoes Raymond Williams, who diagnoses a "weakening of purposive social thinking"[8] as a direct consequence of the experience of advertising. Williams criticizes advertising in which "objects are not enough but must be validated in fantasy by association with social and personal meanings which in a different cultural pattern might be more directly available."[9] In 1961, Leo Löwenthal states that a "product of popular culture has none of the features of genuine art, but in all its media popular culture proves to have its own genuine characteristics: standardization, stereotype, conservatism, mendacity, manipulated consumer goods." Popular culture is advertising in the sense that "the products themselves eventually take on the character of advertising."[10] Elaborating this point, Williams argues that on television there is an "organic relationship between the commercials and other kinds of material." Ads determine "the character of a dominant culture, in which needs and satisfactions are mediated, over a wide range, in terms of commodities. . . ."[11] Look "more closely at the programmes in which these commercials are embedded and even much of the fare on BBC, where there are apparently no commercials at all, and you still get the distinct impression that something is being *sold*," echoes Potter, and introduces the well-known concept of an amorphous occupying power that colonizes our culture.[12] In this light, it seems logical that in his later plays Potter abandoned the technique he employed in 1972 in *Follow the Yellow Brick Road* of reenacting the artificial graphic separation of his fictitious ads from the other levels of discourse.

Dennis Potter parts company with Arnold, who gave up on the masses and recommended authority against a working class culture he could not see other than "raw and half-developed";[13] with the Leavisites, who upheld a minority culture against mass civilization; with Adorno, who declared modernist art autonomous from the material presence of late capitalism. He seeks to reunite the potentially disintegrative social and ideal poles of Raymond Williams's concept of culture—for dons and coal miners. Commentators who see Potter primarily as a postmodernist may convincingly realign him with new humanism and an ethics of *Bildung*,[14] but others have articulated the need to historicize Potter,[15] or to locate him firmly within the British tradition of opposition against the detrimental effects of industrialization connected with the names of Thomas Carlyle, Frederick Denison Maurice, or Charles Kingsley as a "Christian Socialist," albeit "with a running edge of apocalyptic disgust."[16] Of course, to Potter, the Christian Socialist, advertising is both the Antichrist and the Arch-Capitalist. And it is from both Christianity and socialism that Potter derives the obligation to fight the "suffocatingly dead materiality of things"[17] in defiance of prevalent cultural skepticism. Potter's purchasable products, whether on the video shelves, selected as pay-per-view, or separated by ad breaks in transmission, still seek an ironical "redemption of faith" against a "redemption of purchase."[18] Potter continually pits his attempts to retrieve an intact Hoggartian working class culture, derived from sounds and images of his youth in the Forest of Dean, against a mass culture dominated by ubiquitous consumerism. And yet, even his disdain of New York quoted above entails the opposite story, a story that tells us not just about cornucopias of tinsel, but also about earthly versions of Paradise. Notably in *Lay down Your Arms* (1970) and *Lipstick on Your Collar* (1993), Potter attaches value and redemptive power to rock 'n' roll, jukebox cafés, petticoats and permissive sexuality as signs of a change in the cultural climate from the stuffy class-ridden England beset by dusty Empire fantasies to a more Americanized and free youth culture.

Discussions of mass culture are essential in nearly all of Potter's works, from the sixties' *Alice* and the *Nigel Barton Plays* through to the cathartic pulp fiction of *The Singing Detective* (1986) and his trilogy of metamusicals, in which one may find a recontextualized reversal of the MTV aesthetics.[19] In *The Singing Detective*, Potter's picture redresses Hoggart's view of gangster-fiction writing that is "in a large measure dead, full of trite simile, weak imitation of tough American talk, and flatly photographic description," with tentatively conceded "crude force" that has "in parts a kind of life."[20] Potter extends Hoggart's faith in more positive enjoyments to exactly the kind of "typical radio dance-music and crooning" that has, as Hoggart laments, replaced the traditional club-singing.[21] On the same impulse, Potter rejects Adorno's view that "music standardization is pseudo-individualization."[22] He echoes Hall and Whannel's claim that pop songs "dramatize authentic feelings." Potter also seems to agree with their final indictment that much of the popular music is "not very good."[23] In employing songs as complex narrative instruments, however, he implicitly opposes Hall and Whannel's verdict. It should also be noted that Potter's personalized popular objets trouves are targets in a bygone cultural war—Al Bowlly's music imbued with the hope of redemption is less provocative to Potter's viewers than more contemporary vehicles of advertising insipidity.

While creating texts that in their complexity and richness reflect the influence of semiotics and structuralism, and provide a field day for such a reading, Potter rejects the theoretical framework of structuralism, semiology and post-structuralism altogether—not because he thinks semiology is milk pudding,[24] but because it denies his neo-Romantic, humanistic ideal of individuality. For the same reason, he poses as popular culture's and mass media's chief philistine, waging war against the excesses of high modernism and its academic life-support machinery.[25]

ADVERTISING VS. CREATIVITY

Advertising is a natural antagonist to Potter as socialist (in that it seeks to spread capitalist consumption), as Christian (in that it preaches a rival gospel of salvation), as humanist (in that it teaches an antieducational curriculum), and as artist (in that it claims to aestheticize commodities). Drawing the working classes away from rallies and agitation, commercialism imbues them with a false consciousness; drawing Christianity out of the chapels, it commodifies belief; drawing idealism out of human beings, it materializes morality; enslaving the arts under the yoke of salability, it corrupts and compromises free expression. While addressing advertising in almost every one of his plays, Potter makes his critique most explicit in *Follow the Yellow Brick Road* (1972), *Double Dare* (1976), *Blackeyes* (1989), and *Cold Lazarus* (1996).

In all of these works, Potter juxtaposes creativity and its corruption in advertising; in other words, he posits the idea of an autonomous intrinsic self versus a manipulable extrinsic self.[26] Whereas ads provoke human beings to consume, Potter offends them to make them act as human beings. He intends form to follow function; whereas in ads form is to follow value. In *Follow the Yellow Brick Road,* this conflict is located in the paranoid out-of-work actor Jack Black, at the same time a material, ideological and mental victim of the culture industry. As an indication of his paranoia, he feels he is being followed by the camera of a left-wing TV playwright bent on exposing his false utopia built from a view of the world that is contaminated by the commercials he has acted in. The central metadramatic irony is that his paranoia is not unfounded, but an "appropriate" reaction to the filming of Potter's play.

Follow the Yellow Brick Road exposes the materialistic ideology of advertising, which tries to persuade us "that we can achieve certain desirable goals in life through possessing things in a cycle of continuous and conspicuous consumption."[27] Potter uses both characterization and the formal device of incorporating fictitious mock ads in a secondary discourse of flashbacks and fantasies. Jack Black painfully experiences the consequences of falling prey to consumerist ideals: his paranoid hatred of the TV establishment brings him impotency, mental anguish and physical pain; as a result, his wife betrays him with his agent Colin; the girl at the center of his visions of purity, the agent's wife Veronica, turns out to be corrupted with infantile materialism; his pain and paranoia eventually make him attempt to murder his wife. Colin and Veronica, on the other hand, are a cardboard couple of "one-dimensional men" in a bourgeois nightmare of commodification exemplified by luxurious apartments, designer TV sets, excessive cooking, decadence in the form of moustaches, pet dogs fed with wafers of mint chocolate, and, of course, cynicism, arrested development, and casual sex. The iniquity of an uncaring old-fashioned NHS doctor in his practice is contrasted with an anodyne that consists in a combination of psychiatric drugs and the objectified fantasies of the commercials. In relentless irony, Potter has Black star in an ad for the psychiatric drug Mogabrium:

> *(Jack, in white coat and earnest spectacles, holds up his pretty phial of capsules. He speaks from the epistle to the Philippians with the eye-snapping, hard-sell telly-ad voice known to us all.)*
> JACK *(Brisk)* Whatsoever things are true, whatsoever things are honest, whatsoever things are lovely.— ... Whatsoever things are of good report, if there be any virtue, and if there be any ... *(He dries.)* Oh, shit! Sorry everybody![28]

In this characteristically inadequate rendering of religion as cultural anesthetic, Potter expresses his view of advertising as a surrogate religion, which is at the heart of his attitude toward the commercial world and stock-in-trade of analyses of advertising. Indeed, Stuart Ewen has argued that the mass media reinvest "the every day lives of formerly everyday people with a magical sense of value, a secularized input of the sacred."[29] According to Ewen, the idiom of the marketplace is style, the word that Potter hated, especially when applied to his plays.

It has been argued that rather than selling consumer goods, ads terrorize us, hijacking our shortcomings and ideals, and holding them ransom. We pay with loss of real identity, our sense of belonging, and buy an imaginary *Ersatz*.[30] Potter's Jack Black is a case in point. Acting in and buying the surrogate world of consumer goods, he insists on praising the moral standards, cleanliness and happiness in the ads, while his social relationships disintegrate. It is while he is busy acting in the "Waggytail Din-Din" ad that his wife betrays him with his agent; and Veronica, feeding her pet dog and calling Jack "waggytail," can also think only in terms of the product's subtext. Potter makes this explicit when he inserts Black's lines in the ad after the actor has been pushed into a pond by a great dane ("I haven't even opened the tin yet!"), and has them framed by Veronica's repeated offer "Unzip me, Jack!"[31] Consumer goods and social relationships are similarly connected in the first of Potter's mock ads. It projects Black in a nightly raid of the pantry, which renders him oblivious to the luxuries of jewelry and female beauty that he passes coming down the stairs. He ends up in the pantry, the camera zooming in on a pack of Krispy Krunch cereal in the ad, but in his imagined version the zoom is on the revelation of his wife in bed with his agent. Ads are his diseased life, and, by way of Mogabrium and the machinery of the TV studio, also offer a surrogate relief.

In *Double Dare*, the writer Martin suffers from schizophrenic—and again ironically adequate—precognition. He arranges to see the actress Helen in a hotel, only to kill her in a schizophrenic delusion that invents her alter ego as Carol, a prostitute who is to be strangled by her client, while simultaneously developing this scenario for his play. His misconceptions are induced by a TV commercial that has Helen recline to simulate fellatio on a Fraggie flake bar, and of a popular TV play with soft-porn tendencies that casts Helen as a Catholic girl introduced to lovemaking.

Martin's murder in the context of a metadramatical irony accounts for a deeply unsettling experience, which uses his schizophrenia as a metaphor for a deformed and diseased society, which in turn results from the increasing inability to differentiate between the vicarious wish-fulfillment in the fictional sphere of advertising and the requirements of real social interaction. Potter makes Helen confront Martin with this point:

The I that is me and the I that is the character. Whore, actress. Yes? They get
mixed up, don't they, Martin? One being me and the other being a whore which
is also me. Which, let's face it, is still the way, the secret, half-hidden, sneaky
way that writers, directors and even audiences want to think about me.[32]

Martin's erotic fantasies are fueled by the idea that the film's lovemaking might
have been real and that Helen was aware of the erotic subtext of eating the
chocolate bar. "Commodities sell fantasies and fantasies sell commodities,"
says Goldman.[33] Unable to differentiate between Helen as a subject and Helen
as a television image, Martin turns her into Carol, the prostitute, the commodity, the object, and commodification, which so often in Potter cannot but
lead to death.

Finally, in *Blackeyes*, we see Potter largely unchanged. While specifically
addressing the recent tendency for models to take over from screen stars a cen-
trality in the cultural adoration of femininity images, Potter again juxtaposes
commodity values and the values of creativity, this time postmodernistically
decentered. There are at least four writers competing for the story of the
largely mute, exploited fashion model Blackeyes. Having physically abused his
niece Jessica when she was a child, writer Kingsley abuses her a second time
by turning her experience as a fashion model into research for his exploitative
novel *Sugar Bush*. Jessica tries to reclaim her own history from Kingsley's
story, but is seen failing at the task; and Jeff, an advertising copywriter, supplies his own vision of his next-window neighbor, Jessica's alter ego. There is
significant variation in these accounts, especially in the narrative closure:
Kingsley eliminates his Blackeyes by writing her suicide, and Jessica, in turn,
kills off Kingsley before copying Blackeyes' fate. Jeff, who moves between the
discourse levels, introduces Inspector Blake—long believed to have been invented by Jessica—as a male revenger. Jeff's advertising consciousness also
supplies corrupt visions of a happy ending. He appears to be a representative
of a new kind of feminist man, but in fact conceives romantic encounters—twi-
light strolling on a cliff with Blackeyes, hands clasped together, kissing and
laughing—that as commercials would seem to lack only a product brand. As
Blackeyes walks away from the banal happy ending Jeff has devised for her,
the fourth author, Potter himself, rejoices in his omnipresent voice-over, only
to be left behind like the others.

MALE GAZING

One should note the switch in the metadramatical perspective from *Follow the
Yellow Brick Road* via *Double Dare* to *Blackeyes*. While *Follow the Yellow
Brick Road* uses the self-reflexive irony to locate the sphere of oppositional

practices in itself—Jack Black hates the ubiquitous camera of the BBC-television play—Potter turns to a critique of the possibility of "oppositional writing" in *Double Dare*. Here, the creativity of the author Martin is blocked and corrupted by a commodified notion of women. As a recent biography of Potter delights in revealing, he apparently suffered from Martin's condition of writer's block himself, and, moreover, he invited actress Kika Markham to see him in a hotel.[34] By making his fictional author a contaminated, schizophrenic Potter-derivative in the metadramatical *Double Dare,* Potter exposes and purges this contamination of creativity on the nonfictional outside. Among other things, the self-reflexivity in *Double Dare* is a means of validating Potter's epistemological position in the politics of culture. *Blackeyes* has a similar agenda, but it is even more skeptical about the (television) playwright's capacity to supply a culture pervaded by the perversity of commercialism with an oppositional practice. This time, Potter confronts the nonfictional subtext even more directly. In his own voice-over he is deconstructed as a would-be feminist and, in effect, he declares himself complicit with his victimization of Blackeyes. In a sense, the play deserves the feminist uproar. Moreover, it seems to ask for it—even if the accusations of exploiting women deeply wounded Potter. In the final analysis, Potter seems to say the same thing as his feminist detractors, albeit in different prose and different function: Yes, I have authorized this, and, as you can see, my male gaze is corrupted by the culture of advertising.

The distortion of gender relations is at the heart of Potter's critique of advertising. From Friedan to Tuchman, content analyses have exposed what has come to be termed the symbolic annihilation of women in advertising.[35] One of the prime techniques in drawing the viewers' attention to products is using sexuality to tap the affective potentials. When Potter addresses sexualized eyes drawn to the television screen, he inevitably refers to male eyes, disregarding the growing market for the aestheticization of the male body and its use in sexualizing advertisements. He recreates the stereotype of the alluring, enticing female body that caters specifically to the male gaze (with additional resonances in the pressure put on female viewers to meet standards in looks and availability). In both *Double Dare* and *Blackeyes,* the sexualization of advertising is even more blatantly exposed than in the "waggy tails" and "krispy" betrayals of *Follow the Yellow Brick Road*. This time, it is a Fraggie bar that acquires the status of a penis in intertextual conference with a simulation of fellatio—a marketing strategy that has been very popular since the beginning of the seventies. Fellatio serves Potter as an image for the ultimate subversion of women under the male will. At the same time, the scenes illustrate an implicit threat to masculinity that, according to Mulvey, is countered by the fetishization and perpetual passivity of "woman as image." Strategies of minimizing the female threat may, in part, account for the fact that in recent years bodies in ads seem to have become less active, more distant from each other,

although ever more stylish and immaculate. In *Blackeyes*, however, Potter re-
activates the Fraggie bar spot for his model Blackeyes and, in one of the most
controversial scenes, sends his character to an audition where she simulates fellatio on a bottle of body lotion in front of a group of jeering executives (again
in metadramatical irony: when asked which company sent her, Blackeyes answers "PfH," Potter's and Kenith Trodd's former production company, Pennies
from Heaven). Complicitly catering to the male gaze, Potter's camera circles
the object of its desire in one of the characteristic long takes, which in this instance was meant to expose the camera's voyeurism.

While Potter enables Helen in *Double Dare* to rationalize her role in the
twisted man's world exemplified by the schizophrenic Martin, he makes Blackeyes a mute, inarticulate character—just an empty shell, a surface, a deconstructed subject, a "poststructuralist text" awaiting an inscribing gaze, "at the
mercy of the reader's pleasure."[36] Feminist gazes have not proven very merci-
ful with Blackeyes, not just because the exploited advertising model was seen
as a stereotype in a cardboard version of the advertising industry complete
with idling lecherous old men, bitchy models, bland copywriters, and soulless
drug-addicted photographers or directors. She has been regarded as a perpet-
uation and even radicalization of femininity as conceived of in a phallocentric
popular culture: all passivity, all body, all sexuality, all inarticulation, or, as
Potter's voice-over states: "She's been only an object of desire, her thought, her
opinion, her dreams not been given speech."[37] Jenny Diski recently reiterated
her criticism: " . . . I had thought that art was to do something about stereotypes beyond reproducing them for our further perusal."[38] While Diski clearly
disregards the voice-over-generated moments of self-accusation, Potter indeed
fails (or rather succeeds, for this is what he implies in his voice-over) in his desperate attempts to claim the body of actress Gina Bellman for his narrative.
She "bursts through the world of illusion,"[39] but rather than walk away from
Potter's self-confessed male perspective (as his ending has it), she remains in the
dark eyes of the male beholder or in the angry voices of female critics. If one
sees Potter fail in his postmodern strategy to participate in the commodification of female sexuality in order to denounce it from within, then it needs simply a label and a price tag attached to the body lotion Bellman fondles to turn
Blackeyes, the critique of commercialism, into *Blackeyes,* the commercial.

MAPPING THE FEELD:
GOOD(S) CULTURES

In the dystopian *Cold Lazarus,* produced posthumously in 1996, Potter comments with clever precognition on the postmortem packaging of his own pri-
vacy. "No biography!" is the desperate (and futile) scream emanating from the

frozen brain of Daniel Feeld, the writer-character in the companion piece *Karaoke* (1996) and one of Potter's frequent Potter-impersonators. The representatives of crass capitalism in *Cold Lazarus* are the media magnate David Siltz of Universal Total Entertainment, and Matilda Masdon, head of a biochemical industry corporation. While Masdon wants Siltz to instill her target groups with fear via a Masdon-sponsored thriller series,[40] thus creating a market for her anxiety-blocking drugs, Siltz is keen on exploiting the preserved residues of authentic human feeling (compare the name: "Daniel *Feel*d") in a twenty-fourth century marked by globalized glittery boredom and universal gritty terrorism. Feeld's head is preserved in liquid nitrogen in order to make his memory a commercial resource, to be tapped in a cryogenic lab on a so-called Living Wall (reminiscent of Bradbury's *Fahrenheit 451*).

To Potter, such an alliance is as natural as it is unholy. Daniel Feeld's undead head at the hands of the entertainment industry is described as "Separated from God"[41] in the script, and Potter's Christian Socialist rejection of materialism, indeed, looks like an increasingly alien concept in the Westernized society of 1999, both thoroughly secularized (as illustrated by the rise of fundamentalisms) and effectively consumerized (as testified to by socialism's rearguard fight). Potter's attitude to advertising seems similarly outdated. He sees advertising as antihuman and antisocial, but not primarily as antisocialist. His analysis of advertising is not an economic or materialist one, but one that stresses the effects on individual psyches and social relationships. He does not contrast "penny-off perfection"[42] with impoverished working class households, but "Pies in the Sky" with unhappy, twisted, torn psyches and blocked or struggling writers. Potter's alternative values are expressed in the flawed moral scruples of the scientist Fyodor, whose name points to a literary antidote. Fyodor turns out to belong to a group of dissidents, whose acronym RON ("Reality Or Nothing") ironically subverts the Reaganite rule of entertainment. Fyodor puts his "hope in us as citizens rather than simply consumers."[43] Eventually, the scientists agree to destroy the head they do not want to torture "in the name of mass entertainment!"[44] Potter's vision of a "real" and deep truth is to be found in Dostoevsky's literary landscapes of internal struggles and corruption, but, of course, it is also the song "Hush, hush, hush, here comes the bogey man!" that accompanies Daniel's deliverance.

Steeped in the kind of criticism that prevailed in the fifties and sixties, Potter's critique is reductive as it does not go beyond a theory of the male gaze; as it juxtaposes a real, manipulated, male viewer to a false, fictional, commercial world; and as it demonizes the power of advertising. Potter paradoxically operates within a Puritan framework that attacks advertising for its supply of vicarious pleasures. Postmodernism, however, has been rather wary about concepts of originality and individuality[45] and less critical of both vicarious pleasures and lack in depth. Martin Esslin's late-seventies exhortations to (1) acknowledge advertising as a form of (banal) Aristotelian drama, and (2) counterbalance it by supporting serious and intellectually challenging work seem rather dated today.[46] Potter acknowledges, but cannot wholly escape the critique of Mark Poster, who attacks the validity of reading ads "through the representational mode of signification . . . as an offense, a manipulation, a set of falsehoods, deeply disgusting and even morally dangerous," because such a reading refers "to the adult, white, male metanarrative of reason."[47] Scholars in cultural studies have for some time now discussed whether "the lure of popular culture is the lure of libidinal pleasure," and if this "provides its potentially liberating psychic aspects."[48] In fact, in its powerful ability to keep the signifiers floating and fashion moving to such an extent that history catches up with itself, advertising has metamorphosed from punchbag into paradigm. For Baudrillard, the hyperreal, the aesthetic hallucination of reality, marks not just specific communication processes but the society at large.[49] The modernist alternative, on the other hand, described by Andreas Huyssen as a "nightmare of being devoured by mass culture through co-option, commodification, and the 'wrong' kind of success," has been related to "male fears of an engulfing femininity," pointing to "patriarchal, misogynist, and masculinist" trends in modernism.[50] As the dissolution of gender identities has changed the arts and will continue to do so, it may as well continue to change advertising.

Increasingly, the culture of goods is even viewed as a good culture. Summing up the argument against Potter's fierce vision, it may be argued that:

1. The yardstick opposition of the "real world" as opposed to the "ad world" is flawed because they have merged in the hyperreal.

2. Consequently, it is unclear to what extent both the style and the content of advertising either reflect what goes on in a society at large or actively shape the cultural climate.

3. Consequently, one may not simplistically oppose real against artificial needs, and advertising may, indeed, provide aesthetic, sensual, or cognitive pleasure, especially as it has grown more sophisticated and intelligent than it used to be, and is more complex than a mere attempt at selling flakes with fellatio.

4. Advertising may be not nearly as powerful a cultural factor as its detractors and proponents have made it out to be—since viewers, and of course academically trained reviewers, may be more resilient to ads, better trained in reading them, or simply may have grown tired of their ubiquity.

For all that, however, Potter certainly moves in our cultural heartland as he rides the consumerist aesthetics of the media in his quixotic attack, trying to reclaim identity from the postmodern world. Advertising is still "an apparatus for *reframing meaning* in order to add value to products."[51] Why shy away from cynicism and paradox? Looking for meaning beyond products, one might as well consume the valuable products labeled "By Dennis Potter."

NOTES

1. Dennis Potter, "An Innocent Abroad," *Sunday Times Magazine*, 8 January 1978, p.35.

2. Matthew Arnold, *Culture and Anarchy* (Cambridge: Cambridge University Press, 1960), p.164 [1st ed. 1869].

3. F. R. Leavis, *Mass Civilization and Minority Culture* (Cambridge: The Minority Press, 1930), p.11.

4. Denys Thompson, ed., *Discrimination and Popular Culture*. 2nd. ed. (Harmondsworth: Penguin, 1973), pp.18, 20.

5. Dennis Potter, *Waiting for the Boat. On Television* (London: Faber, 1984), p.24.

6. Richard Hoggart, *The Uses of Literacy* (Harmondsworth: Penguin, 1958) 285, 282–283; see also Glen Creeber, "'Banality with a Beat': Dennis Potter and the paradox of popular music," *Media Culture & Society* 18.3 (1996): 502; and his essay in this volume.

7. Potter, *Waiting for the Boat*, p.29.

8. Raymond Williams, *The Long Revolution* (London: Chatto & Windus, 1961), p.297.

9. Raymond Williams, "Advertising: Magic System," in *Problems in Materialism and Culture* (London: Verso, 1980), p.185.

10. Leo Löwenthal, *Literature, Popular Culture, and Society* (Palo Alto: Pacific Books, 1968), p.11 [first ed. 1961].

11. Raymond Williams, *Television. Technology & Cultural Form* (Glasgow: Fontana/Collins, 1974), p.70.

12. Potter, *Waiting for the Boat*, p.29; see also p.23 and compare e.g., with Robert Goldman, *Reading Ads Socially* (London & N.Y.: Routledge, 1992), p.8.

13. Arnold, p.105.

14. See Vernon Gras, "Dennis Potter's *The Singing Detective*: An Exemplum of Dialogical Ethics," in *Why Literature Matters. Theories and Functions of Literature*, ed. Rüdiger Ahrens, Laurenz Volkmann (Heidelberg: Winter, 1996), p.245 (also in this volume); see also Heinz Antor's essay in this volume.

15. See Glen Creeber, *Dennis Potter: Between Two Worlds. A Critical Reassessment* (Basingstoke, Hampshire, New York: Macmillan/St. Martin's Press, 1998), p.196.

16. Julian Barnes, "Not for Laying Down," *New Statesman*, 7 November 1980, p.33.

17. Dennis Potter, "Introduction," *Brimstone & Treacle* (London: Methuen, 1978).

18. James B. Twitchell, *Adcult USA. The Triumph of Advertising in American Culture* (New York: Columbia University Press, 1996), p.30.

19. See for this a more thorough investigation in Eckart Voigts-Virchow, *Männerphantasien. Introspektion und gebrochene Wirklichkeitsillusion im Drama von Dennis Potter* (Trier: WVT, 1995), pp.239–253 and 270–275.

20. Hoggart, p.230.

21. Hoggart, p.285.

22. Quoted in Dominic Strinati, *An Introduction to Theories of Popular Culture* (London: Routledge, 1995), p.66.

23. Stuart Hall and Paddy Whannel, *The Popular Arts* (London: Hutchinson, 1964), p.312.

24. See Potter, *Waiting for the Boat*, p.27.

25. Dennis Potter, "The Philistine Stigma," *The Guardian*, 15 October 1977, p.7. See also Potter's venomous attack on Samuel Beckett's work for TV. Polemically connecting Beckett's aesthetics to the Holocaust, Potter wrote in the *Sunday Times*: "Is this the art which is the response to the despair and pity of our age, or is it made of the kind of futility which helped such desecrations of the spirit, such filth of ideologies come into being?" For the quote and a defence of Beckett see James Knowlson, *Damned to Fame. The Life of Samuel Beckett* (London: Bloomsbury, 1996), p.636.

26. Stuart Ewen, *All Consuming Images. The Politics of Style in Contemporary Culture* (New York: Basic Books, 1988), p.83.

27. Gillian Dyer, *Advertising as Communication* (London: Methuen, 1982), p.7.

28. Dennis Potter, "Follow the Yellow Brick Road," in *The Television Dramatist,* ed. Robert Muller (London: Elek, 1973), p.382.

29. Stuart Ewen, p.83ff.

30. Judith Williamson, *Decoding Advertisements. Ideology and Meaning in Advertising* (London & New York: Boyars, 1978), p.13.

31. Potter, "Brick Road," p.371.

32. Transcribed from *Double Dare*, BBC-1, writ. Dennis Potter, first transmission 6 April, 1976.

33. Goldman, p.25.

34. See Stephen W. Gilbert, *Fight and Kick and Bite: The Life and Work of Dennis Potter* (London: Hodder & Stoughton, 1995), p.208ff.

35. See Anthony Easthope, *What a Man's Gotta Do. The Masculine Myth in Popular Culture* (London: Paladin/Grafton, 1986), p.134ff.; Carol Moog, *'Are They Selling Her Lips?' - Advertising and Identity* (New York: Morrow, 1990), p.141ff.; Strinati, p.184ff.; Goldman, p.107ff.

36. Raman Selden, *A Reader's Guide to Contemporary Literary Theory*, 2nd. ed. (Hemel Hempstead: Harvester, 1989), p.79.

37. Transcribed from *Blackeyes*, BBC-2, writ. Dennis Potter, first transmission November-December 1989, part IV.

38. Jenny Diski, "Made for TV," *London Review of Books*, 14 December 1995), p.16.

39. Laura Mulvey, *Visual and Other Pleasures* (London: Macmillan, 1989), pp.25–26. Subsequently, Potter created a director (Nick in *Karaoke*) who burdens his actress unseemly with screen presence because he is obsessed with her—beyond the "world of illusion." This may be interpreted as a self-critique of

Potter directing *Blackeyes*. See Dennis Potter, *Karaoke* and *Cold Lazarus* (London: Faber & Faber 1996), p.78.

40. With an obvious precursor in Aldous Huxley, this strategy is also reminiscent of Don DeLillo's *White Noise,* where one finds a subtler critique of the medico-medial apparatus through the pill Dylar aimed at erasing Babette Gladney's fear of death.

41. Potter, Cold Lazarus, p.246.

42. Potter, "Introduction," *Brimstone and Treacle.*

43. Potter, Cold Lazarus, p.308.

44. Potter, *Cold Lazarus,* p.380.

45. See the controversy "Coward and Creeber vs. Cook" about Potter and TV authorship: Rosalind Coward, "Dennis Potter and the Question of the Television Author," *Critical Quarterly* 29.4 (1987):79–87; Creeber, *Between Two Worlds,* 4–7; John R. Cook, *Dennis Potter. A Life on Screen* (Manchester: Manchester University Press), p.7.

46. Martin Esslin, "Aristotle and the Advertisers: The Television Commercial as a Form of Drama," in *Television: The Critical View,* ed. Horace Newcomb (New York: Oxford University Press, 1987), pp.304–317 [1st. publ. *The Kenyon Review,* 1979.]

47. Mark Poster, "Baudrillard and TV Ads," in *The Polity Reader in Cultural Theory* (Cambridge & Oxford: Polity/Blackwell, 1994), p.129. [1st publ. in 1990].

48. E. Ann Kaplan, "Popular Culture, Politics, and the Canon: Cultural Literacy in the Postmodern Age," in *Cultural Power/Cultural Literacy,* ed. Bonnie Braendlin (Tallahassee: Florida State University Press, 1991), p.19. For the continuing discussion about a redefinition of high and popular arts, and especially the charge of "populism" against Cultural Studies as defined by John Fiske et al. see Jim McGuigan, *Cultural Populism* (London: Routledge, 1992); Peter Goodall, *High Culture, Popular Culture. The Long Debate* (St. Leonards: Allen & Unwin, 1995); Graeme Turner, *British Cultural Studies. An Introduction* (London: Routledge, 1996).

49. See Poster, p.113.

50. Andreas Huyssen, *After the Great Divide. Modernism, Mass Culture, Postmodernism* (Bloomington & Indianapolis: Indiana University Press, 1986), pp.53, 62.

51. Goldman, p.5.

Religion and Dialogism

OF ALL THE MANY CHANGES THAT POTTER WENT THROUGH in class, religion, and occupation, the change in religious orientation arguably held the most significance for his writing. Raised in a working class milieu of Protestant fundamentalism with attendance required at two services each Sunday at the local Salem Free Church, the later Oxford scholarship boy underwent some extreme jolts and adjustments. Even so, late in life Potter could still claim that he was a Christian. Though he had jettisoned Christian dogma, he still felt true to its spiritual motivation. His own personal journey, refracted in those of his protagonists, resemble the mythic pattern of the loss and regaining of identity. From a literal acceptance of the Bible in his childhood, to a repudiation of God as a young man with its accompanying nihilism and despair, to a newfound assertion of faith based on a dialogical self/world relationship, Potter's journey undoubtedly makes him a most important literary figure of the last half of the twentieth century. While the details of his historical situation and crisis is parochial, the philosophic terms describing his termini—from essentialism to dialogism—have worldwide application. Not only did he live and suffer through this wrenching reorientation, he was able to articulate it for us through his screenplays. All his plays have the unmistakable imprint of his vision. He is that rare TV writer who is also an auteur.

The fact that literature in the form of an aestheticized ethics can displace philosophy and religion in clarifying the nature of the good life has been announced by such eminent scholars and philosophers as Richard Rorty, Martha Nussbaum, Mikhail Bakhtin, and Wayne Booth.[1] Dennis Potter's work is the concrete exemplum of their theorizing. The death of God, according to Potter, is a fake crisis. What dies is one particular social construct of God that has been reified and turned into idolatry.

Even worse, He has been turned into a vengeful, repressive Lawgiver whose edicts warp the natural sexual proclivities of His adherents. In most of his early plays, Potter's protagonists fall victim to their internalized sense of guilt and sin laid on them by their early upbringing. Potter resembles William Faulkner in his scathing rebuke of this repressive Puritanism. Like all other cultural objects, God should be underway historically and continually in need of creation and recreation. S/He is not a finished entity. In a radio broadcast, *The Other Side of the Dark* (1978), Potter affirmed that "the world is being made right in front of us . . . and in living out our lives [we] give back piece by piece what has been given to us to use and work with and wrestle with. We shape our own lives."[2]

The value of Potter's work lies in first liberating its audience/readers from bogus authorities, be they religious or secular, and then clarifying what the good life for humans really can be. For his contemporaries, he can become the indispensable guide and witness. All the more reason that the vast majority of his work now sealed up in BBC vaults should be made available to the public. We need his living experiential pyschodramas to mirror, via image and actions, our own inner spiritual pilgrimage.[3]

For Vernon Gras, Dennis Potter is a great postmodern writer in how he answers the "questions of our moment." Because all stable foundations have disappeared in the postmodern era, humans have to fall back on the interpretive processes that create these foundations. Because interpretation always takes place within some context or background, these preexisting social relationships will infuse interpretation with ethical values and/or political tendencies. If the quest for the good life "must begin with an individual already embedded in a life world of shared practices, language, and values, how is s/he to find her/his way?" Potter's *The Singing Detective* (1986) shows us how. No longer can we search for formal structures with universal values, but we must instead engage in specific historical investigations that uncover how we constitute ourselves and are constituted into being the subject of our discursive practices. As Gras puts it, "Each of us becomes a split-self who must eventually tear himself away from the residue our historical passage leaves with us, consciously or unconsciously." For Gras, *The Singing Detective* is an exemplum of such dialogical ethics.

Chris Lippard approaches the dialogical in terms of confined bodies and wandering minds. To realize the sense of a coherent subjectivity—a sovereign self—Dennis Potter's characters must free themselves from personal fixations and societal constraints: a theme that remains significant in almost all his drama. Lippard illustrates Potter's postfundamentalist God by briefly explicating *Son of Man* (1969) and *Where Adam Stood (1976),* two plays with explicit religious themes. In Lippard's interpretation of Potter, "God was that which you could not quite get your tongue around, the ineffable thing which distinguished humans from the merely animal." He is always part of an inner personal drama, but explaining Him should be freeing, not confining. In any event, television is admirably equipped to show the interior process whereby people reveal those feelings and fantasies that shape their lives. The tension and conflict between personal confinement (physical and/or ideological) and the need to break free is treated by Lippard in three early works of Potter: *Traitor* (1971), *Casanova* (1971), and *Brimstone and Treacle* (1976).

Heinz Antor selects Potter's only stage play, *Sufficient Carbohydrate* (1983), to continue the analysis of the conflict between the structured and the structuring self. This time, the ethical crisis of the protagonist finds a parallel in a cultural crisis. The personal crisis of Jack Barker, who finds himself adrift and spiritually bankrupt, finds a social parallel in the disintegration of Jack's family and business relationships. Jack's business and family crises also seem inexorably linked to his ethical/religious crisis. Jack is in a quandary. He can't accept the theological metaphysics of the past (his father had been a minister). Nevertheless, even though he can't believe in the boat taking believers over Jordan to the land of the Blessed, he still needs a boat, that tramp steamer he sees going to and fro on the horizon every morning. The boat reminds him of his childhood, that Edenic time filled with yearning and potentiality. The ship on the horizon may eventually provide a tenant for the vacancy left inside his head when God moved out. The freighter has no ultimate destination, no discernable telos. But it reminds Jack that he has lost his compass, that he has forgotten he is on a journey. According to Antor, Jack's final position is a dialogical and open-ended ethics in which we with him must constantly remap our lives and define our positions via communicative exchange. Thus, *Sufficient Carbohydrate* becomes an example of the ethical turn found in recent postmodern philosophizing and literary writing.

Gwendolyn Connelly, in her reading of the novel *Blackeyes* (1987), fixes most of her attention on how the story is told. The novel foregrounds its own telling by following how its chief characters seize and rework the central events, thereby first imprisoning and then releasing the main character, Jessica. This narrative method, says Connelly, is Potter's strategy to show us how we can resist social/cultural discourses that seek to turn us into volitionless subjects under their encompassing authority. *Blackeyes* recounts the strenuous efforts of its protagonist, Jessica, to regain her free agency after being represented as a passive sexual bunny by her uncle, Maurice Kingsley, in his own novel, *Sugar Bush*. It is the fictional portrayal of Jessica and her experiences that forms "the nexus of the dispute for narrative control." How the story is told is being contested. Whoever controls the point of view (the author or narrator) determines how characters are represented in the text. Unless Jessica can disavow Kingsley's version and substitute her own representation, she will remain an object in someone else's discourse. The "doubling" that Jessica experiences at the hands of her uncle is similar to the processes through which we are all captured in our surrounding social discourses. When we fail to interrogate these codes, we become objects in a narrative not of our choosing. To succeed in life, we must proceed dialogically by first demystifying our surrounding discourses in order to be able to reshape our own chosen identity. In an epilogue, Connelly debunks the recent "supposed" sexual scandal about Potter visiting prostitutes. True or not, such details "are hollow and mundane in their biographical context." In fact, the struggle against such "autobiographical hijacking" is central to Potter's sense of humans creating/writing their own self-interpretation.

Building on Connelly's epilogue, John Cook mounts a strong counterattack against the scandal and rumor peddling media (which headlines Potter's alleged "visits to prostitutes" while ignoring or even turning a contemptuous back on his work, especially by Murdoch-owned newspapers). Potter in *Cold Lazarus* (1996, posthumous), says Cook, quite accurately predicted what is happening to him posthumously. He articulated the anxiety that the world from which he was departing in 1994 was engaged in misunderstanding his work—that all too often, his audience made reductionist errors in seeing "memories" of the past as straightforward biography. What Potter in *Cold Lazarus* makes clear, says Cook, is the complex interrelationship between fact and fiction, memory and fantasy. The hostile philistine world of *Cold Lazarus,* which seeks to plunder and exploit for gain the memories of Daniel Feeld, has a clear echo in the present media attempts to gain *direct* and unproblematic access to Potter's own "real life" experiences. Neither of them can be successful in revealing what is crucially important to human meaning-giving. The return to the lost lands of childhood for Potter is to recapture the "aliveness . . . of feeling all things as new." We must "remember Eden . . . in terms of its possibilities and potentialities." That is the continuing message of Christianity to us in the twentieth century when it admonishes us to become as little children. *Karaoke* in tandem with *Cold Lazarus* illustrates: Do we just sing the tune given us by the past, or do we make something new out of it? Don't turn the meaning-giving process into a commodity; don't befoul or dispense with our true human inheritance. Don't turn Pygmalion (imagination) into Pig Mailion (the bottom line). That is Potter's posthumous message. Both Pig Mailion, the villain in *Karaoke,* and David Siltz, the villain in *Cold Lazarus,* reduce all values to money, and pursue it via all available means. With the "Occupying Powers" encroaching in ever more areas of human concern, all the essays in this section ultimately agree with Potter that we need to take heed and change our environment.

NOTES

1. Richard Rorty, *Contingency, Irony, and Solidarity* (Cambridge: Cambridge University Press, 1989); Martha C. Nussbaum, *Love's Knowledge* (New York: Ox-

ford University Press, 1990); Mikhail Bakhtin, *The Dialogic Imagination*, ed. Michael Holquist (Austin: University of Texas Press, 1981); Wayne Booth, *The Company We Keep: An Ethics of Fiction* (Berkeley: University of California Press, 1988).

2. Quoted in John Cook, *Dennis Potter: A Life on Screen*, 2nd ed. (Manchester: Manchester University Press, 1998), pp.124–5.

3. For a good discussion of the moral value of literature as clarification, see Noel Carroll, "Art, narrative, and moral understanding," in Jerrold Levinson, ed., *Aesthetics and Ethics* (Cambridge: Cambridge University Press, 1998).

CHAPTER 6

DENNIS POTTER'S
THE SINGING DETECTIVE

An Exemplum of Dialogical Ethics

Vernon W. Gras

I

DENNIS POTTER, THE BRITISH PLAYWRIGHT, DIED 7 JUNE 1994. Many readers of this article will be unaware of his death or even ask, "Why mention it?" When he died, Dennis Potter had written circa 31 television plays, 6 serials (3 with songs), 8 screenplays (e.g., *Gorky Park, Dreamchild*), 7 adaptations of others' work (e.g., *Christabel, Casanova*), and 4 novels. Not only was he prolific, he was brilliantly innovative. Had he written for the stage rather than TV, he probably would have been well known by now on both sides of the Atlantic.[1] Undoubtedly, his suffering from psoriatic arthropathy, so vividly portrayed in *The Singing Detective*, curtailed a more ebullient pursuit of his career. He stayed close to his birthplace in the Forest of Dean (near Wales) for his entire life. While his recognition in England was steady and he became prominent with *Pennies from Heaven* (1978), recognition in the United States became widespread only with the successful showing of the TV serial *The Singing Detective* (PBS, 1988). Following this success, Potter received an extensive recapitulative showing of his work in 1992 by the Museum of Television and Radio in New York City. Though late in coming, he has been cited recently as "the most important creative figure in the history of British television."[2] In praising his work, Vincent Canby in the *New York Times* admitted that "Mr. Potter's screenplay is remarkable not only for its achieved seriousness and lucid complexity but also for having (in American eyes, at least) achieved production. It couldn't happen here."[3] While Potter's work needs more promotion in general, I have space only to elucidate his masterpiece, *The Singing Detective*. I will affirm that it is a great postmodern work in how it answers the questions of our moment.

II

So, what are the questions of our moment? In the ethical personal field, they make up questions such as: What is truly worthwhile? How do I find it? and How do I make sense of so much pain and chaos that surrounds me?—particularly when traditional religious and philosophical answers have lost their power to persuade and console. In the postmodern era, foundations have disappeared, no matter whether objectively or subjectively pursued. In place of such stable and timeless foundations as God, Platonic Idea, Natural Law, Entelechy, Reason, Moral Duty, or the Collective Unconscious, postmodernism offers ceaseless open-ended interpretation and reinterpretation. Escape from vertigo comes only in the form of a momentary intersubjectivity or consensus, which sooner or later faces inevitable revision. With this loss of foundation comes an inversion that privileges the process over any product. This inversion has been labeled "the interpretive turn" because (1) interpretation has become "a universal and ubiquitous feature of all human activity . . . there can be no appeal to experience, meaning, or evidence that is independent of interpretation or more basic to it"; and (2) "interpretation always takes place within some context or background—such as webs of belief, a complex of social relations, tradition, or the practices of a form of life."[4]

If interpretation takes place within a context already in place, this background unavoidably preshapes the direction interpretation can go. Preexisting social relationships will infuse interpretation with ethical value and/or political tendencies. If any effort to lead the good life must begin with an individual already embedded in a life world of shared practices, shared language, and differentiated values—how, then, is s/he to find her/his way?

To achieve for ourselves some significant identity, each of us must make choices against a background of things already forming a hierarchy of values. Ethical investigations will no longer be practiced as a search for formal structures with universal values, but as historical investigations into the events that have led each of us to constitute ourselves as the subject of our discursive practices. We can no longer embrace a naïve "objectivity" and linguistic transparency that denies the enunciating subject. The hermeneutic realization that we must start with everyday existence ("Dasein") leads us to reconceptualize the role of language. "Heidegger suggests that, instead of seeing language as a tool on hand for designating an independently existing world of objects, we think of it as primarily the medium through which the world is 'made manifest' to us."[5] Language articulates and differentiates the world to us, allowing it to emerge and enabling us to compare and choose. Most of our choosing will consist in trying to perceive more clearly our own experiences, judging them qualitatively while fending off distorted perceptions, seductive delusions, and stultifying self-deceptions. Such use of language must operate in actual concrete situations, remain temporal and open-ended, and through patient self-clarification bring to fruition one's own personal commitments.

Literature provides the purest examples of agents creating self and world through discursive action, so it comes as no surprise that the interpretive turn brings with it an "ethical turn." Literature more than philosophy can best provide an exemplum of dialogical ethics.[6]

III

The title *The Singing Detective* refers both to the six-episode TV series written by Dennis Potter and to a detective novel written by Potter's hero, Philip E. Marlow, who appears twice as an incapacitated author (in the TV series) and as his famous detective namesake (parodied) within the pulp thriller. In fact, the TV series could best be described as a psychodrama in which the sick author's imaginative rethinking of his detective novel—an exercise to keep him sane—becomes embedded with recollections of his youth, morbid suspicions about his estranged wife, and an often hallucinated "take" of his hospital surroundings. The author/hero lies in a hospital bed suffering from psoriatic arthropathy, which blisters the skin and makes his joints swell into immovability. Early on, he laments being like Job—"a prisoner within my own skin and bones." The head specialist suggests that his condition is not merely physical but psychic and spiritual as well. Being confined in a city hospital, however, allows Marlow to escape from the pressures of the commercial world, to recollect his past, and ultimately to come to terms with the crisis in his life. While in a fevered condition brought on by his disease, which puts his body temperature out of control, he mentally begins to rewrite his novel, *The Singing Detective*. In the novel, Marlow assumes an alter ego, a tough detective who sings nightly at the Laguna Club when not solving crime cases. The imagined story begins to interweave with the frame story so that at the end Marlow, the tough detective, enters the "real world" story of Marlow the author, and helps solve his case (release him from his spiritual crisis). The next day, Marlow the author leaves the hospital in the hat and trenchcoat of his persona, the tough detective, having reconciled with his ex-wife, Nicola.

That Mr. Potter means his presentation to function on multilevels is evident from the extensive self-reflexivity found in foregrounding the detective genre as an allegory of human existence, as well as reiterating that characters (even his author/hero) are products of an authorial or socially inscribed discourse. Both in its content and method of presentation, *The Singing Detective* offers us a way out of our current predicaments. Potter's indirect message seems to be that we are all detectives trying to find significance and direction for our lives. In this quest, we seem to have too many clues and few or no solutions. Potter offers to solve "our case."

IV

> Grandad: Look at the hole. Watch the hole, Philip.
> Uncle John: *(Wink.)* That's right. Always keep your eyes on the hole.
> *Aunt Emily sniggers. Mrs. Marlow frowns.*
> Mary: That all depends *whose*, don't it?
> Grandad: Stop that!
> Uncle John: See—look—the needle is going on, round and round—to the hole in the middle—a-a-a-and—hey presto![7]

The parody and send-up of the detective story, with its neat solution and interlocking contributory clues, is a recurring event in postmodern literature. Tom Stoppard's *After Magritte* and *Inspector Hound,* E. Ionesco's *Victims of Duty,* Thomas Pynchon's *The Crying of Lot 49,* and Antonioni's *Blowup* come to mind. William Spanos, in an important early article on postmodern literature, made the undermining of any "final solutions" the earmark of postmodern literature, e.g., "the paradigmatic archetype of the postmodern literary imagination is the antidetective story (and its antipsychoanalytical analogue), the formal purpose of which is to evoke the impulse to 'detect' and/or to psychoanalyze, in order to violently frustrate it by refusing to solve the crime (or find the cause of the neurosis)."[8] The motive for this antidetective story was to disturb the reader or viewer from his or her comforting delusion that s/he was "at home" in the world. Absurdist literature insisted on defamiliarizing our human habitation, estranging us from the world into dread and sometimes despair. The absurdist phase of postmodern literature seems now behind us, but the problem of the "loss of center" still provides the common denominator for postmodernism, whether found in literature, philosophy or science.[9]

From one angle, *TSD* assumes the antidetective posture described by Spanos above. Mimicking the genre of the tough detective thriller, *TSD* parodies cliché after cliché of the detective genre and leaves the initiating mystery surrounding the Skinskapes nightclub unsolved. The initiation of young Philip, age nine, into life's mystery tersely described in the epigraph above, however, is successfully resolved. But not until many years later—it takes place in the last episode of *TSD,* to be exact. Thus, the antipsychoanalytical analogue described by Spanos above, which frustrates solving any psychic crisis, does not take place. Marlow, the author/detective solves his crisis/case.

What makes *TSD* postmodern lies both in the nature of Marlow's crisis and in the nature of the remedy. On the surface, *TSD* operates like a typical Freudian psychodrama, with the uncovering of a childhood traumatic event (the suicide of Marlow's mother) for which Marlow felt guilty and that seemingly turned him into a cynic and misanthrope. But the use of the Freudian psychoanalytical journey has been utilized in the same manner and for the same reasons as the detective thriller. Both are popular literary and TV genres whose conventions are well known to a mass audience. Because of their familiarity, how one cites these genres can lead to an increased clarity, efficiency, and intensity in communication. For example, the viewing of the TV drama is a bewildering mixture of childhood recollections by the sick patient, Marlow, coupled with the actions and characters found in popular thrillers written by Marlow, the pulp mystery hack. Despite a sick Marlow braiding together fiction and "reality" and even dissolving the boundary between them, the viewer finds himself guided by the structural principles of both genres, so that an underlying order is felt in the otherwise confusing progression.[10]

But, what exactly is Marlow' s crisis (if not his mother's suicide)? We have already claimed that the dominant characteristic of postmodernism is the realization—and having to deal with the consequences—of a loss of center. That applies to *TSD*. There is no vertical or depth dimension to escape into. Marlow states this loss of foundation specifically to Dr. Gibbon, the psychiatrist, and with some bitterness:

> I believe in no systems, no ideologies, no religion, nothing like that. I simply
> think—Oh, it's very boring this. Very—I just think that from time to time, and
> at random, you are visited by what you cannot know cannot predict cannot
> control cannot change cannot understand and cannot cannot cannot escape—
> Fate. (Little shrug) Why not? 'S good old word. (p.172)

Earlier, Marlow had admitted to Gibbon that "I would have liked to have used my pen to praise a loving God and all his loving creation" (p.57), instead of writing the trashy pulp that he does write. He is now at the end of his tether. Like Job, he feels that his world is abhorrent but, unlike Job, he reacts with hatred, loathing, and contempt for himself and his fellowmen. His bile and misanthropy find an outlet in the cynical asides of his alter ego, the tough detective; in his railing against his estranged wife, Nicola; in murdering people imaginatively while lying in bed; and in vituperative descriptions or statements about the sex act. Sexual intercourse takes at least five such batterings. Prepared through years of Freudian psychodrama, we know that such repetitions denote neurosis and await the uncovering of its cause followed by a therapeutic healing within the patient. The surprise, however, comes when the healing catharsis is triggered by a different memory than the suicide of his mother. But let us first sample the vituperations. Dr. Gibbon, who has read *TSD*, points out the excess repugnance Marlow has for the sex act, which seems out of place in a detective story!:

> Mouth sucking wet and slack at mouth, tongue chafing against tongue, limb thrusting upon limb, skin rubbing at skin—faces contort and stretch into a helpless leer, organs spurt out smelly stains and sticky betrayals. This is the sweaty farce out of which we are brought into being. . . . We are implicated without choice in the slippery catastrophe of the copulations which splatter us into existence. We are spat out of fevered loins. We are the by-blows of grunts and pantings in a rumpled and creaking bed. Welcome. (p.58)

This revulsion surfaces again in Marlow's (the author's) visit to a prostitute. Following their copulation, Marlow asks her with anger and loathing, "Doesn't it disgust you, what you do? Being paid to stretch yourself out, and let a stranger enter you?" (p.181). This "real life" episode had found earlier fictional expression in his novel, *TSD*, between Mark Binney and Sonia, who play the identical scene (p.59). Again, he informs his ex-wife, Nicola, he wants to make love with her alongside a big mirror so, when he ejaculates, he can spit into his mirrored face. Finally, we also join young Philip in his voyeuristic watching of his mother's adulterous copulation with Ray Binney who, with Philip's parents, entertains at the village pub. It is Philip's revelation that he had witnessed this act that brings about his mother's suicide. Without doubt, Marlow's misogyny and self-loathing is instigated by his mother's suicide and adulterous betrayal of his father. The recurring motif of a female body fished out of the Thames recapitulates his mother drowning herself in that river. But Marlow's protective misogyny lies embedded in a broader nihilism that finds its origin elsewhere.

This nihilism finds its most graphic portrayal in the deaths of two patients, Ali and George Adam, one after the other, in the hospital bed next to Marlow's. Both deaths are sudden and plausible, though unexpected. Ali's death is filled with pathos. His cardiac arrest follows hard upon his declaration that none of them will ever get out of there (the hospital). After his death, the candy that was to give a momentary pleasure lies scattered over the floor. Marlow weeps openly for him. George's death is even more depressing. Suffering from mental loss, George is reduced to being a dirty old man, to the old Adam in us, our common heritage as sexual animals. Recounting his World War II experiences, George gesticulates obscenely and with relish his sex acts with the young Frauleins—"come out of *holes*, these krauts, wouldn't they? Holes in the ground. In the rubble and that—know what I mean? . . . Lovely bits of stuff. Good knockers on 'em. Well—couple of fags it was for a shag. Couple of fags, eh? and up with their dresses, dahn with their knickers—Eh?" (p.108). A bit later, there is another doubling of sex with "holes in the ground." During Marlow's recollection of his mother's adulterous copulation with Ray Binney, their passionate ecstatic gasps merge with those of George dying from cardiac arrest. Sex and death climax simultaneously to be followed with Raymond's laughing "one more done, then!" (p.114). But the most intense identification of the two holes comes in the associative word game Marlow plays with the psychiatrist:

Gibbon: Passion
Marlow: Pretence
Gibbon: Woman
Marlow: Fuck
Gibbon: Fuck
Marlow: Dirt
Gibbon: Dirt
Marlow: Death (p.177)

Potter articulates Marlow's crisis in sexual and religious terms, directly and obliquely. Whether consciously or not, he accepts T. S. Eliot's framing of the problem and even echoes some of his imagery.[11] For Eliot, the spiritual dessication of the modern wasteland was expressed in the meaningless cycles of the seasons. April is the cruelest month because spring's renewal could no longer reverberate symbolically. Time had become a flat, meaningless repetition without depth or transcendence. To its eternal cycle of birth, copulation, and death, Eliot envisaged two reactions: the paralysis and velleities of Prufrock, or the mindless animalism of Sweeney. Neither alternative was adequate for Eliot, who eventually retreated to "the still point of the turning world." Potter in *TSD* links sexuality and spirituality much in the Eliot manner. But he cannot envisage salvation in Eliot's traditional fashion, outside of time. Being a postmodern writer, Potter accepts temporality, historicity, absence of center, and the social construction of worlds. But he concurs with his modernist predecessors, in the necessity to provide a solution for this loss of center beyond mere "demystification." This is why *TSD* is a more significant work than so much postmodern literature that focuses exclusively on loss.

In the epigraph to this section, young Philip is introduced to a phonograph player by his grandfather and uncle and told to keep his eye on the hole while the record plays. Under the control of the hole (the turning point of this world), the record spins on its axis-rendering song, the needle attracted in its forward progress by the hole at the center. Sexual and religious allusion attach to "the hole" when taken as either our place of origin or destination. In these respects, the hole also controls what the majority of popular songs sing about (love and death). Enigmatically, it is young Philip's initiation into adulthood. Humans journeying between these two absences or "holes" and attracted by their mystery give vent to song. They try to fill in the mystery with interpretation. While this is a generic human task, the poet or writer has been recognized as life's preeminent decipherer since Homer, e.g., "Sing, O Muse, the wrath . . . ," etc. Updated to present times, the job description of the contemporary writer can with some accuracy be formulated as "the singing detective." The title thus refers to Marlow, who fronts a small band when not sleuthing; to the author, P. E. Marlow, who has to solve his personal crisis; to Potter, who wants to show us a way out of the postmodern condition; and ultimately to the viewer who, by singing along imaginatively, translates the plight and escape of the author/detective into his own contemporary task.

V

Potter believes suffering to be an inescapable element in the relationship of present to past, and that each of us has to learn how to deal with our inheritance in life-specific terms. Like Philip, we all have to mature into detectives in order to find out how the past is still victimizing us. The relation of present to past invariably is a suffering, a victimization of the present "I" by the structured "I" of the past. To be able to escape this historically structured self, we need the freedom to dialogue with that past. Losing the power to dialogue, to construct our self and world, is a pathological condition. We sink into spiritual illness that Potter expresses through a physical disease, psoriatric arthropathy. We can and do become locked in ourselves very much as Marlow was locked in his body, a prisoner confined to a limited space with ever less movement and no egress. Only by freeing ourselves from the limitations imposed by the past and enlarging the parameters of the self in a postmodern version of *Bildung* can we survive.

For postmodernism, authority (whether religious, political or scientific) can only grant temporary legitimation. Finite standpoints can only have circumscribed authority. Evil, as Potter has us experience it, lies in the self-privileging of some people who believe themselves superior to other people. Often allied with social institutions like school, hospital, church or government, these people tell others what to think, how to behave and who they should be. Social institutions tend to beget individuals who echo the values that preserve those institutions, i.e., the social status quo. When this tendency becomes too strong, individuals lose the power to shape themselves. Whereas the viewer is asked to identify with the hero, Marlow, who liberates himself by turning into a writer/detective, Reginald and Mr. Hall, two other ward patients, provide examples of failed dialogue in a comic mode. Reginald is reading the pulp novel, *TSD*, in parallel synchrony to the watching viewer. Barely literate, he finishes reading the story (in circa three months) as Marlow successfully limps out of the hospital on Nicola's arm. Having come to understand how his own and others' past deeds have contributed to his personal crisis, Marlow exits, freed from his debilitating hatred and bitterness and more in control of his future. Reginald, on the other hand, consumes the trashy pulp thriller filled with graphic descriptions of violence and gore to its "happy ending," in which the detective solves the crime and gets the girl. "Lucky devil," comments Reginald as he, too, prepares to return to the outside world. (p.249) Having indulged in some literary escapism, Reginald, a petty thief, will return unregenerated to his former activities. Mr. Hall, an unctuous and proper little shopkeeper, epitomizes the extent to which British society can inhibit when it finds the right material. Mr. Hall is frozen in English propriety. He panics at calling attention to himself: it's improper to shout, to complain about the tea, to be open about needing the bedpan, to use direct language in place of euphemisms, to associate with the criminal element. He can only utter social banalities, whether in praise or blame, but he is far too inhibited to ever assert himself publicly. He might have provided an occasion to vilify the repressive English social system if he were not so laughably ridiculous. As fellow reader and spectator, Reginald and Mr. Hall become foils to the readers/TV viewers who distance themselves from these failed surrogates, whose example teaches them how more fully to imitate the dialogical transformation of the writer/detective.

Other representatives of authority, less victims than victimizers, are not so laughable. Representatives of authority in school, hospital, and government—the schoolteacher, Dr. Finlay, and the two mysterious men—range from having to be taken very seriously to being almost extravagant parody. The harsh school disciplinarian embodies the worst that society, in the guise of the older generation, can do to the younger. In fact, she is identified with the scarecrow (a death symbol) and made to resemble Hitler, the supreme Fascist. Using physical and psychical abuse, she coerces her young charges into fearful obedience. It is her sadistic misuse of religion and the cane that induce Philip and his entire class to bear false witness and betray young Mark Binney, a slow, backward boy. He never regained the psychic strength to overcome their false charges, coming even to believe in his own guilt, and finally, ending in the insane asylum. Having joined with those who crucified the innocent Binney is the source of Marlow's trauma:

> I sat in my desk, perjurer, charlatan, and watched and listened and watched and listened as one after another they nailed that backward lad hands and feet to my story. I have not seriously doubted since that afternoon that any lie will receive almost instant corroboration and almost instant collaboration if the maintenance of it results in the public enjoyment of someone else's pain, someone else's humiliation. (p.212)

Later, in the hospital, Marlow re-experiences the causes of this betrayal when Dr. Finlay yokes medical and religious authority together to force some hymn singing on the defenseless ward patients. They have little choice—either sing along or passively endure the imposition. Characteristically, the doctor imposes his will, convinced that it is for the patients' own good. Self-appointed, the doctor-evangelist knows best.

In the last example, the two ominous and mysterious men have political connections to Whitehall. Presumably, their undercover intelligence work, bumbling as it is, has its source in the British government that gives them license to kill when secrets vital to the national interests are at stake. In consequence, two "prostitutes" are assassinated (one probably a Red agent) and Marlow, a too-intrusive private detective, is set up for a hit. Ultimately, it is Marlow, the detective (with Potter's help), who cashiers the two undercover agents.

In all these cases, the exercise of an overweening authority is condemned as a social abuse of individuals who should have the freedom of self-development. When such possibility is abrogated, as in the case of young Mark Binney, it amounts to *the* fundamental crime against humanity, the one unforgivable offense within Potter's postmodern perspective. Thus, Marlow's guilt and self-loathing have their origin in this traumatic event, from which his mother's sexual betrayal of his father and subsequent suicide conveniently detracts.[12] It allowed him to redirect his self-loathing upon others, especially women. He heaps upon them the shortcomings of the world and seeks to hide his self-betrayal in his illness and a bitter misanthropy. Nicola aptly describes his condition:

> You smash up people's lives—you're rotten with your own bile! You think you're smart but really you're very very sad, because you use your illness as a weapon against other people and as an excuse for not being properly human—ach! You disgust me! You sick little creep—You poisonous, malformed, cynical oaf! (p.218)

An alternative ending looms ever more threateningly in the last two episodes. As Marlow's hate and paranoia seem to tip the scales in that direction, Potter uses extreme self-reflexive devices to help viewers draw the analogy between characters in a play being scripted and his "real-life" hero, Marlow, losing control while being driven into increasing isolation by his past disillusionments.

VI

Self-reflexive writing draws attention to itself as created, instead of being an unnoticed, transparent representation of "what just happens." Foregrounding the script destroys the illusion that we can escape language into some world in itself. It focuses on the problem of how humankind reflects, constructs, and mediates its experience of the world. Such backing-up from action itself to the script controlling the action emerges from postmodern consciousness of how language constructs and maintains our version of reality. In commenting on its own construction, such writing probes the fictionality of "real life," making clear that life and art are both products of discourse. Implicit in this expose by postmodern writing is the need to free ourselves of unconscious dependencies, of inherited values and practices controlling present behavior without the agent's full awareness.

To bring TV viewers to self-awareness that their own predicament/possibility parallels that of Marlow, Potter utilizes many defamiliarizing techniques to interrupt any passive habitual consumption. The entire *TSD* makes use of antirealist techniques, e.g., having his characters lip-synching popular songs; parodying the film noir genre with its dark lighting, ominous music and abnormal camera angles; including comic features from Warner Brothers cartoons (the iris camera closure with "that's all folks"); and including allusions to the Keystone cops and Laurel and Hardy buffoonery when his two "intelligence agents" always exit running and whose inept bumbling and final rebellion unearth the real murderer (P. E. Marlow). But it is when posing an alternative ending, especially, that Potter reveals the necessity of breaking the hold of the past in order to control one's future.

Paranoid and suspicious of his estranged wife, Nicola (who has been asked to help on his case by Dr. Gibbon), Marlow has created a scenario of treacherous connivance between Nicola and Mark Binney (now turned by him into a 1986 film producer, Mark Finney) to steal his screenplay of *The Singing Detective*. As all the scenes between Finney and Nicola are the product of Marlow's paranoid delusion, the scenes reflect the mind that is scripting them. Binney even says that "I feel almost as though he has made all this up," (p. 147) and then he and Nicola continue to voice a description of their own creation:

> Binney: I have this awful—I have this awful dash he stops himself comma and all but shudders full stop
> Nicola: Darling dash question mark (p.149)

Meantime, Nicola casts shadows on the wall of a parrot and rabbit, which is what they have become—no longer free persons but manipulated victims.

Just before Marlow's cathartic breakthrough, the "real" Nicola, with some remnant of affection, informs him that a production company is interested in his screenplay, *The Singing Detective,* and that he should take the offer. Once she leaves, Marlow's general hostility wells up again fiercely: "You think I fell for that? She thinks I fell, hook line and sinker. And look what'll happen! Look what I'll do. Rot her thieving, narrow, poisonous soul!" (p.205) Thinking murderously about what he has in store for Nicola, Marlow affirms that "all shall be well." Turning to Noddy, Marlow then asks "You agree, don't you?" To which Noddy's unceasing nod-nodding seemingly acquiesces, while his palsied condition ironically countermands the agreement. Noddy is the picture of what Marlow will become if he continues on his present hate-filled course. He will end in rage and verbal impotence, with all loss of communication. In the film script, but not shown in the film, Noddy remembers Judges 16: 26–30 with wish-fulfilled animosity:

> And Samson took hold of the two middle pillars upon which the house stood, and on which it was borne up—And Samson said, Let me die with the Philistines. And he bowed himself with all his might, and the house fell upon . . .

Cackling with glee, Noddy watches Marlow resume writing with his splinted hand and slowly write "Blood." Shortly thereafter, Marlow has his two imagined thieves fall out with Nicola, murdering Finney by sticking a knife in his throat. She then commits suicide by jumping into the Thames and is fished out like her three predecessors (Sonia, Amanda, Lilli-Marlene/Mrs. Marlow). Meantime, in the pulp thriller, Binney lies murdered in the same gruesome manner. The two intelligence agents show up but, unlike Nicola and Finney, refuse to remain victims of their scriptor. As they view the bloody last message of the victim, Binney, which says "Who killed Roger Ayckroyd?," they humorously parody Potter's serious intent. They "absorb, ponder, act" and unearth the true culprit, the true "killer" who (as in the Agatha Christie mystery) happens to be the narrator hiding away in the hospital.

In the final shootout, the real culprit, the paranoid misanthropic author, receives his just deserts—a bullet through the head—from his alter ego, the tough detective. This brings an end to their long partnership. The writer of cheap detective thrillers has moved on to more important concerns, to interpreting and making sense of his own life.

VII

In his interview with Alan Yentob of the BBC, Potter stated that he has no idea where "the world is moving to" and doesn't care. But he wishes to show concern for "the sovereignty" of the human being who exists behind all the selves that time and social involvement always produce.[13] He reaffirmed that our lives are detective stories with superfluous clues and no final solutions. Only when we correctly perceive how the past still operates in the present can we comprehend the values built on that past, so that we can know ourselves better than before and take a hand in our destinies. By uncovering clues about ourselves and reassembling the pieces, we build a more adequate self. Potter believes human finitude inevitably leads to suffering. Each of us becomes a split self who must eventually tear himself away from the residue our historical passage leaves with us, consciously or unconsciously. But like a postmodern Aeschylus, Potter asserts that man can learn through suffering, and that continual disengagements and reinterpretations are not only man's lot, but challenging occasions for emancipatory sleuthing. Out of a dialogical investigation by the historically split self, between its present and past, a new self can emerge, with wider parameters and to whose endless regeneration and *Bildung* Potter commits his writing.[14]

NOTES

1. Graham Fuller, ed., in the introduction to *Potter on Potter* (London: Faber and Faber, 1993).
2. Fuller, introd.
3. Quoted in *Contemporary Literary Criticism* 58 (Detroit: Gale Research, 1990), p.397.
4. See the introduction to David Hiley et al., eds., *The Interpretive Turn* (Ithaca: Cornell University Press, 1991), p.7.
5. Charles B. Guignon, "Pragmatism or Hermeneutics? Epistemology after Foundationalism," in Hiley, p.99.
6. This is the verdict of both Martha Nussbaum in *Love's Knowledge* (New York: Oxford University Press, 1990); and Mikhail Bakhtin in *The Dialogic Imagination* (Austin: University of Texas Press, 1981).
7. Dennis Potter, *The Singing Detective* (London: Faber and Faber, 1986), p.128. Future references will be abbreviated *TSD* and cited pages included in the text.
8. William Spanos, "The Detective and the Boundary: Some Notes on the Postmodern Literary Imagination," *Boundary* 2 (Fall, 1972), pp.147–68.
9. Some general works covering these areas would be Kenneth Baynes, J. Bohman, and T. McCarthy, eds., *After Philosophy* (Cambridge, Mass.: MIT Press, 1987); Hazard Adams and L. Searle, eds. *Critical Theory Since 1965* (Gainsville: UP of Florida, 1986); Richard Rorty, *Contingency, Irony, and Solidarity* (New York: Cambridge University Press, 1989); and John McGowan, *Postmodernism and its Critics* (Ithaca: Cornell University Press, 1991).
10. Rosalind Coward in her article "Dennis Potter and the Question of the Television Author," *Critical Quarterly* (Winter, 1987) states: "There is no clear unilinear narrative development; scenes are juxtaposed rather than being connected in any linear 'cause and effect' sequence" (p.85). But there is a clear linear action even though the logic of sequences combine by association in fantasy,

dream, or paranoid projection. *TSD* is a psychodrama in which the "sick" consciousness in which the action moves will either resolve its problem or fail to do so. Marlow, with some help, heals himself even though a bad alternative ending threatens at the end of the fifth episode.

11.   Compare *The Wasteland* overtones in this excerpt: Binney: "This is the dead time, isn't it? Dead time in a dead city. You can feel the Nothingness pressing down on you. Pressing down on the whole dirty place. It looks cold out there. The river looks as though it's made of tar, sludging along. Full of filth" (p.59).

12.   Most critics refer only to Philip's mother's suicide as the traumatic event. That this event contributes to his cynicism and misogyny must be admitted, but the cathartic breakthrough comes, nevertheless, with his admission that he was victimizer as well as victim. Only then can he love again, forgiving those who made him suffer as he weeps over his own false witnessing. For a typical reading, which also includes a fine account of the origins for the various stunning effects in such a complex production, see Joost Hunningher, "The Singing Detective: Who Done It?" in George W. Brandt, ed., *Television Drama in the 1980s* (Cambridge: Cambridge University Press, 1993), pp.234–57.

13.   I find in both Potter's work and scattered interview comments a concern for his audience that finds theoretical support and expansion in Charles Taylor, *The Ethics of Authenticity* (Cambridge: Harvard University Press,1992). For the interview comments, see Graham Fuller, passim.

14.   For a lucid exposition of this updated concept of Bildung, see the last chapter of Georgia Warnke, *Gadamer: Hermeneutics, Tradition, and Reason* (Palo Alto: Stanford University Press, 1987).

CHAPTER 7

CONFINED BODIES, WANDERING MINDS

Memory, Paralysis and the Self in Some Earlier Works of Dennis Potter

Chris Lippard

> I ... wish we could talk over the many prisons of life—prisons of stone, prisons of passion, prisons of intellect, prisons of morality and the rest—all limitations, external or internal, all prisons, really. All life is a limitation.
>
> —Oscar Wilde[1]

> Through thick and thin I clung to a hard nut of individuality, deep down in my childish nature.
>
> —Edmund Gosse[2]

> Human actions trace no perfect circle or square; as historical events they escape axiomatic definition.
>
> —Ihab Hassan[3]

DENNIS POTTER KNEW SOMETHING ABOUT CONFINED bodies and wandering minds—this is the condition of his best-known creation, Marlow in *The Singing Detective,* and was so often that of Potter himself, constantly balancing drugs with the pain of psoriatic arthropathy, so as to still allow himself to write. The onset of Potter's illness directed him away from a political career in which he had already lost interest, and from the world of public affairs he turned to a different public soapbox, one that enabled him to reach many people but was itself confined, truly a box—television. Throughout his long career as a television writer, Potter made especially cogent use of literal and

metaphoric confinement, and attempted in many of his works—undogmati-
cally, and with due regard to the complexity of life and of the self—to plot possible ways out. In this essay I will examine the dichotomy between the
humanist and postmodern elements of Dennis Potter's work, focussing on the
variously confined characters in three works from the 1970s.

For Potter the struggle within television was always accompanied by an
equivalent subject matter, the struggle within the self—an exploration of individual sovereignty and its confines. Potter's work is balanced between two
strands of contemporary thought: the postmodern and the humanist. While his
work commonly presents the diffracted self and uses many of the strategies we
associate with the former, most of his comments on writing and the self emphasize his sense of belonging to a humanist tradition that acclaims the importance of individual self-knowledge.

To realize the sense of a coherent subjectivity—a sovereign self—Dennis
Potter's characters must free themselves from personal fixations and societal
constraints—a theme that remains significant in almost all his drama. To seek
to understand one's own identity is the task that one must undertake in order
to function satisfactorily; to achieve this self-awareness his characters must not
only "come to terms" with their pasts, but must be aware that past and present lie, intertwined, alongside each other. This relation of different time periods is something many of his characters signally fail to achieve—for example,
Bernard and Jean, in *Cream in My Coffee,* return to the seaside hotel of their
honeymoon, but succeed only in opening up old wounds that leave them lonely
and disoriented. On the other hand, it is the triumph of Marlow, in *The
Singing Detective,* to reach at least some awareness of how the different times
and events of his life intersect and determine each other, and thereby to break
from the confining influence of his past. Ihab Hassan, discussing Hans-Georg
Gadamer's *Philosophical Hermeneutics,* refers to "[t]his active pastness of the
self, this vital historicity of understanding," and Potter's work is a fine illustration of this view of life.[4]

There is, however, a second threat to the individual's sovereignty: the appeal and power of controlling paradigms of thought and life. As humans, Potter suggests, we fall short when we involve ourselves too completely with one
set of assumptions or pattern of thinking at the expense of our own highly individual circumstances and responses. The idea of abandoning self to system
operates on several levels in his life and his writing. Willy, the economically
and intellectually impoverished young protagonist of Potter's *Where the Buffalo Roam,* lives in a world he creates from his wholesale assumption of the
values of American western movies. Unfortunately, he must also live in the
drab industrial landscape of Swansea, where no buffalo roam. Willy dies in the
hopeless attempt to match his value system to his circumstances. Arthur
Parker, in *Pennies from Heaven,* craves a world true to the songs he sells and

behaves accordingly, even though he sometimes realizes the disparity between his passion and the realities of life in thirties England. As he is about to leave for the West Country to hawk "Roll along, Prairie Moon," his wife inquires "there's not a prairie in Gloucester is there?" to which he is compelled to reply, "No. There's a desert."

In political terms, Potter began to write plays after he felt that he was "invalid" as a politician. Psoriasis yielded him a personal route via television, to the confrontation of social problems. Thus, while he remained consistently hostile to Thatcherism, which attempted to redefine personal freedom by attacking communal values, Potter turned away from direct involvement with the Labour party or the politics of the left, and was highly suspicious of the overarching solutions offered by Marxism.[5]

Against the dominance of systems, Potter advocates individual creativity. From the writer's perspective he bemoans "the destruction of humanism" in his preface to *Waiting for the Boat,* the 1984 collection of three of his plays.[6] Comparing contemporary intellectual thought to oil clogging the feathers of an albatross, Potter claims that much of it works to stifle humanistic culture. He valorizes individuality of utterance, using the powerful metaphoric rhetoric of which he is a master to link ideological "paralysis" to the verbal poverty of such thought.[7] He argues that:

> The overwhelming thrust of contemporary critical ideologies, whether Marxist or Structuralist, whether in the fractured syntax of the semiologists or the muted woof and warp of intertextuality et al., is consistently away from the singular or individual and in lumbering, flat-footed, tongue-tied motion towards the universal and the systematic.[8]

There is a strong strand of resistance to "theory" in Potter's writings and interviews, yet much of his own work is explicitly intertextual and allusive, ripe for the kinds of analysis he here decries. For example, Potter bases his remarks in the preface on a speech he made in Dublin, in which context the repeated reference to paralysis suggests an allusion to Joyce's *Dubliners.*[9] The symbol of the befouled seabird evokes Baudelaire's metaphoric comparison of bird to writer that structures his well-known poem "The Albatross." The phrase "muted woof and warp of intertextuality" in fact, taken on its own, does not sound condemnatory and is allusive as well as metaphoric.

It is impossible not to feel that Potter invites exactly the kinds of commentary he claims to despise. Many of his plays embody his divided allegiances—to the intellectual and the popular, the high modern and the postmodern, the democratic and the self-referential—that dismissive stances such as those in the above quotation seek to deny. Potter's "betrayal" of his own infrastructure was fairly consistent. Earlier in the same introduction he also makes the Wildean comment: "I do not believe what writers say about themselves, except when they think they are not saying it about themselves."[10] The content and rhythm of these comments, qualifying and requalifying, reflects a humanism that is based on concepts of freedom to adapt and of balance as the keys to individual fulfillment.

Potter's humanist God is also best seen in terms of personal sovereignty. For him religion was the wound, not the bandage: a reminder that humans have spiritual needs, that they are often holes, not wholes.[11] God was that which you could not quite get your tongue around, the ineffable thing that distinguished humans from the merely animal. In *Son of Man* (transmitted as *The Wednesday Play,* in April 1969), Potter's Christ is a man whose God burns inside him, tearing at him. He is set apart from his fellow men both by this "passion" and by his power over words, but he remains fully human, a carpenter who recognizes the quality of the timber on Calvary.

In contrast to the heartfelt experience of a man who suffers his divinity, which Potter portrays in *Son of Man, Where Adam Stood* (1976) looks at the highly organized religion of an evangelical Christian sect in the mid-nineteenth century. Potter's play is adapted from Edmund Gosse's autobiographical *Father and Son,* a record of Gosse's strict religious upbringing under the watchful eye of a father who believed in the literal truth of the Bible. The elder Gosse (Alan Badel) is a widely renowned naturalist, whose unbending religion prevents him from giving credence to Darwin's discoveries, and who constructs his own theory to account for the evidence of evolutionary forces in the world.

Edmund (Max Harris) is too young to challenge his father's logic on such points but he does resist the constraints on his life, adapting—though perhaps more chameleon-like than Darwin-like—to his environment. Coveting a fully rigged model ship in a shop window, Edmund is instructed by his father to pray for guidance from God. Gosse confidently expects his son's prayer to result in a sober rejection of the frivolous toy. When Edmund tells him that God has said that he should have the ship, the father, trapped by his own methods, must indulge him.

The interior language of prayer, in which the Plymouth Brethren of *Where Adam Stood* believe so strongly, discounts the individual before the wishes of God. Rejecting this kind of confined communication, Edmund eventually writes, in *Father and Son,* an account of his father's beliefs, rooted in a time and a place, which locates the God inside the man rather than portraying man as a facet of God. For Potter, as for Edmund Gosse, God is part of an inner personal drama, His explanation a facet of our humanity that must be freeing, not confining.

The search for such a God provides the kind of "interior drama" that Potter wanted to write for television. The domestic setting of television-viewing afforded access to the interior of the home, and Potter hoped and believed that this environment would, in turn, allow him to address the audience's most deep-seated concerns. Shortly after the broadcast of *Where Adam Stood,* he described what he thought was the subject of good television drama:

> I'm much more concerned with interior drama than with external realities. Television is equipped to have an interior language. Certainly one of the strands in television drama is that of the interiorising process, the concern with people's fantasies and feelings about the shape of their lives, and about themselves. It seems very important to me that television should be concerned with that, because the people watching it are watching it in a very peculiar way, with all their barriers down.[12]

Alone or in small groups, in their own homes, the distracted television audience is also, Potter suggests, unusually receptive, unguarded and thus susceptible to the writer's ends. His emphasis in the following statement is rather different: television's distracted viewers may be harder to "reach" than in other media, but the effect on reaching them is all the greater precisely because of the normally quotidian nature of the experience:

> When you watch television you don't dress up for it, you don't go out for it, you don't pay for it, the lights are on, and you do things and you talk, and all that is largely to the detriment of the experience—but if something is working it can be extraordinarily powerful because it sits right in the middle of all that mundaneness.[13]

The humiliations and embarrassments of the human condition, our preconceptions and pasts, constitute the pervasive limitations of life, the confines of the human. Such is the interior drama that humans endure. Good television drama, Potter contends, by catching people unaware, explores this territory at the heart of the viewers' everyday existence.

I now want to illustrate how Potter attempts to break through the mundane in three texts that offer additional complications to the theme of personal confinement. In *Traitor,* the eponymous character lives alone in a spartan Moscow apartment; in *Casanova,* the protagonist's life is presented via his time in prison; while in *Brimstone and Treacle,* the protagonist is not human, and the central figure, trapped in a body that no longer functions, is not sentient.

TRAITOR

In *Traitor* (1971), former British intelligence officer Adrian Harris (John Le Mesurier)—apparently a version of Kim Philby—now fled to the Soviet Union, is visited by four Western journalists, eager for a story. Harris's existence in Moscow is clearly a sad one, and he is entrapped in several senses. In the first place, his physical environment is a soulless, isolated apartment at the top of an apartment block in which the elevator doesn't work. As he talks with his visitors, Harris strides nervously about the apartment, at one point rushing out onto his small balcony, only, it seems, to be thwarted of any other place to go.

Harris's rigid and unloving upbringing in England has instilled in him a hatred of its class system that exists uneasily with a continued love for his country, sans flag-waving and public (i.e., private) schools. Although the memories that he recalls to himself and to his guests are horror stories of English repression—his father remaining seated a few feet away, ignoring his son's screams while he calls for a nanny to tend to the boy; a sadistic schoolmaster who torments him because of his stutter—a small picture of a Constable painting on the wall of the apartment is a reminder of the England he yearns for, one separated from the stifling veneers of its social organization. As the traitor tells his guests, "nowadays almost all belief is prickled and speckled with desperate irony, and necessary complexity." Still, trapped in his "miserable little room," Harris's life is, in another sense, now very simple—and rigidly constrained. We find out at the end of the play that his apartment is "bugged," and we witness throughout his thrall to the bottle. As the reporters labor up the stairs at the start of the play, we see Harris, in his apartment, compulsively rearranging the objects on his desk, and trying to decide how much to hide his drinking. His consumption of "White Horse" scotch is accompanied on the soundtrack by a song about a "milk white steed" that introduces a picture of a falsified chivalric England tied to the Arthurian legend with which his archaeologist father is enraptured. But the white horse is also evocative of the English countryside, which still draws him so powerfully. Many such horses are cut into the chalk hills of southern England, but Harris will now come no closer to them than the bottles his visitors encourage him to drink so that he will give more and more of himself away.[14]

The power of this play resides in the sympathy we feel for a pathetic, intelligent man who has made an understandable, but perhaps unforgivable—certainly unforgiven—mistake.[15] Forced to recite William Blake's poetry by the schoolmaster, the young Harris cannot get out the word "nibbled." "What did the lambs do?" repeats the master, until finally Harris, his tongue paralyzed, bursts out with "Pee-ed themselves." This first act of defiance against English authority contains the seeds of his ultimate dilemma, because Harris's treachery loses him not just the harrowing petty fascism of the English public school, but the lambs and fields of his birthplace and the highly conscionable, radical patriotism of Blake.

What repulses Harris about England, then, are the small terrors and savage inequalities of the class system. As well as his own past, we see historical footage—accompanied sometimes by Blake's "Jerusalem," long a working-class mantra—of urban poverty and of the Jarrow crusade for jobs.[16] He tells his visitors: "I am a traitor to my class, yes; to my country, no. No, not to England."

In fact Harris is like Potter in his yearning for an Englishness separable from and opposed to monied interests and hierarchical exploitation. Potter has since made several direct references to his pleasure in England and the English, and words such as the following from his last interview with Melvyn Bragg echo the sentiments of the exiled Harris:

> I feel the pull of tradition and I love my land, I love England, and when I'm abroad, I genuinely feel homesick. I've always loved my country, but not drums and trumpets and billowing Union Jacks and busby soldiers and the monarchy and pomp and circumstance, but something about our people.[17]

Benedict Anderson, discussing the development and growth of nationalism, records that nations, like other communities "are to be distinguished, not by their falsity/genuineness, but by the style in which they are imagined."[18] In this way, we are able to conceive a relationship with other people in a national group. Potter's "imagined community" seems to have been created by extending his conception of the social cooperation and community values that he recalled from the Forest of Dean, where he grew up, in the decade following World War II.[19] Like Potter's perhaps, Harris's version of England is based on what Raymond Williams would call a "residual" culture, one that gradually dissipated before the "emergent" and opposing ideology of Thatcherism, in which the aspects of the country that he scorns are reasserted.[20]

In his rejection of a culture in which England "is treated as a mass hunting-ground by the rich," Adrian Harris imagines a socialist rather than a national community. His nostalgia and the mise-en-scène of *Traitor*, however, show that England remains for Harris the more deeply imagined community. Reacting against his father's sense of an England sustained by Arthurian legend, he has sought, and been confined by, a very different but equally elusive Camelot.[21]

CASANOVA

Potter's serialization in six episodes of the life of Giacomo Casanova, based on the extensive twelve-volume *History of my Life* Casanova wrote in the few years before his death in 1797, was broadcast on BBC2 in November and December 1971, starting its run barely a month after the showing of *Traitor*. Casanova's time imprisoned under the leaden roof of the ducal palace in Venice ("the Leads") occupies a relatively small section of his memoirs—five chapters of the sixteen that comprise volume 4—but becomes the focus of Potter's extremely loose adaptation.

Languishing in jail, where he is supposed to reflect on and amend his wickedness, Casanova (Frank Finlay) recalls his past exploits with both joy and regret. Rather like an illness, the enforced inactivity of jail compels the prisoner to take stock and to use his memories to escape present circumstances. Casanova relishes his sleep because in it he can reclaim a past, unsullied by the present. From the second episode onward however, there are at least as many flash-forwards to what Casanova does after his escape from the "Leads" as there are flashbacks to the time before his arrest. In the post-imprisonment sequences, Casanova, having once been deprived of his freedom, is determined to use it well. To be free is the essence of his life, which now has two purposes: to be happy, and to store up memories for the confinements of old age. He explains: "I want to remember everything, to savor it all once more and I hope to regret nothing, [to be] able, even in my dotage, to acknowledge that I used my freedom as though it were precious." *Casanova* continually shifts back and forth in time by cutting on the closing and opening, locking and unlocking of doors, relating Casanova's sexual liaisons to his incarceration. As the protagonist does, the audience learns the shape of Casanova's life from the temporally discontinuous actions, dreams, and memories that are laid next to each other. (Potter was to bring this technique to its full potential in his similarly multilayered six-part masterpiece, *The Singing Detective,* fifteen years later.)

Potter later remarked upon the importance of struggling with what it is to be human as we grow older; otherwise life becomes a steady degeneration from the passions of adolescence.[22] Casanova, however, strives to do the one while continuing the other. Although he regrets some of his actions as he grapples with what his life amounts to, he does not turn away from a dissolute life; rather he is reconfirmed in his amorous exploits, seeking to preserve those youthful passions not only in memory, but in old age, where they seem inappropriate and faintly embarrassing. Even on his deathbed, he makes a deal with the attractive woman who reads his memoirs back to him, allowing him to stroke her breast. His sensuality is, however, a confinement as well as an assertion of freedom, in that it does not allow him to achieve that balanced approach to his humanity that can accept aging and death. When he really falls in love, the libertine is unable to escape the memories of past insincerities because every compliment he pays with meaning, he has previously paid without meaning. Thus the panoply of previous pleasures denies him the possibility of a deeper, more serious attachment.

In prison, however, Casanova learns that while systematic and logical thought can explain very little, a determined reliance on the self will ultimately realize his goal. He was arrested in July 1755, possibly at the instigation of playwright Abate Chiari, on a series of vague charges of profligacy, corruption and atheism. In the first episode of Potter's serial, as Casanova is led through door after door along the labyrinthine passages of the palace/jail, a list of the charges is read out, including such items as "cheat at cards" and "unbeliever." He never discovers the true reason for his imprisonment, nor how long he is to be there, but he does learn not to fret about such things. What his jailer Lorenzo tells him on the day of his arrest—that it "is better to hope than to know"—turns out to be excellent advice. By the second episode, Casanova, despite occasional bursts of frustration, is able to tell his cell mate, Schalon, who wants to know why they are treated as they are, that "nothing makes sense. The more you try to explain things, the less you understand." To retain his sanity, the prisoner must focus on himself, seeking to understand *how he can,* not *why he must* function in these circumstances. Not that Casanova ever gives up the hope of freedom: it is his constant focus. He begins planning an escape immediately after he stops questioning why misfortune has befallen him, and his guileful skill as a seducer serves him well in his new role as a prisoner. When his first escape route—a hole in the floor—is discovered, he persuades Lorenzo that it is only his negligence that has allowed him to proceed so far and that, in his own interest, the jailer should not report him; he then begins the search for a new means of escape. In his memoirs Casanova writes that: "when a man takes it into his head to accomplish some project and pursues it to the exclusion of anything else, he must succeed in it despite all difficulties"; and, indeed, he eventually orchestrated the only successful escape from the "Leads."[23] Casanova goes on to add that good fortune is also necessary for success. Potter's script retains all these elements, and the mix of skill, determination and luck is the same that working class writers need, as Raymond Williams—and Potter himself—suggests, in order to escape a laborer's destiny.[24] Potter, however, accentuates the role of writing—something over which *The History* passes quickly—both in preserving Casanova's sanity in jail and in his escape.

To Casanova's means of temporarily escaping his situation—memory and sleep—books are added when he is granted access to a few sanctioned volumes. Their lack is one of the greatest hardships for the educated prisoner to bear, for they offer a connection with another human mind and thus an escape from solitude or unstimulating companions. Although Casanova is delighted to be allowed to read, he is ecstatic when he finds he can write. In the final episode of the series, the prisoner is brought mulberries on doctor's orders for the sake of his physical health. (His symptoms include nightmarish fantasies that have replaced his previously consoling dreams.) Casanova is at first only mildly pleased with the treat, but he soon discovers that the fruit is a panacea for something that ails him severely—the lack of ink. With a shriek of joy, he jams his finger into the fruit and then smears words on the inside cover of a book with it. Thus he is able to communicate with fellow prisoner Father Balbi, explaining, in the margins of the books they are allowed to exchange, the plan of escape he has hatched but that the less closely watched Balbi must set in motion.[25]

The final episode of *Casanova* cuts between Casanova's formulation of his escape plan and his final days as a librarian at the castle of Count Wallenstein, where he struggles to complete his memoirs before he dies. Although the castle itself reminds him of his imprisonment—his walk through doors and corridors to his room is cross-cut with his similar walk upon arrival at the palace in episode one—Casanova's decrepit body is now his new jail, the confines of which he will "escape" but to no new philandering. We have seen Casanova reject prayer as hypocritical soon after his arrest—he abandons his prayer in favor of thumbing his nose at God or at his fate—and there is no sense that he now believes in a spiritual afterlife. In life he has adapted God to his own purpose, proclaiming that, "He has given us nothing which is not designed to make us happy," and, in death, he clings instead to his stacks of written pages, his memorial in the material world. The series ends with his death and his escape: the final images show him standing, outlined against a dawn sky, in long shot above the rooftops of Venice, finally on the right side of the lead. The sense of space, accentuated by the long rays of the just-rising sun, makes this image powerfully evocative of freedom. We do not, I think, even need to have seen the series to be able to read it in this way, so mythically resonant is the symbolism. The contrast with the many shots in the cramped confines of the cell, however, clearly emphasizes the effect. Closing on such an image imparts a triumphant feeling to the end of the text, even though the reminder that life too must finally escape comes just before it. Indeed, Casanova's death is also an escape, in the sense that he is free of the sexual appetites that he has pursued in freedom with almost the same single-mindedness that he has sought escape while imprisoned.[26] *Casanova* shows us a man who becomes a very good prisoner, escaping his confines mentally as best he can, and finally breaching them literally. About the validity of the rest of his life, dominated by his supreme valuation of freedom—from marriage and other potential restraints on his behavior as well as locked rooms—we may well remain unconvinced. Has Casanova examined his life sufficiently deeply? *Casanova*, I think, provokes us to ask the same question of ourselves.

BRIMSTONE AND TREACLE

Just as *Casanova* ends with freedom achieved, so does *Brimstone and Treacle*, but this time freedom is the consequence of a sudden and malevolent presence. Casanova uses sex as a way to breach the limitations of the human; for him it is the nearest thing to transcendence. In *Brimstone and Treacle*, sex also brings about renewed life, and the manner in which it does so has made the script Potter's most controversial. *Brimstone and Treacle* may be grouped with his television plays *Angels are so Few* and *Schmoedipus*, and the feature film, *Track 29*, in a subgenre of Potter's work that focuses on visitations from figures who are, or appear to be, angels or devils. In each case, the supernatural character claims some special relationship to, or need from, the house he calls upon.[27] In *Brimstone*, Martin (Michael Kitchen), an exaggeratedly well-spoken young man, dupes Mr. and Mrs. Bates (Denholm Elliott, Patricia Lawrence) into believing that he was once a close friend and would-be lover of their daughter, Patricia (Michelle Newell). Patricia has been catatonic since being hit by a car two years before and requires constant attention that she receives mostly from her mother. Taken in by their visitor's kindness and professions of love, however, Mrs. Bates leaves Patty alone with him. Martin abuses and sexually assaults her, but when he attempts to repeat the rape the following night, Patty wakes, screaming, from her coma, apparently recovered. Martin escapes into the dark to go in search of another victim.

Patty's parents differ in their attitudes toward their daughter. While her mother regularly sees signs of improvement and continues to talk to her as if she can understand, her father disdains what he sees as a deluded and unrealistic attitude in his wife. For him, Patty has passed from the human realm and her continued existence, trapped in an unresponsive, "in-valid" body is horrific. "Caged up, cooped up inside your own head. It's always been one of the worst nightmares for me," he declares. Since Mr. Bates, ashamed of his daughter's condition, refuses to have anyone in to care for her, Patty's imprisonment in her body also effectively confines her mother to the house where she feels trapped and underappreciated. As he finally persuades her to leave for an hour to have her hair "done," Martin points out that she is hardly able to go: "that's what comes of being locked away for such a long time. It gets to be like a disease."

Mr. Bates does get out of the house, to go to work, but his dismal view of the present is fed by a diseased, nostalgic view of the past. Potter's plays are pervaded by nostalgia, which he uses to open up the past both within the drama, for his characters, and, sometimes, for the audience at home. However, he also regards it as a degraded or "second order" emotion, one that displaces any sense of the individual's genuine relationship to his or her history, and confining the present in its potent grip. (We have seen how this holds true in *Traitor*.) Ostensibly a kind of remembering, nostalgia, for Potter, is in fact "a means of forgetting the past, of making it seem cozy, of saying, 'It's back there—look how sweet it was.'"[28]

Mr. Bates's nostalgia for the world he used to know is really the desire to return to a time when he felt in control and before his life was marked by his daughter's tragedy. He tells his visitor: "[a]ll I want is the England I used to know, the England I remember as a young man. . . . I simply want the world to stop right where it is and go back a bit." His unbalanced attitude to the past makes Mr. Bates opposed to any change. In its benign form, this conservatism results in opposition to fluoridation and decimalization, but it also leads him to a reactionary and racist view of immigration. Martin, well suited to play devil's advocate, embarrasses his host by enthusiastically taking his opinions to their logical, Nazi-like conclusion: "England for the English. Irish, blacks . . . put them into camps . . . round 'em up from the ghettos and push and prod and hunt 'em down." Mr. Bates, of course, recoils from the pain and violence that his racism implies—but the implication is clear: an inappropriate vision of the past degrades and dooms both the individual and the society. Whereas for Potter's Casanova, under the "Leads" and on his deathbed, memories constitute a necessary and productive illusion of freedom. Using nostalgia to prop up one's view of the world can be appalling, the equivalent of a sickness. "You should always look back on your past with tender contempt," Potter remarked on at least two occasions, adopting a typically ambiguous, carefully balanced view of life.[29]

Brimstone and Treacle is relatively unambiguous in establishing Martin as human only on the surface.[30] He is a dark angel: we can smell the sulphur on him. Seemingly dedicated to old-world values of love and obedience to his elders, he claims to relish housework and despises "stains or dirt of any description." He professes an undying affection for Patricia, who he claims to have always loved despite her own comparative indifference. "She will always be, for me," he tells her parents, "the girl the songs sing about." Martin is embarrassingly sentimental about his feelings; like treacle he is cloyingly sweet—but we soon see the brimstone underneath. Allowed to spend the night in Patty's old room, Martin rubs himself with her underwear, an action that begins a marvelously witty, visually exciting, but intensely disturbing musical sequence. To the sounds of "That Old Black Magic" and a reworded "Diamonds are a fiend's best friend," Martin cavorts around the house, revealing his cloven feet and accompanied by billowing smoke, flashing lights, fish-eye lens shots and the crowing of a male voice choir. As the routine continues, he moves downstairs, his eyes gleaming red and orange, and peels back Patty's clothes. Although no sexual assault is shown, Martin's intentions are sufficiently clear and at the end of the play, as he repeats his performance, she wakes only when he is already astride her.

These sequences were influential in convincing BBC director-general Alasdair Milne to ban *Brimstone and Treacle* only days before it was to be broadcast in 1976. The play remained unseen for 11 years, finally screening on 25 August 1987 as part of a celebration of Potter's work following the success of *The Singing Detective*. In a letter, Milne referred to *Brimstone* as "diabolical," which, Potter commented, "it was . . . but not of course in the sense that he meant."[31] The diabolical subject that the play treats was also, Milne apparently feared, presented in a diabolical manner.

The choreographed assault scenes provide just one example where the tone of the play might cause such offense.[32] *Brimstone* is also loaded with a sharp, flip innuendo. For example, Martin, asserting that Patty needs love, assures her mother that he is "going to love her every day." Delighted, Mrs. Bates responds: "surely she must pick up some of the vibrations." And Martin counters: "oh, I'm sure she does." Finally, the play refuses to condemn its devil, and the "happy ending" of Patty's awakening questions conventional morality by submitting that evil acts can bring good results—and, presumably, good acts, evil results. The viewer may be reminded of the quotation from Kierkegaard with which the play begins: "There resides infinitely more good in the demonic man than in the trivial." Introducing the play at a retrospective of Potter's work in New York in 1992, Kenith Trodd, its producer, suggested that *Brimstone* "tries to shatter and shred any easy sense of wholeness and oneness," and, somewhat hyperbolically perhaps, that the play is "the most unsentimental of any modern drama I know, written in the English language." For all these reasons, *Brimstone* was judged by the BBC (and some critics who saw the rather less compelling 1982 film version starring Sting) not as the work of a humanist, but as an attack on the human itself: its degradation before a diabolical verbal and visual wit and moral ambiguity.

Potter, on the other hand, clearly believed that both his subject and his manner in *Brimstone* address something essential to our humanity. Before he picks up and "dances" with the helpless Patty, prior to assaulting her, Martin turns directly to the camera and addresses the audience: "switch over or switch off if you are delicate but we all have some horns and a tail." The use of nonnaturalistic techniques such as the direct address and the musical sequences attempt to catch a level of audience attention that will prevent channel-changing and puncture the mundane. Potter writes that:

> to use non-naturalistic devices in a naturalistic medium is a way of making people put the lights out, draw the curtains, sit around and pay attention . . . If it works, it works in a way that draws you right into that box. . . . Non-naturalism and its use of the inside of your head is more likely to remind you about the shreds of your own sovereignty.[33]

POSTHUMANISM

Potter's consistent use of nonnaturalistic devices, complex narrative structures, even the techniques of magic realism, align him not only with the tenets of modernism with its ties to psychological depth and humanism, but also to the postmodern sensibility that he resisted and attacked. In Ihab Hassan's list of the characteristic tendencies of the cultural moment in the introduction to *The Postmodern Turn*, every item, it seems, corresponds to an element in Potter's work:

> Indeterminacy and immanence; ubiquitous simulacra, pseudo-events; lightness and evanescence everywhere; a new temporality, or rather intertemporality, a polychronic sense of history; a patchwork or ludic, transgressive, or deconstructive, approach to knowledge and authority; an ironic, parodic, reflexive, fantastic awareness of the moment.[34]

Potter's humanism endeavors to be without illusions, sentimentality, or nostalgia. Despite the fact that he is writing "inner dramas," concerned with what might, perhaps, best be called the spiritual, Potter's drama is also deeply rooted in the body, and especially in its sexual functions (or malfunctions). Consistently, in Potter's work, it is memory that links mind and body. In a significant number of archetypically postmodern texts, such as those of Philip K. Dick, the memory can be captured and repackaged, and this notion has proved inviting for Hollywood. The most advanced replicants in *Blade Runner* (based on Dick's *Do Androids Dream of Electric Sheep?*), for example, believe themselves to be human because they can recall childhoods they never actually experienced. In Potter's posthumously produced *Cold Lazarus,* the protagonist's cryogenically frozen—and now activated—head is able to recall its past, but not to control its dissemination: he/it suffers the indignity of having his/its memories "televised" for popular entertainment. Memories without human subjects are now resonant in our postmodern culture, but the reverse is hardly true—as people we are the meeting points of our pasts. This preoccupation with memory is a thread that runs through, indeed structures, the great majority of Potter's writing, being intimately tied to the writerly, (post)modern nature of his narratives.

While the term humanist needs qualification, Potter's approach to his material is not a transcendental one, nor is it a postmodern abandonment of the subject. Hassan, expressing his dissatisfaction with the postmodern term, argues for a reconceptualization of the cultural moment in relation to humanism. Like Potter, he is adversely impressed by the suggestions of a lack of depth that cling to "postmodernism" and wants to address what "it reaches for[,] something larger, something other."[35] Hassan labels this tendency "posthumanism," and the word fits Potter very well. Like the characters that appear in his visitation scripts or who are confined by the conditions of their life, Potter writes about—to employ another of Hassan's terms—the "inconclusively human," dramatizing, suggesting, inciting, but rarely resolving, the conflicts and tensions of such a "posthuman" world.[36]

Potter contended that the emotional power he believed his work contained was the result of "the contest between [his] real self and [his] invented self."[37] It is not the unified self of traditional humanism, then, but achieving a balance between conflicting versions of the self, that produces effective living and writing. Memory, misused, unacknowledged or unrestrained, threatens this balance and invites emotional or spiritual paralysis.

For Potter, the self he called real was usually the psoriatic sufferer, while the invented self was the individual who existed aside or beyond the pain and its constraints. For him, the primary balance his life as a writer required was that between health and illness, but the metaphor of the contest or the balance is widely applicable to his thought and work. He also adopted the standard metaphor equating mental health with the achieved balance: "[t]he object of mental health is to have in balance all that you strive for and want to do."[38] For Potter everything hung in the balance or must be balanced. He remains a Janus figure; emotionally and intellectually committed to the past in terms of class allegiance and democratic values, he was also committed to radical experimentation and invention as an artist. In his work he is both premodern and postmodern, popular and elitist, nostalgic and unsentimental and, like all of us, both real and invented.

NOTES

1. Richard Ellmann, *Oscar Wilde* (New York: Alfred A. Knopf, 1988), p.505.
2. Edmund Gosse, *Father and Son* (London: Penguin, 1949/1907), p.140.
3. Ihab Hassan, *The Postmodern Turn: Essays in Postmodern Theory and Culture* (Columbus: Ohio State University Press, 1987), p.xv.
4. Ihab Hassan, *The Postmodern Turn* (Columbus: Ohio State University Press, 1987), p.158.
5. Both *Traitor* and *Blade on the Feather* critique Soviet Communism (as well as many aspects of British culture and society). Potter is contesting specific applications of Marxism in these texts; nevertheless, the humanist or posthumanist thought and strategies he employs in his work suggest a more general opposition to traditional Marxism.
6. Dennis Potter, *Waiting for the Boat* (London: Faber, 1984), p.26.
7. Potter, *Boat*, p.26.
8. Potter, *Boat*, p.26.
9. "Paralysis" is the first word in the first story of Joyce's collection *Dubliners* and sets the tone for the stories that follow.
10. Potter, *Boat*, p.13.
11. Potter says that religion is a wound, not a bandage, in his 1978 television interview with Bernard Levin, and repeats the phrase—acknowledging that he is doing so—in his final interview with Melvyn Bragg in 1994.

12. George W. Brandt, *British Television Drama* (Cambridge: Cambridge University Press, 1981), p.175.

13. Dennis Potter, *Potter on Potter* ed. Graham Fuller (London: Faber, 1993), p.122.

14. Guy Bennett, a thinly disguised Guy Burgess, in Marek Kanievska's *Another Country* (1984) shares Harris's preference for whiskey over vodka. Kanievska's film is told as a chronological narrative aside from a framing story in which an American reporter interviews Bennett as an old man in Moscow. To her, he explains his treachery. Bennett begins by asking the journalist's question for her: "why would someone of [my] class turn around and kick it in the teeth?" His answer is to describe the rottenness and hypocrisy involved in his public (i.e., private) school's suppression of his homosexuality. *Another Country* is full of the signifiers of upper-class Englishness: military parades, punting, cricket in lily-white uniforms and a belief in hierarchies that makes two select school prefects into "Gods" each year. The film is entirely sympathetic to Bennett, but it does not, I think, show enough of him in Moscow for viewers to speculate on his new situation. The distaste for vodka can only carry so much symbolism.

15. Le Mesurier is especially impressive in the central role. He would have been well-known to British viewers for his role as Sergeant Wilson in the long-running and extremely popular situation comedy about the Home Guard in World War II, *Dad's Army.*

16. The Jarrow crusade remains one of the most powerfully symbolic events in the history of British working-class protest. In 1936, 200 unemployed workers marched 300 miles from Jarrow on Tyneside to Westminster after the closing of the shipyards had left three-quarters of the town unemployed.

17. Dennis Potter, *Seeing the Blossom* (London: Faber, 1994), p.17.

18. Benedict Anderson, *Imagined Communities* (London: Verso, 1991), p.6.

19. The Forest of Dean is geographically a very clearly defined area, a wedge bordered by two rivers. Across one of these, the Wye, lies Wales, and in the Bragg interview Potter noted his "natural," geographically determined hatred of the Welsh: "I'm a border person, and that's the way it is" (6). He later adds: " . . . yet many of my friends are Welsh." The "hatred" itself is, of course, a mythical or "imagined" fiction by which to operate.

20. Raymond Williams, "Forms of English Fiction in 1848," in *Literature, Politics and Theory,* ed. Francis Barker, Peter Hulme, Margaret Iverson, and Diana Loxley (London: Methuen, 1986), p.1.

21. Potter's other play about traitors is *Blade on the Feather.* At its climax the traitor, Cavendish, offers an explanation not simply of his own actions, but also of the strange congruence between his class and political treachery:

     I was born into a class that loves what it owns. And we don't own quite enough of it any more. That is why all, all, not just some but all, of the renowned traitors working for Nazi Germany or for Stalin's Russia, all come from my class.

     There is little logic behind Cavendish's contention; rather, it is the reaction of a sulky child. Deprived of the "Englishness" he believes he should own, he sells out. There is no sense here of any socialist commitment—however misguided—such as it is hard not to see in Adrian Harris's treachery. Things have already moved too far towards equality: for Cavendish, perhaps for everybody, the sense of Englishness and traditional patterns of ownership are inextricably bound up, and, rather than have them taken from him, he will undermine them himself. His imagined community càn only *be* imagined in terms of rigidly fixed class distinctions; without them there is no England. In discussing *Blade on the Feather*, Potter argues, somewhat elliptically, that this emphasis on property, pervasive in the upper classes, cuts them off from the more deeply held qualities of their countrymen, what he terms the "English condition": "There is that patrician element in the English upper-classes which makes them willing to sell out anything to anybody at any time. Even though they appear to foreigners to be the ultra-English, they are—to me anyway—the least English-like of all the English" (Fuller, p.43). Potter thus reverses Matthew Arnold's assertion of the Englishness of the upper (and professional) classes as against a working population salvageable for England only through "Culture."

22. Potter says this most clearly perhaps in his *Levin Interview* with Bernard Levin, broadcast on BBC2 on 16 April 1978.

23. Giacomo Casanova, *The History of My Life*, trans. Willard R. Trask (London: Longmans, 1967/1797), 4:222.

24. Discussing D. H. Lawrence, Williams notes: "It is only by hard fighting and, further, by the fortune of fighting on a favorable front, that anyone born into the industrial working-class escapes his function of replacement." Raymond Williams, *Culture and Society, 1780–1950* (London: Penguin, 1961/1958) 202. These words about Lawrence are equally applicable to both Williams, himself, and to Potter.

25. In *The History*, Casanova mentions his discovery of ink only when he comes to the description of his illicit communication with Father Balbi. He writes, simply: " I had let the nail of the little finger of my right hand grow in order to clean my ears with it, I cut it to a point and made a pen of it, in place of ink I used the juice of black mulberries" (264).

26. John Cook has suggested that Casanova's exploits parallel Adrian Harris's in *Traitor*. Both men are "possessed of the same spiritual yearning. . . . Utterly secular, even profane, in their actions and settings, both [*Traitor* and *Casanova*] smuggle spiritual themes out to a mass audience, under the guise of the spy play and costume drama respectively." See John R. Cook, *Dennis Potter: A Life on Screen* (Manchester: Manchester University Press, 1995), p.160.

27. Potter has described his psoriasis as such a visitor. In a remark that recalls Robert Frost's "Bereft," in which the narrator holds the wind-buffeted door of his house, Potter comments: "[t]he wind had got into my house again, as it were, and the tiles were falling off me" (Fuller, p.124).

28. *Potter on Potter*, p.22. *Blue Remembered Hills* (*Play for Today*, 1/30/79), in which he reprises the technique of children playing adults but sustains it for 72 minutes, is perhaps Potter's most direct treatment of nostalgia as well as one of his most riveting single plays. Its title comes from A. E. Housman's nostalgic and sentimental paean to his childhood memories.

29. *Potter on Potter,* p.98; Potter, *Blossoms,* p.13.

30. In the 1982 film version of *Brimstone and Treacle,* directed by Richard Lon-craine from Potter's script, Martin's status is less clear. Although the film stays fairly close to the television play, it has several notable differences. Sting as Mar-tin lacks the smarmy charm that characterizes the features of Michael Kitchen, who seems to have more both of the brimstone and the treacle about him. Patty (Suzanna Hamilton) is a strikingly beautiful woman in contrast to the contorted, tormented portrayal by Michelle Newell. The "dance" sequence is less extrava-gant and uses Police songs, while Mr. Bates's offensive politics are omitted.

31. *Potter on Potter,* p.52.

32. The incorporation of the rape into a musical number in *Brimstone and Treacle* recalls the choreographed beating of a man and raping of a woman to the sound of "Singin' in the Rain" in Stanley Kubrick's 1971 film of Anthony Burgess's *A Clockwork Orange* (1962). As in *Brimstone and Treacle,* the lack of fit between the familiar and happy song and the violence emphasizes the horror of what is happening. Alex (Malcolm McDowell) uses his cane in imitation of Gene Kelly's umbrella, reenacting the original in a grotesque parody of the musical genre. The violence in the movie is much more explicit than it is in *Brimstone,* but both se-quences involve nonchalant—and androgynous—young men attacking the help-less. The musical accompaniment perhaps suggested to some viewers that these sequences were treating rape without appropriate seriousness, and most viewers are liable to be made very uncomfortable by such scenes. Adding to the notori-ety, neither Alex nor Martin is unequivocally condemned within the text; in fact both texts reveal the difficulty of simply pitting good against evil. *A Clockwork Orange* received an "X" certificate in Britain.

33. *Potter on Potter,* 30. The assertion that television can be a productive experience for the viewer unsurprisingly recurs from time to time in the work of Britain's TV dramatists. Its power is pleasingly rehearsed by the newly-widowed Harry in David Mercer's *Rod of Iron* who tells his estranged sons, "twenty years of my eyes glued to the box have raised me up. . . . I have walked on the Mars, seen the Indian holy man under his Baobab tree. . . . I have become a celestial navigator."

34. Hassan xiv. We might add the propensity for listing, a trait common to many of Potter's characters that reaches its comic climax in *The Singing Detective,* in Marlow's desperate bid to prevent his ejaculation by thinking of all the most boring things about life in mid-eighties Britain.

35. Hassan, p.xvii.

36. Hassan, p.82.

37. *Potter on Potter,* p.10.

38. *Potter on Potter,* p.22.

CHAPTER 8

IS THERE A SHIP
ON THE HORIZON?

Notes on the Ethics of Dennis Potter's New Humanist Postmodernism in *Sufficient Carbohydrate*

Heinz Antor

SUFFICIENT CARBOHYDRATE WAS DENNIS POTTER'S FIRST and only play produced exclusively for the stage rather than for television. When it came out in 1983, it was reviewed badly by many theatre critics who thought that a writer of TV scripts could not live up to their standards. The film version of the play came out in 1987 and was entitled *The Visitors,* and it "has been generally over-looked"[1] ever since. It is the purpose of this article to show that this evaluation is untenable and that on the contrary the play is a very serious and subtle work of art that engages with some of the important questions of contemporary social life and with key issues of postmodernism, notably the question of ethics in an age that has been characterized by the philosopher Alasdair Mac-Intyre as being one "after virtue."[2]

The play is set on "a small, unspoilt Greek island"[3] where the characters spend a holiday away from home. In the isolation of this Mediterranean solitude, Potter confronts two men and their worldviews with each other. Jack Barker is an old-fashioned British liberal humanist, who works for Greenace, a Norfolk food manufacturing company that was founded by his grandfather but is now directed from Indianapolis along pragmatic and utilitarian lines. This new approach is embodied by Eddie Vosper, Jack's American colleague, who is willing to do away with traditional values in order to maximize the company's profits. Soon there is a bitter conflict between the two colleagues' ways of thinking that transcends the concrete level of discussing the company's future and involves more general issues. Right from the beginning, we are confronted with the question of whether we need an ethical framework that should direct our actions, and if so, what would be the values that could provide us with such a frame.

In the discursive space opened up by this fundamental question of the play, Jack holds a fairly conservative position. He is a rather old-fashioned and in many ways inflexible character, which is symbolized in the first scene when, in spite of his having traveled to a hot climate, he is shown wearing "his striped pyjamas—which he would insist on wearing in bed even on the Equator itself, let alone this Greek island."[4] Jack is in rather a bad mood at the beginning of the play because he feels that he has reached a moment of crisis in his life. He is dissatisfied with the way Greenace and Eddie Vosper try to reorganize the company founded by his grandfather. For the Americans, according to Jack, profit comes before quality, and money is more important than ethics. While Eddie, for example, advocates biogenetically manipulating the mushrooms Greenace produces so that they all grow to the same size and can be cultivated and harvested on an industrial scale, Jack violently rejects this idea as an irresponsible dilution of the high standards of quality to which he aspires. He can only counter Eddie's economic pragmatism with an aggressive reassertion of the values he feels bound to:

> JACK: A mushroom is a mushroom is a fucking mushroom! They don't and they *won't* come in standard sizes—right? Not *real* mushrooms—*proper* mushrooms—they happen to reproduce in varying sizes because of their genetics— . . . But you and your lot want to change all that. Nature's not bloody good enough for you. It's all bloody biotech and microbes and membrane filtration and protein separation and— . . . Well, this is where I make my stand! My grandfather's company used to put proper food on the shelves before fucking Greenace bought us out—and that's where our future lies. Quality! Who wants to eat out of a fucking test-tube![5]

Jack rejects the methods employed by the new American management of Greenace as a kind of dishonest manipulation. He still believes in objective authenticity, genuineness and fixed qualitative standards one should try to live up to. He is highly critical of the credo of do-ability inherent in Eddie's stance, a belief in the unlimited potential of human agency that can easily turn into the doctrine of a radical "anything goes" that rejects limits to human endeavour.

The above scene is not only to be seen in the context of how best to manage a food manufacturing company. It also has to be read in a wider context, for the taking over of the traditional British company by the American firm is the objective correlative of what goes on in the realm of ethics in the postmodern age. We live in the decentered period of postfoundationalism, in which stable and timeless concepts such as God, natural law or moral duty seem to have lost their status as ultimate norms; instead they have been replaced by the poststructuralist process of the infinite deferral of meaning, which is open-ended and can only lead to a ceaseless series of reinterpretations of the world and that cannot provide a basis for an absolute moral law. The dispute between Eddie and Jack over how to grow mushrooms is nothing but an example of this in the field of ecological or environmental ethics. Eddie refuses to let his actions be hampered by the outward constraints of general ethical norms not devised by himself. He prefers to conform to the economic rules of utility and profitability without any regard to the old liberal humanist values that have become increasingly problematic in the age of postmodernism.

Potter uses the paradigm shift from the old ethos of Jack's grandfather's company to that of the new American management as an example of the major issue at stake in his play, namely the question as to whether and how man can live a full life in an age in which it becomes more and more difficult to find acceptable ideals and in which many—Eddie among them—seem to prefer to do without them. That this is actually so is shown, among other things, by the title of the play, which designates Jack's formula for the negative ethical consequences of Eddie's position. When the quarrel between the two is taken up again in act 2, Jack pretends to have a proposal for Eddie as to how the food-processing business could be made even more effective and profitable:

> JACK: Instead of using dipotassium phosphate and sodium caseinate to replace milk in coffee and extra microbes to help *whippability* we ought to add blood and nerve tissue to our hamburgers. Human blood. Human tissue. Adequate protein. Sufficient carbohydrate.
> EDDIE: What are you talking about?
> JACK: People like to eat all sorts of things, Eddie, from snails to bullocks' testicles. But what they really want, what people really want to get between their teeth and slowly chew and swallow is other people. People want to eat people. They dribble at the mouth at the very thought of it. Have *you* got wet lips, Eddie? And blood on your teeth—eh?[6]

Eddie's economic utilitarianism and his disregard for the natural setup of his surroundings is, to Jack, tantamount to complete absence of values. This is why he describes Eddie's world of functionality and utility, which is only governed by the laws of demand and supply and maximizing profits, as breaking the ancient taboo against cannibalism. In Eddie's world, he implies, it is only personal interest that counts, no matter how great the damage to others may be. Jack accuses Eddie of following the Hobbesian anthropology of *homo homini lupus*, a bleak concept of man that is incompatible with Jack's idealism. Eddie, in turn, makes fun of Jack's views and derisively calls him the "Aristotle of the food-processing business" and "Plato among the pizzas."[7]

Jack still works in what used to be his family's own company, but he does not make a secret out of his opposition to the new philosophy pursued by Eddie and his like. Reminiscent of the behaviour of Jimmy Porter in John Osborne's *Look Back in Anger* (1956),[8] he rails at his colleagues, turns up in a drunken state at work, and "goes up and down the corridors kicking the radiators."[9] This is why he is regarded as a drunkard by many in Greenace, and the management of the company try to get rid of him by carefully suggesting early retirement. It is Eddie's task to find out during the holiday on the Greek island whether Jack would be willing to leave Greenace. Jack suspects right from the beginning that the free holiday paid for by the company must be:

> a kind of *test* or something to examine either my loyalty or my suitability or both. A sort of commercial McCarthyism. Just because I pee on the seat. (*Sniff.*) And a few other places. . . . Who the fuck do you think you are, Eddie? Mrs Thatcher? Come on. What is it you want to say?[10]

Jack here reacts like an angry old man. To him, the way Greenace is managed now also implies a disregard of individual freedom and in particular of his own freedom of conscience. He feels the methods employed by the new leaders of Greenace to be a direct attack on his personal integrity, which he values higher than the commercial aims of the company. He compares Eddie to Margaret Thatcher because to him, Thatcherist monetarism is the medium through which American pragmatic and economic utilitarianism has entered British life at the expense of liberal human values, such as respect for the individual and due regard for the needs and wishes of others. The new approach practised at Greenace makes Jack associate it with a big machine that is to function as flawlessly as possible, and which can be used against anybody who might jeopardize its effectivity: "There always are wheels within wheels,"[11] as Jack says to Eddie's second wife Lucy. In such an organization, the values of the individual and the traditional ethics advocated by Jack can no longer be accepted because they are incompatible with the overriding aim of profitability.

To Jack, the development at Greenace mirrors the development of the world in general, which he thinks is becoming ever more shabby. In the first scene of the play, he admits to Eddie's son, Clayton, that this includes even himself, and that consequently he finds himself in a sorry state:

> JACK: When you get older, Clayton, you'll think you are getting wiser. But you only get shabbier. Believe me.

CLAYTON: Oh, come on.

JACK: No, no. Take me, for example. Insomniac, because I've nothing what-soever to dream about. How's about that, then? Don't you think that's sad, young man?[12]

Jack feels the necessity of dreaming, of having values to live up to and of pur-suing aims that endow his life with ideals and with a meaning. Instead, every-thing seems to have gone stale for him. He does not find himself within a satisfactory meaningful order any more. Rather, he confronts the contingency of old patterns and norms falling apart. That the old qualitative standards of his grandfather's company have disappeared are just one example. The disin-tegration of family patterns—Jack's wife Elizabeth commits adultery with Eddie and thereby not only betrays Jack but also violates his humanist ideals—is another case in point. Jack suffers intensely from this situation. His hard drinking is a symptom of how difficult it is for him to cope with what happens. In his plight, he tries to reestablish a new orientation for himself by having re-course to several strategies. One of these is the construction of a negative image of America as the symbol of everything he rejects, as becomes clear in the following exchange with Lucy:

LUCY: . . . This is his [i.e., Clayton's] first trip outside the states.

JACK: I feel it's mine, too!

LUCY: What?

JACK: This tiny island has no Coca Cola signs, no muzak, no hamburgers, not a sniff of cocaine or a single sud of a sodding soap opera, no muggers, noth-ing—no amenities whatsobloodyever. It's as though America lived in vain. Everywhere else I've been—especially ye olde England—is a pocket-sized imi-tation of the Land of the Free— . . . I know which side my homogenized, processed, New and Improved monosodium-glutamated food additive is but-tered on. Greenace Incorporated pays my ample salary and arranges this ade-quate holiday—So what do I care if your countrymen leave their litter all over this planet and even on the far side of the sil-ver-y-moon? I simply say to my-self Pardon me, boy, is this the Chattanooga Choo Choo and sit back with my arse in clover and my head as empty as Donald Duck on one of his better days. Quack. Quack. Quack.[13]

To Jack, the Americanization of the Western world is a process character-ized by a growing consumerism, by the destruction of our environment, and by an entropic cultural homogenization that equalizes everything and renders individual cultural manifestations such as different value systems impossible. He regards hedonistic mindlessness as the anesthetic used by this system in order to stifle any critical response, so that in the end the individual subject is submerged in the general and vulgar ideology of economic utilitarianism. To

Jack, therefore, people are not so free in the Land of the Free, and he consequently uses this stereotype of America as the embodiment of everything he rejects. Potter, to a certain extent, uses his own ambivalent attitude toward
America here. As he stated in an interview with Graham Fuller, European culture to him is the answer to questions such as "Is this culture? Am I right?"
whereas in America, "[i]t's a case of 'There's the goods, do you want to buy
them?'"[14] At the same time, however, Potter also admitted to admiring America for its "genuinely populist culture" and for its New World "rewriting of the
book."[15] In Potter's definition of European culture, just as well as in Jack's reaction to the increasing Americanization of the world, the ethical question of
what is right and wrong, what makes our lives worthwhile, and what values
should we cherish, is the dominant aspect.

But although Jack is the dominant character of the play, his attitudes and
opinions are not to be accepted uncritically. Rather, in a manner that is typical
of Potter in general, what Jack wants becomes the subject of a critical dialogue
between him and the other characters in *Sufficient Carbohydrate*. Jack's relatively conservative liberal humanist ethics, then, are put to the test, and it will
be interesting to see the outcome of this experiment.

At first sight, Jack does not create a very good impression with either his
fellow vacationers or with the audience in the theatre. Just like Jimmy Porter,
he rants and raves on stage and behaves in a thoroughly bad manner. Not even
his wife Elizabeth is willing to support him in his aggressive stance toward
Eddie and everything he stands for. She doesn't accept his ethical claims, anyway, and she even provokes him further by pretending to be simply bored by
his tirades. As Jack himself states, she treats him like "some snotty-nosed little
schoolboy at the back of the class who hasn't turned in his homework on time.
Well—I *haven't*—and I'm not going to!"[16] Jack's answer makes it clear that he
does not intend to conform, and he thereby insists on keeping his individuality. Elizabeth, on the other hand, thinks that her husband refuses to leave a
sinking ship, as she confides to Eddie and Lucy in a conversation about the values advocated by Jack:

> ELIZABETH: But of course we don't *really* believe it [i.e., Jack's ethos]. Not
> even Jack.
> LUCY: (*Laugh.*) Don't be so sure!
> ELIZABETH: No, no. He doesn't. It's just that he is going to seed even faster than
> dear old England itself. I think he knows the game's up for him and his sort—[17]

Elizabeth doesn't take her husband's ideals seriously, and it is no coincidence
that she talks about a game in this respect, because to her, all the things that
are of the utmost importance to Jack are indeed nothing but a game. She does
not accept traditional norms such as marital fidelity, for example, and has an

affair with Eddie, who also conveniently prefers to look at both his job and his private affairs as playing games in the ludic postmodern space of the liberating "anything goes." Elizabeth cannot love her idealistic husband anymore because his yearning for ethical orientation is incompatible with her egoism. Consequently, when Jack goes missing early in act 2 and it is not quite clear whether he has committed suicide and drowned himself in his drunkenness, she thinks more about the insurance money she would sue Greenace for in case of Jack's death than about the loss of her husband.[18] But shirking responsibility, pursuing hedonistic pleasure and avoiding ethical considerations very quickly produce negative consequences for both Eddie and Elizabeth, as further events in the play show.

Eddie has taken Clayton, his sixteen-year-old son by his first wife, on the holiday trip to the Greek island. But father and son hardly know each other, since Eddie is too busy pursuing his utilitarian games and committing adultery for him to have much time for the boy, whom he has only seen four times in the past three years.[19] Clayton, who is in the difficult phase of late adolescence anyway, a period of life that is characterized by a feeling of uprootedness in between infancy and adulthood and by a yearning for values, role models and self-definition,[20] is filled, as he says himself, with a feeling for "the pain in the world. And the *dirt*. And *lies*. And the— . . . Sad. Just sad, I guess."[21] These thoughts in him are provoked by the lines of John Keats's "Ode to a Nightingale," which Clayton can quote by heart and which for him symbolize his own feeling of unfulfilled yearning and his suffering from the decenteredness of the loveless world of his father, in which he does not feel at home. The poetry of Romanticism becomes a symbol in the play for the idealistic, organic existence at one with the world and not yet prone to the fragmented existence that becomes palpable in the way Eddie behaves both in his job and at home.[22]

To Clayton, the world is fallen and polluted both in a literal and in a moral sense. That is why he likes the view of the sea, because its wide expanse suggests to him something of the purity he is after. "It's *clean* out there,"[23] as he describes it himself. It is significant that Eddie cannot understand this remark by his son and that Elizabeth only tells him that "we're not too keen on blue at the moment."[24] The two adults, exponents of the ethics of arbitrariness and irresponsibility, do not bother to take Clayton seriously; in this respect the boy is much closer to Jack and his idealism than to his own father. It is only consistent that Jack can understand Clayton much better than Eddie can when the boy quotes Keats. Jack immediately realizes what Keats means for Clayton, and therefore even apologizes to him for his initially rather gruff behaviour:

> JACK: Then I'm sorry I talked down to you. Truly sorry, old lad, for being such
> a patronizing old fart. I didn't know there was a kindred soul suffering here
> under the same hot tiles.[25]

Clayton and Jack are fellow sufferers in a world gone to the dogs and in which there are no values that can provide a satisfactory orientation. Eddie, on the other hand, does not seem to be worried by this loss of a center. When Clayton starts to recite the "Ode to a Nightingale" and Jack tries to make him continue, Eddie simply tells his colleague to "[l]eave the kid alone,"[26] as if he was not interested in his son being inculcated with any cultural values or ideals. It soon turns out, however, that Eddie has only pretended not to know the poem—in fact he even knows it by heart—only in order to humiliate Jack. In a stage direction, Potter says that "Eddie has been playing with [Jack],"[27] and thereby once again introduces the notion of the game here. When Jack complains about being thus humiliated by his colleague, Eddie cynically answers that he prefers "a good balance sheet"[28] and, significantly enough, reverts to the logic of economic utility that is so typical of his thinking even in its imagery. Eddie is not interested in quality, neither in the food manufacturing business nor in literature nor in the realm of ethics. Although he does know Keats, he recommends Sydney Sheldon and Arthur Hailey to his son, who he thinks "can do worse than open a good meaty book now and then."[29] Jack, who can understand Clayton's longings, immediately draws a comparison between Eddie's literary recommendations and the junk food Greenace produces under Eddie's management.[30] The latter, however, cannot understand that what is really at stake for both Clayton and Jack is the question of quality, value and norm. He therefore simply wonders why his son often can only answer his remarks by a dismissive shrug, which irritates him immensely. Father and son simply do not link up with each other, because Eddie completely ignores the most fundamental needs of his son. Together with Eddie's brutal utilitarianism and his contempt for ideals, this obtuseness is effectively summed up in a scene in which he complains about Clayton's adolescent behaviour and where Lucy tries to defend her stepson:

> LUCY: (*looking at* EDDIE, *with an edge*) There's something there. There's something different about him. He's got a lot of sensitivity. He looks, and he sees. And he thinks.
> EDDIE: *That*'ll help him a bundle. (*Provocative*) I said, that's no good to him. Unless he wants to be some kind of professor or something, walking about with his head down and a heap of books under his arm. It's great to make up little rhymes about nightingales or tomtits. But it won't pay the rent, will it?[31]

Not only does Lucy ineffectively run up against Eddie's brash and unfeeling pragmatism in defence of Clayton, but she also becomes a victim herself of her husband's brutal egoism and his disregard for the emotions of others. When, at the end of act 1, Eddie openly flirts with Elizabeth and it gradually becomes clear that the two are having an illicit affair, Lucy looks for both revenge on Eddie and for a pair of comforting arms in Clayton's bed.[32] Things thereby take an unexpected turn that is so serious that it cannot be disregarded and shrugged off even by Eddie and Elizabeth any more. At the beginning of act 2, however, we see the two exponents of the game of "anything goes" still unwittingly playing on, with Elizabeth and Eddie trying to evade the consequences of their more or less open adultery of the previous night. They don't want to be made responsible for their actions in divorce proceedings, and they don't want to be forced to accept the ethical framework implied by such a value as marital fidelity. This is why Elizabeth once again has recourse to the postmodern metaphor of playing:

> ELIZABETH: Listen, if we *all* behave as if it *was* a game—mmm? As though nothing much happened. It's a good way of dealing with things. Sort of pretend it never happened.[33]

But they soon have to realize that their playing games has already had serious consequences. When they hear the result of their actions, i.e., the Clayton-Lucy affair, Eddie immediately reacts by referring to traditional norms and talks about incest. He is not willing to accept Lucy's excuse that she felt both physically and emotionally hurt by the events of the previous evening and therefore went to Clayton's room:

> EDDIE: What's that to do with it! Why'd you have to involve *him*! He's not playing games. He's too vulnerable! For Christ's sake, Lucy! You're—you're *disgusting*—! That's practically *incest*.[34]

It is only when he is confronted with the negative consequences of his own behaviour, of his playing around with the feelings of others, and of his egoistic hedonism that Eddie all of a sudden is willing to accept the existence of moral rules. But these are to be respected only by others rather than by himself. Eddie wants Clayton to be excluded from the irresponsible games he has been playing all the time, and he has to learn the hard way that this is impossible. He finds himself bound up in a social network of mutual relationships in which the shirking of responsibility for one's own actions inevitably falls back on oneself sooner or later. The moral disgust Eddie displays toward Lucy, then, is not acceptable coming from him of all people. Even Elizabeth realizes this when she tries to stop him by drawing his attention to the inconsistency of his argument:

> ELIZABETH: Don't be such a bully! What's good enough for the goose is good enough for the gosling.[35]

The situation is only saved temporarily when Lucy says that she did not actually have sex with Clayton, although this remains doubtful and may be another version of Elizabeth's game of pretending it all never happened. Elizabeth, at least, swiftly takes her up on this and says:

> ELIZABETH: (*Cutting in*) It was the same with us. Wasn't it? Eddie? Nothing happened.[36]

But the time for playing games, for deception as well as for self-deception, is over. Eddie now is really concerned about Clayton. The boy has fallen in love with Lucy, and when she tells him that the events of the previous night had better be forgotten, in his disappointment, he retires into a cave by the shore "where a wounded animal would go to lick its sensibilities,"[37] as Jack puts it. Jack himself is no longer willing to play Elizabeth's game of hushing everything up, as he still was at the end of act 1.[38] Things have gone too far, and Jack finally openly confronts Eddie and Elizabeth with what their adulterous affair actually meant to him:

> JACK: Do you go to the theatre? Or the cinema? Be bop a loo bop. Eh? . . . Because I've been wondering where the hell you've got the idea that adultery is a little piece of adult behaviour that doesn't matter very much any more. It's just an entertainment, right? Something up there in lights to make us snigger and chortle, all we sophisticates. Don't you know the endless— endless—ache of it—? . . . Or maybe it's something you picked up at work, is it, Eddie? A bit of seasoning salt to add to the diet, sprinkled on what we otherwise couldn't swallow. Things difficult to digest like—love and duty and commitment and—[39]

Jack here, out of his own indignation and vulnerability, pits all his moral seriousness against Eddie's irresponsible stance of "anything goes" and deconstructs his colleague's immoral self-service mentality of seemingly enlightened adult entertainment as an empty pose that cannot hide the emotional havoc it wreaks in the souls of others.

What we are ultimately confronted with, then, in this play, is the disintegration of all traditional patterns, be it in the food manufacturing business or in the structures of family ties and personal relationships. Taboos are broken, and everything seems to fall to pieces. But this is not only done in order to produce "an adultery drama set on a Greek island and embodying a clash between British and American cultural values,"[40] as Graham Fuller has it, although these elements are certainly there. Rather, we are presented with the question of how human beings react when faced with the contingency of chaotic situations in which old patterns that have supported us so far are no longer valid. We also confront the question whether we really need such patterns or whether we can do without them. Eddie and Elizabeth, with their rejection of conventional norms and their economic as well as personal hedonism, at first seem to indicate the latter possibility. But their behaviour, based on the philosophy of a radical postmodern "anything goes," soon proves to be impracticable and unsatisfactory not only to others, but even to those who practise it themselves. Eddie's and Elizabeth's refusal to accept the need for human values and norms, for explanatory patterns that make life worth living to them and humankind, is implicitly condemned by the way the plot develops.

This, however, does not mean that Potter presents his audience with a conservative plea for an uncritical return to old liberal humanist values. Jack is a far too ambiguous character in this respect. Although one can understand much of his anger, he is not shown in an altogether uncritical light. His ranting tirades are rather ineffective, and he sometimes cuts a rather ridiculous figure. His physical attack on Eddie in act 2 ends with him on his backside floored with "*a look of comical astonishment on his face.*"[41] This not only illustrates his lack of realistic judgement, but also proves how little he achieves by the way he expresses his discontent. When he realizes at the end of act 1 that it was due to Lucy's warning him against Eddie's and Greenace's plans that the whole plight of his business and private affairs was finally detected, he fiercely lashes out at her, kicks her and hurts her. This may be recognizable as a reaction to the pain he suffers as he confronts the fragments of his previous life. He reacts with the fierceness of a wild animal at bay, but in its brutal inadequacy, the attack on Lucy loses him some of the audience's sympathies. In an earlier scene, Jack had already admitted that his choleric outbreaks of violence do not change anything and only hurt himself. When Lucy asks him whether he really kicked the radiators along the corridors of Greenace out of anger at the outcome of a policy meeting, he replies:

JACK: Yes. That's right. I did. And hurt my foot.
LUCY: Did it help any?
JACK: (*Sepulchral*) No-o-o.[42]

Nevertheless, Jack's behaviour must not be judged rashly with reference only to a number of such incidents. His position is much more complicated. He is indeed a decentered man, and he cannot stand the lack of a meaningful dimension in life, the loss of a pattern that would allow him to lead the good life of fulfilment. Jack's father was a clergyman, but Jack himself can no longer accept the faith of his father. In the following exchange with Lucy, he rejects the theological metaphysics of his family background:

JACK: I used to have to listen to an enormous number of extremely turgid hymns when I was a boy. My father was low church. (*Sigh.*) Very evangelical. An awful lot of those bloody dirges were about the boat crossing over to the

other shore. On the far side of the Jordan. Where all our loved ones were wait-
ing—the ones who've gone before. What a bloody thought!
LUCY: Ain't it.
JACK: Do you know what's *really* there? On the far side of the Jordan. (*Sniff.*)
Refugees.
LUCY: And terrorists.[43]

Jack obviously suffered from the excessive piety of his parental home, and
he criticizes his father's religion for its unworldliness by pitting the very real
plight of Palestinian refugees in Jordan in the early eighties against the beatific
and to him totally unconvincing, vision of eternal life that, in the metaphoric
geography of his father's Christianity, was separated from this world by the
River Jordan. Lucy's reply about there being criminal terrorists as well as innocent refugees on the far side of the River Jordan, however, provides a reminder that Jack's way of looking at the matter may be a little one-sided.
   And indeed, even if Jack cannot believe in the boat from the dirges sung
in his father's house, he cannot quite do without a substitute for it. For he constructs for himself the idea of another ship passing to and fro every day on the
horizon. The old freighter, however, soon turns into much more than a part of
the local infrastructure and becomes a symbol of everything for which Jack
yearns. In the first scene, he explains to Clayton what he believes he can observe every morning, and already hints at its further significance to him:

> JACK: Every morning about half past five an old black freighter trundles across
> the horizon over there. . . . I wasn't up on our first morning here, but I've seen
> it on the last four mornings. It must be the cargo boat which tramps across
> from Brindisi and puts in to the Greek mainland at about seven o'clock. It re-
> minds me of my own childhood because it brings back all the sea stories I used
> to read as a boy marooned in a country vicarage. Ahoy, there! Et cetera. Trou-
> ble is, it reminds me of something else too. Something delicious or terrible
> or—which I've either forgotten, or haven't yet had. Something gone for ever
> or awaiting me for ever.
> CLAYTON: I know the feeling—
>   . . .
> JACK: When it passes, the ship, the light is even more opaque than it is now.
> Sort of—marbled. And cool. There are a few wisps of mist curling about an
> inch from the top of the sea, and yet the water is still that impossible blue—
> It's all like when the world began, and God Saw That It Was Good—(*Bitter
> little laugh.*) A chalice full of the warm South. The sea slap-slapping itself. The
> little olive trees catching hold of the rocks. Space. Air. And an uncertain
> smudge which sort of—*solidifies* out of the ache in the mind and very slowly
> becomes a black freighter dragging itself across the edge of the world—For a
> moment—a whole minute—it's all so perfect you want to reach out and—pull
> it into your soul. You want to pick it all up—and *eat* it.[44]

The freighter, it is implied here, might be less a physical reality than a mental construct created by Jack's mental suffering from the state of the world he has to live in, a world without a center, one without values and without an overriding explanatory pattern that could make his existence meaningful and bearable for him. The ship, to him, is an idealistic vision, which initially can only be glimpsed in a haze and seems to remain ungraspable. It is delicious and terrible at the same time because it holds the promise of a telic existence without making it absolutely clear what the telos might be. The old freighter almost takes on the qualities of Platonic Ideas, because Jack cannot remember what it is it reminds him of. It is no coincidence that the ship romantically reminds him of his childhood days. For, as the great romantic poet William Wordsworth showed in his *Ode: Intimations of Immortality From Recollections of Early Childhood,* the child is still closer to the Platonic world of Ideas and therefore still has a smattering of what this world may look like. Jack, who in a stage direction is described to be *"full of vague, unhappy yearning,"*[45] would like to retrieve some such thing as the dimension represented by Platonic Ideas. In particular, he is in need of an ethical pattern to fill the gap he has experienced both at Greenace and in his private life. The ship symbolizes for him the world before its fall into the imperfection of what he is surrounded by, i.e., a universe in a state of Edenic purity and goodness, as the Biblical allusion in his words shows. He also quotes from Keats's "Ode to a Nightingale" and thus links his own ideals with those of Clayton. The boy says he can understand the way Jack feels because the two are kindred souls. The man who has lost his bearings and the adolescent who is still in search of his own identity and values suffer from the same lack of center. Neither can feel at home in his surroundings, which are totally uncongenial to his needs. When Jack admires the "impossible blue" of the sea through which the old freighter ploughs its way, this connects him yet again with Clayton, who likes the purity of the sea and is only rewarded by Elizabeth's trite remark about her not being interested in blue. When the ship passes, it is still cool, which, in the context of the whole play, is also significant. For throughout *Sufficient Carbohydrate,* Potter uses the description of the stifling and oppressive heat, which makes the days on the island almost unbearable, as an objective correlative of the lack of direction, values and beliefs from which the protagonists suffer. In scene 2 of act 1, for example, Eddie wonders how the ancient Greeks managed to philosophize in such heat:

EDDIE: Imagine squatting down on some hot rock or other and working out Transcendence or a new theory of Justice with goddam insects biting your arm and the sweat trickling into your eyeballs.[46]

Jack's ship is a fit vehicle for Transcendence and Justice, then, because it makes its way through the cool and pure atmosphere of early morning before the heat of the day—and that of moral infection—can spoil the Edenic air of ideality. This also implies, however, that the mists have not yet risen and that one cannot actually be sure whether one can see the ship—whether the old freighter is there or whether it is only an illusion. The smudge on the horizon is still uncertain, and when it solidifies it does so out of the ache in the mind, so that we might simply be confronted with a case of wishful thinking. When the freighter can be clearly seen, the euphoria of this experience lasts only for a short moment anyway. The glimpse of the ideal, then, takes on the quality of an epiphanic moment, which is bound to be short-lived. Indeed, Jack is anything but sure whether the ship exists or not. When the curtain rises on the first scene, we see him *"looking rather miserably out to sea,"*[47] doubting the existence of the old freighter and fretting about not being able to cater his need for the meaningfulness of an ethical framework:

> JACK: No. You're not there. You're not there, are you? No. Definitely not. No. Never. Never. (*Fractional pause.*) Why not? Why aren't you? Boring old bugger![48]

Jack is also dissatisfied with his own way of coping with the dilemma. His is the typical plight of the English liberal humanist who cannot make up his mind and subscribe to a definite ideology or world picture, which threatens to leave him just as much without explanatory patterns and without reliable ethical standards as the exponents of a radical early postmodern "anything goes," i.e., Eddie and Elizabeth. In a conversation with Lucy, Jack makes it clear to her how unpleasant this state of affairs is to him:

> JACK: I haven't got the resolve to be anything very much, one way or the other. My Yea is not exactly a Yea, and my Nay is very rarely a Nay. I'm English, you see. I'm helplessly, compromisingly bloody well damned well English. . . . My hot is not hot and my cold is not cold. Just a sort of lukewarm grey sludge. Indistinguishable, I should imagine, from the colour of vomit. . . . I'm talking about this dank little room bob-bobbing about on top of my shoulders. The inside of my head, darling. I'd give a lot to find a suitable tenant, but there's none to be had.[49]

The ship on the horizon in the play takes on the symbolic function of the desperately sought tenant Jack has such great problems in finding. Eddie, not interested in a value system save that of economic utility and personal hedonism, cannot take Jack seriously. Therefore, when he hears about Jack's ship, he makes fun of the idea and ironically asks where the ship is going. Typically enough for him, he can only think about the ship in practical terms, i.e., as a vehicle that must be going somewhere. At the same time, Eddie unwittingly asks the question of teleology that vexes Jack so much. The latter answers:

No, I don't suppose it would be worth your while to wake up especially to see it, Eddie. You're quite right. It's only going there and back. . . . Actually, the bloody ship probably isn't there. A ship of fools. I probably didn't even see it. It was only a speck. A smudge on the horizon—or on the back of my eyelids.[50]

Jack is confronted with a double dilemma. Not only can he not be sure the ship is actually there, i.e., that there is an ultimate truth or value system that can heal the decentered world he finds so insufferable, but even if the old freighter is actually there, it only goes to and fro—it has no ultimate destination. This metaphor, therefore, puts teleological thought in doubt as a tenable approach.

Nevertheless, Jack is never willing to give up the possibility of the ship's existence. He wants it to be there, and he also uses it as a means of escape from depression. When he is confronted with his wife's infidelity with Eddie and their refusal to conform to the value of marital fidelity, it looks for a moment as if Eddie was about to speak openly about the dissolution of established personal patterns. But Jack quickly says that he does not want to talk about it, and suggests they should talk about his old freighter instead, thereby using the symbol of his ethical idealism as an instrument with which to quell the tide of moral depravity and personal treachery.[51]

Nevertheless, despair is always only just around the corner for Jack. When Eddie's and Elizabeth's affair has come out in the open, he tells Lucy about how, in the early morning, the ship had just gone out of sight, and he was hoping for it to return, i.e., for a moment of Christian revelation. Jack was yearning for an experience that would enable him to go back into the fold of his father's belief without the sickly sides of the latter's Evangelicalism, and to find himself comfortably cradled in a meaningful universe once again. What he got instead, however, was something completely different:

And so I said to myself—Hold still. Keep quiet. Don't move. Don't think. Most of all, don't get down on your knees, and don't ask for anything. Wait— just wait. And if, after all, after everything, if there is, is, really is, truly is a God, a loving God in his loving Creation, then he will reveal himself between the bones of my head.
All I had to do was *wait*.
And I waited. For the word. The sense.
Watching the very last black traces of smoke from the old freighter, as far as the eye could see.
And—
Nothing came.
(*He slaps at his chest bone again, in discomfort and his voice is thicker.*)
No. Worse. Something came, winging across the water, or dropping out of the sky, from everywhere, all around me, inside my nose and at the back of my

throat. I could smell it and taste it. Disgust. It was disgust. Nausea. Rotting,
slimy, stench. The maggoty corpse of—what?
Guess what. Guess who.[52]

Jack then begins to weep. His anguish here is the reaction to the disappointment of all his hopes. Instead of a Christian revelation of universal meaning, he has an experience of almost existentialist revulsion and despair at a
world totally deprived of any deeper meaning, and indeed, Jack's nausea here
is reminiscent of the very similar reaction of Jean-Paul Sartre's Antoine
Roquentin to the meaninglessness of life in *La Nausée* (1938).

A little later, Jack tells Eddie about another reaction he displayed when he
saw the ship. After the disaster of Eddie's and Elizabeth's open gesture of adultery, Jack fell asleep on the rocks of the island. When he woke again, he tells
Eddie, he could see the ship:

JACK: . . . I don't think there was ever before such a sight that filled me with
such (*little pause*) absolute (*little pause*) grief.

Jack here recognizes the discrepancy between what he wants and what the ship
symbolizes, on the one hand, and the state of the world he observes around
him on the other, which is totally incompatible with his needs and with his
ideals.

Athough the existence and the effectiveness of the ship and of Jack's ethical yearnings are shown to be in a rather precarious state several times
throughout the play, Jack does not give in, and he does not abandon his quest
and his scanning of the horizon. Toward the end of the play, he tells the other
characters that the ship takes up an old childhood dream of his, and at the
same time takes on much greater significance than his fellow vacationers
might at first have thought. As a child, he imagined himself to be "an old
tramp steamer like that one out there."[53] The decisive thing about this fantasy was that whereas the old ship took out "*ordinary* baubles" and "*usual*
beads," it always came back with "cinnamon and coriander and silks,"[54] so
that it made Jack look out optimistically to a world full of wonders waiting
to be discovered by him. Sometimes the going may have been hard and the
deck may have been awash with waves, but often the going was good, and it
was always worth his while to venture on the voyage. Jack finally realizes that
the ship fantasy tells him something very important and very serious about his
own life:

JACK: It took me a long, long time to realize that I actually *was* on a journey.
Even just sitting there, or lying awake, anywhere, everywhere, no matter
what, I was on a journey. And then, when I understood this, I went and for-

got it. Somehow or other I lost the sense of it. Lost my compass. That's why I'm glad I can see that battered old boat out there, trundling along from one end of time to the other.[55]

To Jack, it is important to rediscover the sense of being on a journey, i.e., of not having arrived at a final destination, but of still going on. The boat in his metaphor may be old and battered, it may only trundle along rather than swiftly plough the waves in order to reach an ultimate port of call as quickly as possible, but all this does not matter to Jack as long as it keeps going and does not stop. To him, it is the journey that matters, not the arrival. He now can see that Eddie's typically functionalist and utilitarian question of where Jack's ship is going is the wrong kind of question to ask. What is important to Jack is neither to stay down inside the ship and subscribe to a single edifice of thought, nor to give up the search for values in the postmodern age "after virtue," but to stay up on deck and look out for the new:

> JACK: If we were on board, rolling a bit as we braced our feet on the deck, we'd have a stronger sense of being on the journey. Like now. Right now. It's a bit stormy, and a bit misty. Eh, Clayton? . . . Well, that's what it's like on a voyage, old son. *The* voyage. We don't necessarily know exactly where we are going. Mind you, it would be a pity if we did, because then we'd never be surprised by unexpected islands or the visiting albatross. Look at that old boat! I think they're all up on deck. There's not much point in staying down below in the hold. That's like sitting in a cave. Christ—we know what's down there—the stuff we brought with us, the lumber. Got a bad smell. It doesn't always keep, does it? . . . It only came back to me a little while ago. The image of myself with my head in my hands, cowering in the bowels of the black freighter. Seeing nothing new with a fresh eye. Things make you want to do that sometimes. You feel you have to hide.[56]

It is significant that Jack here rejects the idea of knowing the symbolic ship's philosophical destination. It may be going somewhere, but the exact name of that place remains a mystery. Jack, then, does not reject teleological thought as such, but he is against an all too concrete teleology that amounts to closure and to a new foundationalism. He wants to preserve openness and the possibility of having a new and hitherto untried look at things. Jack advocates getting rid of the old philosophical ballast that has gone stale and no longer holds true, but that does not mean he reverts to a new kind of nihilism. He rejects the conservatism of those who do not want to face the deconstruction of the old world picture, but he also criticizes those who, like Eddie, deny the existence of his ship and think they can do without any serious ethical endeavor whatsoever by freeing themselves from all value structures.

Jack, a one-time liberal humanist, has learned the lessons of poststruc-
turalism and postmodernism, and yet does not throw overboard his ethical
ambitions. Having become a new postmodern humanist, he cannot go back to
the old orthodoxies even though he's not willing to subscribe to an early postmodern "anything goes" or do without meaningful patterns. Jack thus respects
the anthropological setup we all share, for man is a pattern-building animal
and always wants to construct meaningful consistency out of contingency.[57]
Whereas Eddie can only cynically shrug off such attempts at creating meaning,
simply measuring them against his own personal hedonism, Jack takes them
seriously without turning back to old, anachronistic value systems. He has to
recognize that his project is open-ended, that one cannot say where the journey will take him, but he gladly accepts this as the best available alternative.

Jack has recognized the invalidity of both moral conservatism and ethical
arbitrariness. When he says that staying down below in the hold of the ship is
like sitting in a cave, he expresses his dissatisfaction with traditional world pictures and value structures; to him these fall short of the mark, because they
only approach the ideal at one remove, as if we had accepted to remain in the
Platonic cave without ever trying to get a direct view of the things that cast the
shadows. One may sometimes feel tempted to retire into the cave, to go down
below deck or, in philosophical terms, blindly subscribe to one of the old, familiar philosophical systems because one feels so confused by all the surrounding contingency. But this ethical stasis cannot be a satisfactory solution
for Jack in the long run. On the other hand, Eddie's anti-ethics of noncom-
mitment cannot be accepted by him either. As an alternative to both these dead
ends, he suggests a third way in his final recommendations to Clayton:

JACK: . . . you have to get back on deck, and brace yourself, before you can see
where you are. You can get some idea by the smell of the wind or the position
of the stars. They're the sound of other people's voices. People who are on a
voyage too. They kind of feel lost at times, Clayton. We can't help it. It's the
nature of the vessel, old son. And the peril of the journey. But—you're not
starting from here, you're already on the way.
(*Pause.* CLAYTON *looks at him.*)
CLAYTON: It's a mess though. A real mess.
JACK: We don't get time to look at the shape of our lives, the chart of our tran-
sit. Or rather, we *do* get time, plenty of time, but we don't care to use it. That's
why I'm glad to see that old freighter out there. (*Laughs suddenly, and calls—
with glee*) ahoy there! You cunning old bugger!
(*Little pause. Then* CLAYTON *laughs.*)[58]

Jack here presents a model of dialogical ethics based on listening and responding to other people's voices. He acknowledges that there is a deep need
for self-definition in every one of us, a desire to know one's own position, a

yearning for a philosophical framework that allows us to draw an ethical map and determine our own whereabouts in it. This, Jack indicates, is only possible by referring to others. Alterity is the most important instrument of self-constitution, as Jacques Lacan has also shown in his poststructuralist approach to psychoanalysis. Jack's recommendation to Clayton is to practice ethical plurivocity and keep the dialogue going with other people. This may be hard at times, as Clayton's complaint about "the mess" confirms. But this is no reason for capitulating in front of the task of constantly remapping our lives and defining our positions in an ongoing ethical undertaking only made possible in the discursive space of ceaseless communicative exchange with others. We must not give in, but doggedly pursue the project of dialogical ethics. This is exactly what the ship on the horizon stands for and what makes Jack so glad to be able to see it. The old freighter goes to and fro just as we all must keep going the ceaseless interchange of voices and opinions in the process of ethical heteroglossia that allows us to define and redefine our selves and our positions time and again.

Jack's approach is the only one that provides both a way out of the aporias of his earlier liberal humanist stance and an answer to the utilitarian pragmatists such as Eddie. Jack has now learned that what he complained about in his liberal humanist phase, i.e., his inability to subscribe to one particular cause or always to give definitive answers, need no longer be seen in such a negative light now, since it is part of the dynamics of dialogic ethics always to renegotiate positions by comparing them with those of others. He has also found an alternative to the ethical nihilism of Eddie and Elizabeth. To Eddie, since the ship does not have an ultimate destination known to us, the old freighter and what it stands for do not exist. But this, to Jack, is tantamount to a denial of life itself. And indeed, in an earlier scene, Eddie and Elizabeth are depicted as zombies, i.e., as examples of the living dead, for when Lucy suggests they might all go to the taverna because this might put some life into them, Elizabeth, in a defeatist manner, simply answers: "Impossible!"[59]

At the end of the play, Potter clearly directs our sympathies in favor of Jack and his new postmodern humanism. After having depicted the sometimes ridiculous and often ineffective consequences of Jack's earlier liberal humanist idealism, and the destructive results of Eddie's and Elizabeth's rejection of values, he allows Jack to present at great length his symbolic model of the ship as a possible answer to both approaches. Jack has learned to accept the ineffectiveness of striving for final answers, while at the same time respecting the necessity of the ceaseless search for ideals and meaningful patterns. What is new in Jack's model is the combination of courage and modesty, the courage to go on believing in the existence of the ship and of wanting to stand on its deck, and the modesty not to expect it to have a final destination that can be known or found out by us. Jack hereby offers a way out of the impasse between the inconsistencies of the old liberal humanism and the bleak triviality of the early postmodern "anything goes." Potter, in *Sufficient Carbohydrate*, therefore presents us with a comparatively early literary version of the ethical turn of recent postmodern criticism.[60]

The end of the play shows that Potter actually embraces the views voiced by Jack in the final scene. Not only does Jack manage to convince Clayton and make him smile in spite of the mess the world is in, he also enables Lucy and Elizabeth to see the ship in the end.[61] Eddie is the only one who will not come around and who insists that Jack's ship does not exist. But he is interrupted by the "[s]*ound in the dark, of ship's hooter, long and plangent.*"[62] No matter whether the ship is actually there or not, its hooter can be heard several times throughout the play,[63] and this underlines the importance of what the old freighter stands for. Whether the ship has an ontological status of its own or not is not so important. What counts is its epistemological, anthropological, and ethical function as a catalyst for a good and dialogical life.

When Eddie, the exponent of valuelessness, is left isolated at the end of the play, poetic justice is done. Moreover, the audience is confronted with a modest and toned down version of a happy ending in which Jack and Clayton, who have been seeking most intensely for some kind of meaning throughout the play, come together in a smiling embrace of mutual understanding that includes an awareness of the endlessness of the human quest for meaning. This is expressed by Clayton, when he answers Jack's question of whether he can understand what the ship finally stands for by saying that "[t]hat would be one heck of a mouthful."[64] Jack puts this question to the boy in his last speech in the play. In it, he explains the meaning the ship has to him in exactly the same words he used when he first talked to Clayton about the old freighter at the beginning of *Sufficient Carbohydrate*.[65] He can use no other words and can get no closer to the meaning he is seeking through the ship. He therefore has to repeat himself and at the same time gives the play a circular structure while doing so. Consequently, Potter takes up the problematization of linear teleology that has already been expressed by the to and fro movement of the ship and by its lack of a recognizable final destination, and expresses it through the structure of the play itself, which thereby also becomes one without an end in the circularity of the quest expressed by Jack. When Jack and Clayton embrace at the end of *Sufficient Carbohydrate*, they do so *"in a sudden, compulsive, fragile humanity,"*[66] which expresses their shared, urgent need for meaningful patterns and ethical standards, as well as awareness of the precarious status of any such constructions that have to be renegotiated time and again in the dialogical process of ethical plurivocity. Dennis Potter has given a new humanist turn to a postmodernism that, in its antifoundationalism, threatened to drift into the triviality and unsatisfactory bleakness of meaninglessness and the arbitrariness of the resulting philosophy of "anything goes."

NOTES

1. Peter Stead, *Dennis Potter* (Bridgend: Seren Books, 1993), p.116.
2. Alasdair MacIntyre, *After Virtue* (London: Duckworth, 1981).
3. Dennis Potter, *Sufficient Carbohydrate* (London: Faber, 1983), p.9.
4. Potter, p.10.
5. Potter, p.24.
6. Potter, p.62.
7. Potter, p.20.
8. Peter Stead also detects "the kind of dramatic monologue that had dominated the plays of John Osborne" (Stead 116) in *Sufficient Carbohydrate*.
9. Potter, p.25.
10. Potter, p.17.
11. Potter, p.17.
12. Potter, p.11.
13. Potter, p.14f.
14. Dennis Potter, *Potter on Potter,* ed. Graham Fuller (London: Faber, 1993), p.108.
15. Fuller, p.108.
16. Potter, p.18.
17. Potter, p.20.
18. Potter, p.51.
19. Potter, p.48.
20. *Sufficient Carbohydrate* is one of the few works in which Potter deals with adolescence, as he stated himself (Fuller 10).
21. Potter, p.30.
22. On Potter's "ambivalent attitude" toward the Romantics, see Eckart Voigts-Virchow, *Männerphantasien: Introspektion und gebrochene Wirklichkeitsillusion im Drama von Dennis Potter* (Trier: WVT, 1995), p.230.
23. Potter, p.47. The house on the island, conversely, is seen by Clayton as a place which "needs fumigating" (Potter 68) because the adults to him also appear to be unclean: "You've no respect for anybody or anything, none of you! You're dirty! All of you! Dirty!" (Potter 56). These remarks of Clayton's clearly link the imagery he uses with the moral questions tackled in the play.
24. Potter, p.47.
25. Potter, p.33.
26. Potter, p.28.
27. Potter, p.29.
28. Potter, p.29.
29. Potter, p.30.
30. Potter, p.31.
31. Potter, p.35f.
32. Potter, pp.51ff., 66f.
33. Potter, p.46.
34. Potter, p.66.

35. Potter, p.66

36. Potter, p.67.

37. Potter, p.69.

38. Potter, p.38.

39. Potter, p.70.

40. Fuller, p.107.

41. Potter, p.64.

42. Potter, p.40.

43. Potter, p.40.

44. Potter, p.12f.

45. Potter, p.12.

46. Potter, p.27.

47. Potter, p.10.

48. Potter, p.10.

49. Potter, p.41.

50. Potter, p.33f.

51. Potter, p.38.

52. Potter, p.42.

53. Potter, p.74.

54. Potter, p.74.

55. Potter, p.74f.

56. Potter, p.75f.

57. See Heinz Antor, "Ethical Plurivocity; or, The Pleasures and Rewards of Reading," in *Text - Culture - Reception. Cross-Cultural Aspects of English Studies,* ed. Rüdiger Ahrens and Heinz Antor (Heidelberg: Winter, 1992), 27–46; and Antor "The Ethics of Criticism in the Age After Value," in *Why Literature Matters,* ed. Rüdiger Ahrens and Laurenz Volkmann (Heidelberg: Winter, 1996), 65–85.

58. Potter, p.76.

59. Potter, p.34.

60. For further information about this phenomenon see Vernon Gras, "The Recent Ethical Turn in Literary Studies," *Mitteilungen des Verbandes Deutscher Anglisten* 4.2 (1993):30–41.

61. Potter, p.77.

62. Potter, p.77.

63. See Potter, pp.29, 30.

64. Potter, p.78.

65. Potter, pp.13, 78.

66. Potter, p.78.

CHAPTER 9

MULTIPLE NARRATIVES IN DENNIS POTTER'S *BLACKEYES*

Constructing Identity as Cultural Dialogue

Gwendolyn Connelly

THIS ESSAY ADDRESSES DENNIS POTTER'S USE OF A MULTILAYERED narrative structure in his novel *Blackeyes*. It will discuss how the process of narrative reworking that we observe throughout this novel, and that produces the story we find in *Blackeyes,* is Potter's metaphor for a strategy with which we can resist the way social/cultural discourse (and here specifically patriarchal discourse) functions to co-opt and corrupt the formation of personal identity. Lastly, this paper will explore how this metaphor addresses ethical issues associated with the postmodern concept of self-awareness through the foregrounding of discourse/narrative. This process is central to our own successful participation in the ongoing process of creating both self and world in the presence of multiple and competing discourses.

In *Blackeyes,* Potter presents the reader with multiple narrative strands. It is a kind of puzzle, a story within a story within a story. Initially, an unidentified narrator recounts Jessica's frustrated attempts to rewrite yet another narrative, her uncle's novel *Sugar Bush*. Kingsley's novel is a narrative structure that is both present and absent in *Blackeyes*. Its presence is represented in limited quotations, while its alteration and absence signals a process of erasure, critique and amendment that must take place in order for the newer version (*Blackeyes*) to emerge. The best-seller *Sugar Bush* is dependent upon yet another narrative: the "real-life" experiences of Kingsley's niece, Jessica. It is his fictional portrayal of this woman and her life that is at the nexus of the dispute for narrative control. The *Blackeyes* text that we read is the product of Jessica's rewriting of *Sugar Bush* through the assistance of a narrator. It is Jessica who extends the Sugar Bush story by creating D. I. Blake to investigate what he considers to be a suspicious suicide. She provides the list of names for Blake to follow. It is Jessica who corrects and fills in the *Sugar Bush* text with details from her own experience. She finds, however, that she is unable to successfully make the transition between thought, speech and action; she is ultimately unable to put words on paper. Potter therefore provides a sympathetic narrator to record and arrange what she says. This narrator, we later discover (in chapter 23) is Jeff Richards. It is Jeff who provides the narrative continuity between the Sugar Bush narrative, Jessica's corrections, and his own critique. He is the conduit through which Jessica's "amendments" and "scraps of paper" are arranged into the text we are reading as *Blackeyes,* or as Jeff puts it, "Mind you Jessica's amendments to the story suit me very well. I've edited out the most embarrassing and ill-composed bits, but otherwise left it alone."[1] In summary, the narrative structure of *Blackeyes* can be described as follows: Potter (author) writing *Blackeyes* with Jeff (narrator of *Blackeyes*) writing down and arranging Jessica's reworking (adds Blake, modifies ending, etc.) of *Sugar Bush* written by Maurice Kingsley using Jessica's experiences.

What can be gained by telling a story in such an obviously constructed and potentially confusing way? Potter uses this structure to foreground the process and consequences of narrative authority. The way in which a story is being told is what is being contested. Whoever controls the point of view (the author or narrator) determines how characters are represented in the text. Jessica's struggle throughout *Blackeyes* is an effort to shift and redirect the narrative point of view found in *Sugar Bush,* which has produced a distorted representation of her. But the written word has an authority she finds difficult to escape. To allow Kingsley's text to go unchallenged would be tantamount to believing his distortions, thereby granting his representations the status of truth. This is a very real danger for Jessica. The distinction between herself and Kingsley's representations are becoming blurred:

> The trouble was that the strange and lost blankness [Kingsley] had cast over Blackeyes was beginning to fall upon her, too. Jessica was finding it more and more difficult to piece together an alternative account. . . . (Potter, 1989, 17)

Jessica must maintain her distance from Kingsley's portrayals or be trapped by them. She must continually disavow his version and attempt to substitute her own representation. Kingsley's text has produced a doubling, where Jessica is in a position to stand outside of "herself," as she has been portrayed by someone else. It is from this perspective that she gains the ability to see and reject these false images as the first step in assuming responsibility for constructing her own identity.

But how did she lose herself? In *Blackeyes,* Jessica's capture was achieved through a process in which Kingsley merely functions as the agent who both personalizes and enables a larger male discourse to encapsulate her:

> In the book, the bloody book, Kingsley had reduced the girl to a zombie, yet again, turning [Jessica's] matter of fact description into a mute psychosis. How many times, she wondered, would allegedly sympathetic accounts of the manifold way in which women were so regularly humiliated be nothing more than yet further exercises of this same impulse, the identical power. (64)

Jessica's original plan was to provide her uncle with her experiences in order to humiliate him, hoping that whatever narrative he created would result in a public and critical failure. This did not happen. Instead, Jessica finds herself to be held even more securely within another's gaze/narrative. She has literally become an object in someone else's discourse: "And now she considered herself to be little more than words written by a sick old man. . . . A mark on the page: someone else's page" (64).

The ways in which Jessica has been positioned, emptied, and objectified in *Sugar Bush* are symptomatic of how patriarchal discourse operates to create female identity out of male desire in the culture at large. As a historical reminder of the deep-rooted pervasiveness and longevity of this male discourse, Potter foregrounds its literary history with references to both the romance (Nicolette and Aucassin) and the fairy tale traditions (*Rumpelstiltskin*). Escape from the doorless tower for herself and Blackeyes is the task that Jessica takes on. But how is this to be done when the inescapable influence of the confining discourse is at once confirmed and reinforced by the success of Kingsley's novel? A lucrative and powerful market for this type of commodification hungrily awaits each new entry. *Sugar Bush* merely feeds an insatiable cultural appetite for female characters who are nothing more than constructions arising from male desire. So who will listen to what Jessica is trying to say, what she must say to counter the weight of her uncle's narrative claims upon her?

Jessica's salvaging of her own identity begins when she decides that she must rewrite *Sugar Bush* before she begins to believe in the version of herself that Kingsley has created. She decides to focus her deconstructing efforts on the end of her uncle's novel:

> "And now she had to start all over again dismantling his narrative, reclaiming herself." (4)

"Sugar Bush had ended in this way. These were the words Jessica had to make a start with, if she were to prevent a not especially hideous nightmare from leaking so much more nastily into the light of day." (8)

This struggle to maintain her own distinct identity apart from Kingsley's version of her, is what the narrator records as the text of Potter's novel *Blackeyes*. To reclaim herself, Jessica must literally write her own words and mark her own page. Unfortunately, she finds herself incapable of carrying out this task on her own. She knows what she wants to do, but cannot do it. As the narrator explains it: "The few sentences she contrived to get out of her head on to the page were so distorted by indignation or an even worse hatred that one failed to notice their other deficiencies. She seemed to have no idea of how to construct a paragraph, a piece of standard literary engineering as necessary to a writer as—but, no . . ." (135).

This inability on Jessica's part is hardly surprising. She is merely the product of her background, specifically a set of discourses that precluded substantive education in favor of emphasizing form over content. Although Kingsley is clearly incorrect about Jessica not having any brains (45), what he has written about Blackeyes' education is essentially true about Jessica as well, as Jeff points out using both Kingsley's narrative and his own:

> . . . she still had an essentially vulgar mind. . . ."The years in which she had been a model immersed her in the unwholesome and the trashy, where brightness was synonymous with artificial glitter and truth so far out of the question as to be no more than a distant star on a cloudy night" Kingsley wrote. . . . The same could be said about his niece. Jessica's education had been neglected, for her mother thought it more important to be "feminine" (in the old use of the term) than "qualified" (another ancient word). . . . The sort of private school for girls to which she was sent placed more emphasis on being ladylike than becoming human, and considered what it called Deportment to be an asset of greater value than any bookish accomplishment. The wonder was that she could read anything at all. (159)

Just as "real" women must struggle within the cultural confines of patriarchy to tell their own stories and construct their identities, Jessica must work within the narrative framework from *Sugar Bush* to tell her version of the story, the one she knows to be true. She must find a way to make Kingsley's words point to her ending, her truth. She begins by capturing Kingsley in her narrative. His presence provides the previously absent motivation for her actions since he embodies both the specific and general cultural forces that entrap, manipulate and victimize her. Jessica is the victim of Kingsley's sexual abuse, just as Blackeyes is merely a void onto which he can project his desires.

This first step in her challenge to Kingsley's narrative authority does not go unnoticed, as Kingsley looks out the window to see Blackeyes walking down the sidewalk and wonders:

> ... how could she be embodied out there ... ? ... But the half-idea flew up ... that something or someone was interfering with Sugar Bush, or with the private property of his own dreams. (13)

By expanding the narrative frame, Jessica has captured Kingsley. This action is only possible because she sees herself as distinct from her representation in her uncle's novel. He now becomes a character under the influence of her authorial control and Jessica has positioned herself to contradict and correct the "literary voice" that previously held her mute. Although she achieves a significant level of narrative control, she must still continue to use the materials available, in this case her uncle's novel. The frame itself (as with social/cultural discourse) is inescapable, and so Jessica begins working by providing an alternative explanation for Kingsley's ending; for how Blackeyes' hands were injured and why this woman drowns herself in the pond.

D. I. Blake is introduced by Jessica into the *Sugar Bush* narrative (augmented later by Jeff) to dislodge the idea that Blackeyes went to her death without a ripple, leaving no traces of her existence. Blake's character is added to the story to punish the men who mistreated Blackeyes. It is the detective who asks the uncomfortable questions and makes these men squirm.

In Jessica's rendition of the story, Blackeyes roars out of the Kingsley narrative on a motorcycle. Jessica takes advantage of a gap in the *Sugar Bush* text to enable Blackeyes' escape. The ending that Jessica provides, however, is only a further indication of the pervasiveness and inescapability of her surrounding social discourse, in this case the genre of romance. Jessica has Blackeyes ride into "a world made out of half-remembered women's magazine stories, half-ashamed yearning, inadequately digested scraps of an opposing ideology and an inability to describe emotion or landscape or motivation or speech or thought or anything else in original language" (159).

At this point, it is important to note a change in the text of *Blackeyes* that Potter included in the 1988 edition. At the close of the 1987 edition, the Blackeyes character escapes drowning, but Jeff the narrator is poised to "claim" her. This is a cliché "happy" ending that appears to model itself on the problematic and derived discourses of romance and fairy tale that Jessica had so vigorously endeavored to escape. In the 1988 version, Potter completely frees the Blackeyes character even from his own authorial designs by having her literally walk out of the narrative:

1987:
As her lungs filled, she had the satisfaction of knowing that Blackeyes was free. Well, sort of free, anyway, for it is me that is waiting outside her door, ready to claim her.[2]
1988:
As her lungs filled, she had the satisfaction of knowing that Blackeyes was free. Well, sort of free, anyway, for it is me that is waiting outside her door, ready to claim her.
"No," she smiled, without saying it. "No," And walked away. . . .
(Potter 1988, 185)

This revised ending, with its perpetually incomplete final sentence, provides us with a model for narrative release, one that remains open-ended leaving room for self-determination.

For Jessica there remains only the final task of punishing her uncle. This act is accomplished through a type of internarrative exchange. Once Blackeyes is free of Kingsley's narrative, Jessica seems to have taken her place. As she awaits her uncle's arrival for dinner, she finds herself literally enacting the *Sugar Bush* version of Blackeyes' final hours, but with a distinct difference. Although Jessica is unable to completely dismantle her uncle's narrative, and therefore the suicide is inescapable, this time the woman whose body is to be found in the pond will make some waves before she exits. As the narrator explains, the final chapter of *Sugar Bush* cannot be erased without unraveling crucial elements of Jessica's narrative scheme:

> Without Kingsley's last chapter, the inventions Jessica had already made would have no purpose, and the policeman she imagined into life would not be able to be the instrument of her vengeance. (167)

Jessica being the only person who can physically touch Kingsley, is now the only one who can, and therefore must act. She must participate in what Potter refers to as "first order creation." (183) By smashing the throat (voice) of her uncle and the snakes (the symbolic penis) that slither from it, Jessica's first "creative" act functions symbolically to both silence and emasculate Kingsley and, at least temporarily, the discourses he represents. She successfully destroys/disables both the narrative voice (social/cultural discourse) that had held her captive and the snake/penis (male erotic desire) that had victimized her both as a child and as a model. By killing Kingsley, Jessica avenges herself and ends the tyranny of his "literary voice." Her story can now proceed without contradiction toward her redesigned finale.

As we read *Blackeyes*, Jessica's rewriting becomes a record of a sort of ongoing reader-response to her reading and re-reading of Kingsley's text. Jessica's alterations are in the form of a running commentary that continually corrects and fills in her uncle's version of events. As the narrator graphs Jessica's recollections onto Kingsley's text, we are continually reminded of the strategic importance of narrative point of view and control to the construction of truth and to Jessica's task. Such shifts between competing narratives tend to jar the reader out of his/her comfortable position as a passive narrative consumer and force him/her to acknowledge the existence of competing versions, such as the following descriptions of Jessica's/Blackeyes' first audition:

> "Everyone is waiting, said her head, everyone is waiting, is waiting. Tell me what to do." This was Kingsley's account.
> "You pigs," said her mind. "You pigs. You filthy rutting pigs." This is what Jessica knew to be in her head at the time which was the original occasion for the later fiction. (34)

The way in which the Blackeyes character is constructed is representative of the way in which male discourse positions women as objects of the male gaze. The only viable parts in this construction are those that are useful to the observer. Therefore the created image serves solely to reflect male libido, so it is not surprising that Kingsley has Blackeyes state that she does not have orgasms. For such female pleasure is unavailable or perhaps unimaginable within the utilitarian schemes that comprise such patriarchal discourse.

In *Blackeyes,* Potter directs our attention most pointedly toward the way social discourse determines how female images are created by having the female protagonist work as a model in advertising. In this discourse of manipulated consumption, women are reduced to their essential physical likenesses, to images of themselves. These images can be overwritten to market any product. For Potter, advertising and its extensive use of the female image becomes symbolic of all such practices of consumer manipulation through sexual images. This practice has the dual effect of channeling male desire to increase or insure product consumption, while it reduces and restricts female identity within the confines of narrowly defined erotic and voyeuristic representations:

> ... these observers did not give due account for the sensuality of the passive.... Her luminous jet-like eyes said nothing, and so said everything. She was pliable. She was there to be invented, in any posture, any words, over and over again, in ejaculatory longing. (65)

No self-determined construction of identity is permitted to the female in this process. She is flattened and reduced, no distracting details (such as independent thought) are permitted that would interfere with her function as passive recipient of the desirous/consuming gaze.

The struggle that is most clearly brought to our attention in *Blackeyes* is the result of conflicting attempts to construct identity. The "doubling" that Jessica experiences at the hands of her uncle is similar to the processes through which we are all captured in our surrounding social discourses. In our lives these cultural codes function the way narrative does in fiction. When we fail to interrogate/demystify these codes, we become objects in a narrative that is not of our choosing. We allow someone else to write our script. Potter offers us an example of how to reclaim ourselves, how to make our own choices, how to make room for the possibility of authoring our own stories. To succeed, the role we must assume is the one Jessica inhabits in *Blackeyes*. We must become aware of how we are shaped by the social discourse that surrounds and infuses us. Once we can see this discourse as a form of narrative (one written by someone else), we can begin to assert our own agency to construct the identities we want for ourselves. This is only possible when we become aware of the gap between how we have been constructed by social discourse and how we wish to appear. The process of identity construction is dialogical. Just as *Sugar Bush* functioned as a starting point for Jessica to begin her reclamation, so we begin by demystifying our surrounding discourses, to reshape an identity of our own choosing.

EPILOGUE

In April 1997 the first trickle of a later deluge of news stories, commentaries, and book reviews appeared in the British media, promising titillating sexual detail about deceased writer Dennis Potter from a forthcoming biography. This first story appeared in the *Sunday Times* and for the next 17 months prior to the actual release of Humphrey Carpenter's authorized biography, a considerable volume of "I told you so's" and "what did you expect's" sparked defensive responses from Potter's family and other supporters. As a defense, Sarah Potter, who previously acted as her father's secretary, noted that the drugs the writer took to control his psoriatic arthropathy caused impotency. An interesting trump move on the part of Ms. Potter—an admission and exposure, hardly any less personal than the assertions made by her father's former friends and associates that he had secured the services of prostitutes, that he idolized actresses, or that he pursued and was rejected by numerous women during his marriage. The various commentators and reviewers align themselves into basic choruses of those who rush to associate these hearsay confessions with the controversial and difficult sexual themes associated with Potter's work; those who feel justified at last to revile (with authority) the author as a sexual predator; or those who wish to maintain a focus on what Potter left us, the legacy that broke television's potential wide open with his sometimes shocking but always controversial body of work.

Obviously, Potter's thematic repertoire delivers an easy target for speculation about the relationship of the author's real-life experiences, emotional and otherwise, to those tormented fictional characters who make us wince and look away from their on-screen ordeals. But the real core question remains: Do these facts/allegations bring any clarity to our understanding of the work? I think not. There remains an obtuse confusion between art and biography. The fact that Potter used the experiential substance of his own physical and emotional suffering to shape and define his themes and characters has never been in question. The author admitted as much throughout numerous interviews. In the end, such details in themselves are hollow and mundane in their biographical context because the electrical connective tissue, the power of contextual association that makes Potter's work extraordinary—his interpretive context— is missing. Thematically repeated, with differing and uneven results, is his belief that men and women must fulfill their most human capacity by creating/writing their own self-interpretation. The struggle against cultural forms of autobiographical hijacking is central to Potter's sense of humanity as expressed through the work. In relationship to his novel *Blackeyes,* this interpretive activity is central to the character's eventual emancipation from someone else's interpretive scheme. The slippery problem of interpretation, when combined with the illusion of factual reporting, was painfully evident to Potter regarding his very first assignment for television. How easy it was to edit familiar facts to achieve something alien, hurtful and suddenly unreflective of one's own experience. How necessary it was to carefully prepare a narrative context, to present the facts with care. This is the very activity that his characters struggle with during the process of self-narration. The power to use memory and a personal sense of the world to achieve self-awareness. So when the misogyny allegations are flying against "Dirty Den," it is easy to say "why, yes" with a condescending nod of affirmation. But wait, read on—at the end of a self-appropriated narrative there is freedom and redemption, at least for Blackeyes. And maybe for Dennis Potter as well.

NOTES

1. Dennis Potter, *Blackeyes* (London: Faber, 1988), p.159. All future citations will be in text from this edition or from *Blackeyes* (New York: Vintage, 1988 [1987]). They are identical except for the ending. See below.
2. Dennis Potter, *Blackeyes* (New York: Vintage, 1988[1987]), p.184.

CHAPTER 10

"LOST LANDS?"

Dennis Potter, Childhood and the Quest for the Sovereign Self

John R. Cook

IN THIS ESSAY, I WANT TO DEVELOP SOME OF THE IDEAS about Dennis Potter, particularly his relationship to the past and to childhood, that I expressed in my recent book, *Dennis Potter: A Life on Screen*.[1] How we understand the past is crucial to Potter: for him, we cannot make sense of our own lives—find a shape to them—unless we first make sense of our own past. In works like *The Singing Detective* (1986), as well as the feature films *Dreamchild* (1986) and *Track 29* (1988), it is only when protagonists start to excavate, through memory and fantasy, their own lost histories, that they can begin to deal successfully with their predicaments in the present and thereby discover the seeds of psychological renewal. In the landscape of Dennis Potter, to find the real meaning of one's existence, it is vital, first of all, to understand the true significance of one's past.

Ironically, since his death in 1994, such a sentiment has never been more pertinent; for increasingly, how we understand Dennis Potter himself has come to depend, in the popular imagination at least, on how we make sense of his own particular private past: his personal biography. As Gwen Connelly points out in the preceding essay, the 1998 publication of an "official" biography of Potter by controversial biographer Humphrey Carpenter led to a wave of denigration of the late writer in the British media, comparable to that which he suffered almost a decade earlier in Britain, with the television production of his novel *Blackeyes* (1989).[2] As with that TV serial, the derision centered on Potter's alleged attitudes to and mistreatment of women. Sensational "revelations," leaked to the press in advance of publication, that the writer *may* have sought out the company of over 100 prostitutes; that he *may* have wished to sleep with some of his leading actresses; and that despite being happily married, he *may* have been capable of having affairs, seemed to offer ample justification in the press mind that their earlier condemnation of the TV *Blackeyes* as the work of a "dirty old man" had indeed been correct. Here, at last, was the proof: "facts" dredged up from the writer's own private past and authorized, even, for public consumption by his very own estate.

Yet step outside of the British media culture that damned Potter irredeemably for *Blackeyes* and you find a very different context of reception. Away from the din of British press indignation that made even Potter's most sympathetic commentators begin to question their own judgments of the writer at that time,[3] one finds *Blackeyes* being read by American critics, such as Connelly in this volume, not as the salacious, wet-mouthed fantasies of a misogynist, but as an important work with "feminist aspirations."[4] For this British scholar, whose perceptions of the writer have inevitably had to contend with the media mauling Potter has received over the last decade in Britain, the cultural mismatch is not only ironic but telling.[5]

Moreover, Potter himself, throughout his work, repeatedly demonstrated how painfully aware he was of the manifold ways in which the "truth" of what one is trying to say about one's own past and feelings can all too easily become distorted and misappropriated by others. As Connelly points out in her essay, fundamental to the conception of *Blackeyes* itself is the way in which a basically feminist story (Jessica's) is distorted by another (Kingsley), until it comes to seem precisely the opposite of what was intended. And right from his early experience of making a TV documentary about his beloved Forest of Dean, *Between Two Rivers* (1960), Potter learned how, under the guise of apparently incontestable "fact," it was all too easy to misrepresent the "truth" and to hurt others: "They cut it, Dad! They cut it to ribbons!" protests Nigel, Potter's "working class hero" in *Stand Up, Nigel Barton* (1965), after he watches a similar documentary on TV with his father and realizes, with horror and not a little guilt, that he has betrayed him.[6] In the same play, Nigel remembers how, as a child, he also betrayed another boy in school by implicating him in a classroom crime that he himself committed. Then, he sat and watched as all the other children proceeded to back up his story, simply for the sheer sport of persecuting a fellow class-mate. It is a scenario that is reworked 20 years later for *The Singing Detective:* "I . . . watched and listened and watched and listened as one after another they nailed that backward lad hands and feet to my story." Marlow, the central protagonist of *The Singing Detective,* recalls:

> I have not seriously doubted since that afternoon that any lie will receive almost instant corroboration and almost instant collaboration if the mainte-

nance of it results in the public enjoyment of someone else's pain, someone else's humiliation.

Interestingly, what Marlow learns is that the repetition of the lie too many times actually has the effect of turning it into a "truth," which eventually comes to be believed, even by the victim himself: "—what is interesting—is that the boy was *himself* overwhelmed by the weight of the evidence . . . And this poor little sod came in the end to believe that he *had* done it. . . ."[7]

Thus Potter himself was only too aware of how, in certain circumstances, a rabid majority can single out for particular punishment those who dare to be different and of how events can then take on their own horrifying momentum, snowballing out of control until eventually, the victim is nailed "hands and feet" to a version of the past that in the end may distort just as much as it reveals.

Certainly, following Potter's treatment at the hands of the British media in the years since his death, has, at times, seemed eerily reminiscent of some of the darker moments of his plays. As I have outlined in more detail elsewhere, his final, linked works for TV, *Karaoke* and *Cold Lazarus* (1996, posthumous), despite receiving good reviews abroad, were not terribly well received in the U.K., in a manner that seemed to suggest that British media culture no longer welcomed him in the way it once did.[8] In an increasingly commercialized media landscape, dominated by Rupert Murdoch's newspaper and television empire, the values of a Dennis Potter, even a posthumous Potter, sat very awkwardly. In retrospect, the virulent reception that the British press—particularly the Murdoch-owned press—gave to *Blackeyes* in 1989, can be seen to mark the beginnings of this sea change in critical attitude: a decisive signal that the old public broadcasting world in which Potter had once thrived was now under assault from newspapers with proprietors who had their own commercial ambitions in television and who would brook no symbolic opposition (little wonder that in his final TV interview in 1994, Potter joked that he called his cancer "Rupert").[9] And so, in the wake of the critically battered *Karaoke* and *Cold Lazarus*, the stage was set in Britain for the debunking biography.

Yet in spite of the revelatory "facts" that seemed to be so finally damning (and despite the collaboration of some former friends and colleagues in appearing to play along by offering confirmation of already jaundiced press attitudes toward Potter[10]), the authorized version of Potter's past has turned out to be not quite so authorized after all. Having commissioned an "official" biography of her father from established biographer Humphrey Carpenter, Potter's daughter, Sarah, together with his literary agent, Judy Daish, distanced themselves from it on publication. In an interview with *The Times*, Sarah Potter rubbished the allegations about Potter's relationships with various women,

stating that she felt "Humphrey [Carpenter] was too caught up in chasing sensational titbits that would sit nicely in the [newspaper] serialization and sell a
lot of copies." She declared the prostitute allegations to be "utter tosh" and
stated that although Potter could sometimes get sentimental about some of the
actresses he worked with, as a member of his close-knit family, she always
knew "how proper he was with the women that worked for him."[11] If Potter
had had any affairs in his life, she declared, she did not know of them and
"certainly, the candidates that have been pushed forward, they're not the
ones." She herself now regretted the decision, on behalf of the family and estate, to succumb to the commercial pressures for an "official" biography: "I
thought if we do an official one and we're all involved, then it can't go that
badly wrong because they'll see what kind of family we've been." Discussing
it with her father, however, as he was dying from cancer, he had warned her of
how things indeed *could* go wrong: "Dad didn't really want one. There's no
secret to that."[12]

In a way, nothing could more vividly illustrate Connolly's assertion in the
previous essay (with regard to *Blackeyes* the novel) of how easy it is to find
oneself "an object in a narrative that is not of our choosing" and worse, how
that narrative can come to represent the precise antithesis of one's own feelings
about the true significance of the past. In the bleak, black terms expressed by
Philip Marlow in *The Singing Detective,* any lie, if repeated with enough
power and force, will eventually become a truth if it results in the humiliation
and persecution of another. In terms of Potter's own posthumous reputation:
any myth or rumor about the past will circulate and circulate, until in the end,
it comes to be believed and accepted as genuine history by almost everyone—
a convenient justification for previous press criticism of his sexual themes;
even if, as the testimony of his daughter appears to indicate, there is actually
little hard evidence in the end to substantiate it.

Certainly, for someone whose research work predates the writer's death in
1994 and the posthumous denigration of his reputation, the experience of
watching the barely recognizable ways in which the history of Potter's past has
been cannibalized and transformed by elements of the British media for specific commercial (and perhaps even political) ends, has been a fascinating, if
sometimes grim, experience.[13] Whether consciously or unconsciously, the over-
whelming thrust of much British media criticism since his death has been to
dismiss Potter as an overvalued relic of a broadcasting stone age, whose
themes and ideas are no longer "relevant" and who has nothing much to say
to contemporary audiences.[14] In Britain, media interest in his work now principally resides in how much his dramas may or may not "reveal" tantalizing
insights into his private life and his alleged sexual proclivities.[15] In this way,
Dennis Potter takes his place as one more bust on the crowded mantelpiece of
fallen cultural icons—someone the British once thought had something to say

to them, but whose past has been raided posthumously and exposed by biography as having had nothing much to say after all, aside from the "revelation" of a few alleged sexual secrets. Interestingly, however, if one examines closely his final drama, *Cold Lazarus,* one can see this was a future scenario that Potter himself was acutely aware of and whose hostile, commercial motivations after his death, he more or less accurately predicted.

Cold Lazarus picks up where its immediate sister work, *Karaoke,* left off: Daniel Feeld, screenwriter and central protagonist of *Karaoke* (played by Albert Finney), dies of cancer in 1994. Through cryogenics, his head is frozen, and in the year A.D. 2368, when technology has at last made this possible, his brain cells begin to be thawed out. This miraculous resurrection is not, however, the solely disinterested one of science it first appears. In a clear echo of some less than wholesome trends of our own age, there are those in the media world who are out to plunder the screenwriter's personal memories of the past for their own commercial gain. They are all too aware that in the desolate future they inhabit—where the false, privatized opium of virtual reality has become an almost universal public escape hatch from the dystopian grimness of the external world—access to the secret contents of the writer's head will prove financial dynamite. As one character describes the plans of Dave Siltz (Henry Goodman), the Murdoch-like media mogul behind the scheme to plunder the contents of the writer's mind: "*He's* convinced that he'll sweep all the ratings when people out there see [via virtual reality] what it was *really* like to walk and talk and play and screw and eat and drink nearly four hundred years ago."[16]

The interesting, subversive question Potter raises in *Cold Lazarus,* however, is whether direct access to the juicy, personal "facts" of the writer's past can ever be as unproblematic as the Siltzes of the world believe. This is well illustrated by an important scene at the beginning of Episode Two of the drama, in which, as Daniel's memories of childhood begin to be thawed out by the scientists and replayed on a video wall, it quickly transpires they cannot be *literally* true.

The scientists (and we) excitedly begin to view memories of Daniel Feeld's childhood in the tellingly named Forest of Nead (Potter's own spiritually needful Forest of Dean spelled backward). There is a small stone chapel and inside, children's voices can be heard singing the hymn "Amazing Grace." Yet as Potter's script is at pains to make clear, this cannot be *wholly* factual recollection for outside the chapel window, a face is peering in and it is none other than that of the *adult* Daniel Feeld—the middle-aged writer protagonist of *Karaoke* we saw dying in 1994.

All of this puzzles and disturbs the objective, utterly literal-minded scientists. There is something wrong: this cannot be true. It cannot be memory. At first, they blame the neuropeptide drip they are feeding the patient to stimulate his brain cells but then, as they begin to consider the matter more deeply, one of their number, Luanda, comes to some startling conclusions—conclusions that clearly chime with Potter's own authorial viewpoint:

> LUANDA (*interrupts*) But it may not *be* that! . . . I mean . . . don't we sometimes place ourselves as we are now back into the unravelling of an old recollection? . . . I can be as I am now when I dream of my childhood . . .

Emma Porlock, the chief scientist, interrupts: "But that's not the same thing, is it? Dream, memory. Memory, dream." Luanda's reply is significant:

> LUANDA: It's first cousin to it! . . . First cousin. And of the same blood. My dreams are built from the things that happen to me in the waking world. And my memories can also adapt and shape the past. . . . My memory, Emma, is also a tool, an editor, a judge, a jury![17]

This is a key speech—one that has clear resonances not only with *Cold Lazarus,* but with Potter's entire body of writing and thinking on the relationship of the present to the past and, particularly, to childhood.

To take *Cold Lazarus* first: within the specific dramatic situation Potter creates, the speech shows the absurdity of the belief that the contents of the writer's mind being spilled out on screen are literally true; that in dramatizing the past, the writer is somehow giving his viewing audience *direct* and unproblematic access to his own memories. In *Cold Lazarus,* we are presented with a hostile, philistine world in which the most intimate possessions of the writer, his own memories, have been ruthlessly plundered and exploited for personal gain by those whose reductionist, overly deterministic views of what constitutes "reality" have failed to take account of what, for Potter, is clearly the more complex *interrelationship* between fact and fiction, memory and fantasy. Only when his audience, the scientists, realize that "memory" and "dream" may not in fact be separate, deterministic biological entities, but rather spiritual first cousins, do they begin to come to some understanding of the mind of the writer being dramatized on screen.

In *Cold Lazarus,* Potter is clearly articulating the anxiety that the world from which he knew he was departing in 1994 was actively engaged in misunderstanding the nature of his work: that all too often, his audience was making the naïve and reductionist error of seeing the "memories" of the past and of childhood contained in his work as straightforward biography. It is an anxiety most chillingly dramatized in Daniel Feeld's final words before he dies of cancer in 1994; words that haunt the *Cold Lazarus* serial, recurring again and again—perhaps nowhere more vividly than at the end of the very first episode, in which the thawing, severed head of the writer is seen and heard vainly crying out to a world that, apparently, is not listening and that does not want to know his version of the truth. In his original script directions, Potter is at pains to emphasize how this image should be rendered in all its grotesqueness and horror:

> More and more discernible and hideously upsetting, a head seems to float in liquid nitrogen, all wired-up with antennae, neurotransmitters and hair-thin coils of tubes. But the eyes are open, full of terror and the mouth seems to be trying to make word-shapes . . .
> . . . DANIEL (Off, near scream): No biography![18]

Here, Potter's own distaste for biography's plundering of the personal past (also expressed in life, to his daughter Sarah) is vividly dramatized, but the "No biography!" cry cuts in another direction too. It provides a context in which to comprehend more generally, Potter's relationship as a writer to his own past and to what he was often to label the "lost lands" of childhood.[19]

To paraphrase Luanda in *Lazarus*, memory and fantasy are always first cousins in Potterland: his "dreams" may indeed be "built from the things that happen to [him] in the waking world" but at the same time, his "memories . . . also adapt and shape the past." In other words, while Potter is clearly writing out of his own life, constantly drawing upon his own experiences to such a degree that everything he lived through becomes potential grist to the mill of his creativity, crucially, it is only on the page that this morass of experience finds and receives any shape.[20] There is certainly a relationship between Potter's own "reality" and his fictions, but the important distinction that comes out time and again in his writing (and which also distances him from the critical assumptions of biography) is that that relationship is never *one-way*: for not only does reality cross over into fantasy in Potter's work, but so too can fantasy cross over into reality. Far from being distinct, easily quantifiable categories, reality and fantasy constantly interpenetrate each other in his plays, blurring and merging.

Cold Lazarus is a clear metaphorical demonstration of this notion. For their own greedy commercial ends, a future generation raids the writer's mind after death in a quest for his *real* experiences, but what it chasteningly discovers is that those apparent "memories" he has been projecting on-screen, far from being wholly *objective,* can only ever be *subjective.* As Luanda comes to realize, with memory it is impossible to separate out objective reality from subjective fantasy, since memory not only records but also actively "adapts and shapes the past." Memory and fantasy are so inextricably bound up with each other that it becomes fruitless to try and separate the two, since one's recall of factual events is constantly interpenetrated by one's own subjective interpretation of them. Attempt to separate the fiction from the fact—try to take one away from the other—and all you are left with is "nothing and no point."[21] For Potter, it is our very imagination that puts the meaning into our real experiences.[22]

Hence, the cry of "No biography!" that haunts *Cold Lazarus* is not only the writer's plea for understanding but a quite accurate reflection of his own working methods: his writing really *is* "no biography," simply because for Potter, there is just no way of filtering out the recollections of "real" events that have found their way into the fiction from his own feelings about them. Crucially, it is this very act of transforming imaginatively that becomes the only way of making sense of them. We see this in *Lazarus* with the image of the adult Daniel Feeld staring in at his childhood past through the chapel window. The technique echoes Potter's use of adult actors playing children, which he exploited to such effect in earlier BBC television plays like *Stand Up, Nigel Barton* and *Blue Remembered Hills* (1979). With memory, as the scientist Luanda makes clear in *Lazarus,* "I can be as I am now when I dream of my childhood." In other words, being wholly subjective and akin to "dream," memory allows us to superimpose our present selves upon the past and by this very process of imaginative insight, see events from that time more clearly. In Potter's work, it always has to be the adult who makes sense of what the child could not properly understand.

A good example of this comes from another Potter script, which was produced less than a year before *Cold Lazarus* was written. *Mesmer,* based on the exploits of the famous eighteenth century hypnotist, Anton Mesmer, had been written by Potter as a feature film screenplay in the early eighties, but only finally made it into production as a movie in 1993, directed by Roger Spottiswoode and starring Alan Rickman as Mesmer. Unfortunately, due to a contractual dispute between the producers and the film's main financiers, the finished film has never received a proper cinema release (though recently, it *has* had an airing, both in the United States and U.K., on the Bravo cable TV channel).[23] All of this is a pity, for *Mesmer* is one of Potter's finest feature film screenplays—highly expressive of his preoccupations as a writer. In terms of the key themes of memory and childhood, one scene in particular stands out. A key flashback sequence shows the adult Mesmer in his study, remembering himself as a child in the Austrian Alps, when one day, his father came looking for him in the mountains. As Potter's script describes the memory:

A small boy—the young Mesmer—perilously clings on a large rock above the scree, looking down fearfully.
MAN'S VOICE (*Calling, off*): Anton! Answer me! Where are you! . . .
INT. MESMER'S STUDY. NIGHT
Mesmer's eyes gleam . . . as memory contends with love and something like premonition . . .
EXT. ALPINE FOOTHILLS. DAY (MESMER'S YOUTH)

CLOSE. BOY MESMER ON ROCK
Hanging on for dear life, by now too terrified to move, as the scree starts to slip and slide at his feet . . . [24]

The scene strongly echoes one in *The Singing Detective*, where the central hospitalized protagonist, Philip Marlow, recalled himself as a boy hiding up a tree, whilst down below, his father came looking for him in the Forest. Importantly, what is also similar to that work is the sense that it is only the adult's imaginative *recollection* of the event that provides it with any meaning. [25] As Mesmer tells Maria Theresa (a blind pianist who is the one true love of his life) at the very end of the film:

MESMER: When I was a boy I would climb a mountain . . . I could see that all around me, from one horizon to the other, everything was in harmony, in balance—except—except human beings. Except—us. And I wanted—
(*a sudden spasm of real grief*)
I could not bear to do nothing about it. [26]

The adult's interpretation at the end of the film provides us with the context for understanding the earlier flashback recollection of the past. The image of the child, desperately attempting to retain his footing on the scree, trying to hold onto the vision of harmony he once glimpsed from the rock, but that was threatened by forces compelling him to "fall" back into the unbalanced human world, becomes a way for the adult Mesmer not only to make sense of his past, but also to discover a kind of purpose to his life. [27] The memory becomes an act of resolve: the foundation for a determined attempt to try and change things for the better, in terms of bringing the human world more closely in line with the "harmony" of Creation he once glimpsed up in the mountains.

This sense of childhood as a spur to active agency was explicitly discussed by Potter in a number of religious talks he gave on BBC Radio in the 1970s. In retrospect, these are very important because they allow us to trace the development of what can only be termed the "spiritual" ideas that began to dominate his writing from the early seventies onward. For example, in a 1978 talk called *The Other Side of the Dark*, Potter stated:

Looking back with wry amusement, we recall the days when, say, a summer afternoon or an unpleasant school lesson, would appear to go on and on up unto the edge of forever. Because we once seemed to be "making" things for the first time, or because what was in front of us and in our heads was not at once absorbed into the particular matrix of our adult, social, political, or habit-encrusted view of the world—because, in short, we were too new, too ignorant, too obviously "unfinished" to slot every new thing too quickly into its appropriate category—we were able once upon a time, to live out our days minute by minute. One of the strangest, most heartening and indeed irritatingly exhausting things about children, and therefore of what we ourselves once were, is their ability to live almost entirely in the present tense . . .

He went on:

> . . . Yet it is perhaps not quite so difficult. Whenever we play games, or act, or sing, or dance, or make love, we are outside "normal" time, we are in the cauldron of the actual minute, and we have suspended or evaded the claims of any other moment except *this* one. When we are frightened, when we are in pain, when we are excited, and when we are greatly moved, the world stands still. Once again—to our delight or not—all things are as new.[28]

The "lost lands" of childhood do not have to stay lost. We can recapture that sense of aliveness felt in childhood in which "all things were as new" and thereby, as Potter would see it, regain touch with our true "sovereign self": not one's public, "biographical" self, the product of the many drives and imperatives of external, material reality but rather a "true," inner self. It is the self remembered from childhood that lived its days "minute by minute" and therefore felt not only a sense of agency whereby all things were possible, but also a feeling of *wonder*—the glimpse of "harmony" in Creation the child of the Alps felt in *Mesmer*. Likewise, in perhaps Potter's most celebrated work, *The Singing Detective*, it is only when the adult Marlow shrives off his sick and misanthropic "public" persona and learns to live "minute by minute," by reaching back into childhood memory and using its "first cousin" imagination to transform himself into his own fantasy alter ego (The Singing Detective), that he is able at last to recover the "shreds" of his "sovereign self" and leave his hospital bed, "cured." As Potter described this process in a 1987 interview for BBC Television:

> . . . the very act of garnering clues and of remembering, not merely an event but how that event has lodged in you and how that event has affected the way you see things, begins to assemble a system of values and only when that system, no matter how tenuous it might be, was assembled was Marlow able to get up out of his bed . . . which is why [*The Singing Detective*] isn't about psoriasis or psoriatic arthropathy—or detectives, or that particular childhood, but about the way that we can protect that sovereignty that we have and that is all that we have . . . the most precious of all of the human capacities. . . . Out of this morass, if you like, of evidence, the clues and searchings and strivings, which is the metaphor for the way we live, we can start to put up the structure called self . . . [and] we can walk out of that structure, saying at least I know and you know better than before what it is we are.[29]

In a sense, this provides a neat summary of all the various points made in this essay—that it is a mistake, for example, simply to assess Potter's writing in terms of his own biography; of that "particular childhood." Rather, there is an interpenetration of memory with imagination, whereby what is important is not so much a particular event but of "how that event has lodged in you," affecting your whole outlook. As a writer, Potter certainly drew upon his own life experiences, but his quest for "the sovereign self" was much more about the search for buried feelings rather than hidden biographical "facts." Childhood plays the crucial role, here, because for the writer, it is able to remind us of that special "sovereignty"; of a time when we knew what it was like to be free, living out our lives "minute by minute." In this way, if childhood really is an Edenic "lost land," in the country of Dennis Potter, that does not mean it has to stay a forgotten one. As the writer himself put it to me when I interviewed him in 1990:

> You see, I think childhood is to everyone a lost land. . . . The loss of Eden is personally experienced by each and everyone of us as we leave the wonder and magic and also the pains and terrors of childhood into . . . well, it's the same reason why children can write poetry and then stop when they reach, unless they're poets, they stop when they reach puberty. And when the temptations and torrents of the world in a more adult sense come to them, their behavior becomes more restrained. Social conventions become more important: everything, discipline, self-discipline, all those things become of greater relevance. Whereas the discipline is imposed by an adult, when children are amongst themselves, it's all continual fidget and movement, exploration, speculation, wonder, which in a sense to lose that is to lose Eden, is to be expelled from the Garden. And I only use that metaphor as a continuous one because I believe that if when Jesus said "Be as little children," that is what is meant. In other words, be as open and be as innocent as you like. . . . But the knowledge that we have about what it is to be human as a child is something that we necessarily *must* lose but we don't have to lose it totally if we remember. . . . We remember an Eden even though it wasn't perfect . . . but it was an Eden in terms of its possibilities and potentialities.[30]

In his writing, Potter's aim was clearly to remind his audience of those "possibilities and potentialities"; to make viewers recognize their own innate individual "sovereignty" as human beings, waiting to be tapped. This was, as he put it, the "world behind the world": the realization not only that we are "made"—formed by all the external forces acting upon our daily lives—but that in some sense we are also "making," with the awesome power, if we so choose to recognize and use it, to break free of all the restricting social and cultural codes that entrap us.[31] In *Cold Lazarus,* Potter presents us with an utterly hostile future world that, at first, appears to be wholly "made" and conditioned by "external" forces. Thus when its inhabitants start to peer inside the mind of the dead writer, they expect to find more of the same. Instead, what they discover is something entirely "sovereign" and "making," which challenges not only their view of their subject but—liberatingly in the end—the very structures and perceptions of the society that has been oppressing them. By the same token, if British media culture currently does not want to know of Potter other than as the reflex memory of "TV's Mr. Sex,"[32] perhaps this merely confirms *Cold Lazarus*' overall dramatic point of how much "the now totally pervasive assumptions of the market-place . . . have stiffened into something close to natural law."[33] In one way, this all may seem very sad, but in another—given Potter's knowing awareness of the processes of media distortion and misappropriation evinced in such works as *Blackeyes* and *Cold Lazarus*—it could not be more ironic and, to an extent, utterly appropriate. For as both these texts show, it is out of such recognitions that change, perhaps, can spring.

NOTES

1. John R. Cook, *Dennis Potter: A Life on Screen* (Manchester: Manchester University Press; New York: St. Martin's Press, 1995; rev. second edition, 1998).

2. Humphrey Carpenter, *Dennis Potter: A Biography* (London: Faber and Faber, 1998).

3. See, for example, Kenith Trodd's recollection in this volume that *Blackeyes* led to a "bleak rethink [of Potter] for the industry, the public and for me."

4. This was how Potter himself described the TV production of *Blackeyes* at the time of its 1989 British transmission—for example, see Dennis Potter, "Arrows of Desire," interview with John Wyver, *New Statesman and Society*, 24 November 1989, p.18.

5. Interestingly, in interview with me in 1990, Potter himself expressed much the same view that he felt the U.S. critical context for his work was much more "open" than the British—"because they don't know so much about me," he thought Americans were much more inclined to take his themes and ideas seriously and less inclined to sneer at them or to read his work simply as autobiography, in stark contrast with many British reviewers (Dennis Potter, personal interview with John R. Cook, recorded Eastbourne Mews, London, 10 May 1990).

6. Dennis Potter, *The Nigel Barton Plays* (published scripts) (Harmondsworth: Penguin, 1967), p.73.

7. Dennis Potter, *The Singing Detective* (published scripts) (London: Faber and Faber, 1986), pp.212–213.

8. See Cook (rev. second edition, 1998), pp.308–311.

9. Dennis Potter, interview with Melvyn Bragg, first tx. Channel Four, 5 April 1994; published in Dennis Potter, *Seeing the Blossom: Two Interviews and a Lecture* (London: Faber and Faber, 1994), p.14. The year of *Blackeyes*' TV transmission, 1989, was also, crucially, the year of Rupert Murdoch's assault in

earnest on British public broadcasting: first, he launched his satellite service, Sky Television, in February 1989 and then in August of that year, he delivered the annual James MacTaggart Memorial Lecture at the Edinburgh International Television Festival, in which he attacked existing British terrestrial broadcasting as "elitist" and out of touch with popular taste. In part, Potter's own MacTaggart Lecture in 1993, in which he defended public broadcasting from the free-marketeers, was as a specific rejoinder to Murdoch. In the U.K. alone, Murdoch's newspaper and television empire embraces ownership of *The Times*, *The Sunday Times*, *The Sun* and *News of the World* newspapers, plus various *Times Supplements*, as well as British Sky Broadcasting satellite and digital TV channels, not to mention several publishing houses.

10. Gina Bellman, Potter's lead actress in the *Blackeyes* TV series, seems to be a case in point. She claimed in the posthumous biography that Potter had "exploited" her, just as the newspapers had claimed nearly a decade before, despite having gone out of her way to deny this at the time. According to Potter's daughter, Sarah, in an interview for the London *Times:* "She [Bellman] is obviously very damaged by it; I feel sorry about that, but I think her level of bitterness is misplaced—it's probably more to do with the fact that she didn't go on to do other things professionally" (Sarah Potter, "My Dad was not Dirty Den," interview by Grace Bradberry, *The Times*, 2 September 1998, p.15).

11. Sarah Potter, p.15. Humphrey Carpenter is the author of previous biographies on J. R. R. Tolkien, W. H. Auden, Benjamin Britten and perhaps most controversially, the former Archbishop of Canterbury, Robert Runcie. He is also a leading book reviewer for Rupert Murdoch's *Sunday Times* newspaper. Interviewing him in *The Guardian* newspaper, journalist Clare Longrigg commented: "Carpenter is gaining a reputation as a muckraker. Runcie was said to be very distressed by the book, which reported his candid views on gay priests and the parlous state of the Wales's marriage . . ." (Clare Longrigg, "Blue Remembered Thrills," *The Guardian*, 16 April 1997, pp.2–3).

12. For extended discussion and analysis of why Potter was no supporter of the literary biography, see Cook (rev. second edition, 1998), pp.312–313.

13. My research work on Potter began life as a Ph.D. thesis in 1989 and included an interview with Potter in 1990. The main writing up had been completed by September 1992, though final editing and proofing was not completed until July 1994. The thesis was published as the first edition of *Dennis Potter: A Life on Screen* in 1995.

14. For one example amongst many of such sentiments expressed at the time of transmission of *Karaoke* and *Cold Lazarus*, see Mark Lawson in *The Guardian*, 15 April 1996, p.17. On the basis of having only seen one episode of *Karaoke* on video, Lawson nevertheless felt confident enough to write off Potter's posthumous works as not very good, displaying evidence of a sad decline, post-*Blackeyes*. Interestingly, this "product of the past" line finds a corollary in some posthumous academic criticism that argues Potter's entire body of work was irretrievably conditioned by the ideas of Richard Hoggart and the "mass culture" arguments of the 1950s; see, for example, Glen Creeber, *Dennis Potter: Between*

Two Worlds—A Critical Reassessment (London: Macmillan, 1998). To me, this fails to interrogate enough the shifts in Potter's thinking on these matters as his career progressed and the ways in which he came to recognize and critique the external factors that had formed the ideas of his earlier self and how in response, he began to assemble his own individual system of values, moving in the process from anxiety about the world toward a greater sense of personal understanding and equanimity. The danger with the Hoggart theory is that while largely true for the young Potter, it becomes too monolithic and totalizing for a nuanced understanding of the work as a whole, thus making it all too easy for his writing to be dismissed as of no relevance whatsoever to contemporary concerns. By contrast, I would contend (as in this essay) that his ideas about discovering our own individual "sovereignty" and of not being "characters in someone else's script" could hardly be more relevant to us today.

15. Thus Humphrey Carpenter in his biography only ever evaluates Potter's work in terms of how much it seems to "reveal" the writer's life: for Carpenter, the "best" of Potter's writing does; the worst does not. Likewise, in a Carpenter-inspired BBC TV documentary, timed to coincide with the publication of his biography and called, appropriately, *Dennis Potter: Under the Skin* (tx. BBC-2 9 September 1998), extracts from Potter's work were only ever employed as a means of speculating about the relationship of the fictions to the writer's life.

16. Dennis Potter, *Karaoke and Cold Lazarus* (published scripts) (London: Faber and Faber, 1996), p.306.

17. Potter, *Karaoke and Cold Lazarus* (published scripts), p.253.

18. Potter, *Karaoke and Cold Lazarus* (published scripts), p.245. In the finished TV production, the effect of this scene is much more muted both in realization and performance—perhaps because the director, Renny Rye, knew the Potter estate had agreed to commission its own biography and that he and the drama's producers were all being lined up as contributors.

19. See, for example, Dennis Potter, *A Christmas Forest,* radio talk, tx. BBC Radio 4, 26 December 1977. Transcript: BBC Written Archives, Caversham.

20. "Of course, some people boast 'Oh, it's all out of my head' etc. etc. but of course, everything they've experienced and lived through and some of the closest or almost emotional things they've experienced will sooner or later outcrop in a poem or a novel or a play if they're writers. It's inevitable. But to deliberately *choose* to use what *appears* to be like one is in the same order as choosing to use, say, 'the musical genre' or 'the detective genre', in that genres in themselves ie. audience expectations of a certain ritual form of behavior about 'the narrative', is a very powerful, a very potent weapon in the writer's hands" (Potter, interview with John R. Cook).

21. This echoes a description in Potter's first published novel, *Hide and Seek,* in which the main protagonist remembers himself thinking, as a child up his favorite tree in the forest, that "if you took [God] away, then the things, every sort of thing, would have no color, no movement, no smell, no sting, no *point.*" Dennis Potter, *Hide and Seek* (London: Quartet, 1973; repr. Faber and Faber, 1990), p.163.

22. Compare with Arthur Parker's comment to his fellow salesmen in the TV version of *Pennies from Heaven*: "Somewhere the sun is shining—And do you know where? Inside yourself ! Inside your own head . . . Put[s] the real meaning into them songs" (Dennis Potter, *Pennies from Heaven* [published scripts], London: Faber and Faber 1996, pp.69–70).

23. Further details of the precise nature of the *Mesmer* dispute can be found in Maureen Paton, *Alan Rickman: The Unauthorized Biography* (London: Virgin publishing, 1996), pp.181–188.

24. Dennis Potter, *Mesmer*, screenplay, final draft, 5 April 1993, p.55.

25. In *The Singing Detective*, for example, the child Marlow's reconciliation with his father on the Forest floor (after having previously hidden from him) only takes on full dramatic *meaning* within the context of the adult Marlow's recollection of it in hospital. See Cook, *Dennis Potter: A Life on Screen*, pp.235–236, for extended discussion of this.

26. Potter, *Mesmer*, screenplay, p.132.

27. This image of the threat of a "fall" is thematically significant. See, for example, *A Life on Screen* for extended discussion of the motif of the Biblical Fall that runs right through Potter's writing.

28. Dennis Potter, *The Other Side of the Dark*, radio talk, tx. BBC Radio 4, 23 February 1978. Transcript: BBC Written Archives, Caversham.

29. Dennis Potter, interview with Alan Yentob, *Arena*, tx. BBC-2, 30 January 1987. Published in Potter, *Seeing the Blossom*, p.71.

30. Dennis Potter, interview with John R. Cook. Also reproduced in the appendix to this volume.

31. " . . . the minute upon minute in which the mystery I call myself is making and being made" (Dennis Potter, *And With No Language But A Cry*, radio talk, tx. BBC Radio 4, 27 December 1976. Transcript: BBC Written Archives, Caversham).

32. "TV's Mr. Sex" was the label tabloid newspapers such as *The Sun* and *News of the World* used to brand Potter during his career.

33. Dennis Potter, "Occupying Powers," 1993 James MacTaggart Memorial Lecture, delivered at the Edinburgh International Television Festival, 27 August 1993. Published in Potter, *Seeing the Blossom*, p.45. Many of this lecture's sentiments about Britain in the 1990s chime exactly with Potter's portrayal of the future in *Cold Lazarus*.

Media and Values

As attested by the last essay of the previous section, Potter may have been trying to construct his own values and ethics "sovereign" from the market, but his battles on behalf of these were always fought right within the very heart of the consumer kingdom: the contemporary mass media. It was the popular media and, of course, principally television, which were the true wellsprings of his "passion": both his triumph as a writer and, in a way, his tragedy. The final five essays of this volume all explore Potter's relationship with the popular in a little more depth, offering a variety of opinions from a range of media-related perspectives.

Here, the debate widens beyond that of academics. While the work of two academic critics (Brie and Marinov) *is* featured in this section, also included are contributors from other walks of life and from other critical perspectives, whose professional experience and background seem to offer important insights into why Dennis Potter never stinted in putting his work up to the often fierce gaze of modern mass media culture.

Thus the section begins with Philip Purser who, in many ways, can lay claim to being Potter's earliest critical champion. As a leading television critic in the British press from the fifties to the eighties, he watched and reviewed all of Potter's television drama when it was first transmitted and frequently wrote about him for his weekly column in *The Sunday Telegraph* newspaper. In this capacity, he also authored the first major critical essay to be published on Potter in book form: at the time, a casual enough commission but one that, as he readily admits himself, has in the years since brought many a student of Potter knocking at his door in their hungry quest for more morsels of information![1] But Purser was not merely a reviewer of Potter, he also knew and met him as a professional colleague, for during the same period of the sixties and seventies when Potter was establishing his reputation as a major TV dramatist, he was also working as a TV reviewer himself for journals like the old, defunct *Daily Herald,* the pre-Murdoch *Sun, The New Statesman* and *The Sunday Times.*

Hence as Purser asks in his new essay for this volume, to what extent did "Dennis's Other Hat" as TV critic affect his work as TV dramatist and if it did, how far does the parallel career as a journalist offer clues to the plays that were being written during the same period? With posthumous hindsight, it is a perspective that can all too easily be overlooked, yet as Purser's essay reminds us, Potter's "passion" for the medium was always inextricably bound up with "the hit and miss, hurrying traffic of television" he was also avidly watching.[2] As a TV critic reviewing the work of a fellow TV critic many years on, the insights Purser offers on this subject are fascinating, witty and expert.

As the essay makes clear, Potter was always working right at the very heart of the popular, and this is a theme Samuel Marinov picks up in his analysis of how, for him, Potter's three "serials with music"—*Pennies from Heaven* (1978); *The Singing Detective* (1986) and *Lipstick on Your Collar* (1993)— "redefine the genre of musical film." Marinov assesses how each of these serials compares with the great Hollywood film musicals (of which Potter was a declared fan) and concludes by offering his own opinion that Potter's particular "estranging" take on the screen musical genre has certain affinities with the theater of Bertolt Brecht.

A very different perspective on Potter's relationship to music is provided by British academic Steve Brie. In the first study of its kind, he has conducted a survey to try to establish what the British TV *audience,* as opposed to professional critics, may have thought of Potter's use of popular music in his TV serials. In stark contrast to Marinov, his perspective suggests that the music in the dramas may produce "distancing effects" for the audience, but not perhaps "in the pedagogical way" that textual analysts of Potter might think. Instead, the music may operate as a profound mechanism for nostalgia that takes the viewer off on private reveries that may have little to do with making sense of the actual content of the drama. Brie's viewer sample is very small and his results are tentative, but as the first real audience study of Potter, it is important that it be included here—if nothing else, as a reminder to analysts of Potter's texts that they may, as Brie himself puts it, "have taken too much for granted in relation to audience-text-dynamics." Oddly, it is an injunction with which Dennis Potter himself would probably have concurred. He was always keen that his dramas should reach out beyond the "high-brows" to the popular audience, even if simply on the level of reminding them that there *are* other times, places and possibilities beyond the present. As he once expressed it (of *Pennies from Heaven*): "I'm more and more inclined that drama should be open at all points of access so that you can take even the opposite, sometimes, of what is intended. You should be able to use it as sort of working material for what you are responding to, and take from it a lot of things that I wouldn't want people to take from it. But they will, and that's good . . ."[3]

Dennis Potter did not like psychoanalysis[4] and he would not have wanted people to take from his dramas psychoanalytical readings. Nevertheless, because it deals so decisively with the internal landscape of the mind, his work is particularly susceptible to the sustained application of such perspectives. Irving Harrison M.D. is a Los Angeles - based psychiatrist and writer with a particular interest in Potter and in how his work seems to offer insights into the psychological sources of creativity. As part of an ongoing study in this area, Harrison contributes to this volume an essay on Potter's final works, *Karaoke* and *Cold Lazarus* (1996, posthumous)—wittily entitled "The Final Days, The Final Plays, The Final Ploys." Harrison is particularly interested in the idea of the double in Dennis Potter and throughout both final TV dramas, he elicits numerous examples. But at the end of a psychological reading of the final works, he finds himself having to face one central, "profoundly disturbing" question: the artist's mind as a bundle of explicable neurons and psychological tropes versus another, distinctly unfashionable old word. For as these last dramas reach their finale and the "passion of Dennis Potter" finally extinguishes and obliterates itself, rational concepts of the mind evaporate, until all we are left confronting at the end is that awfully awkward, irrational old term: "soul."

After "the final plays and the final ploys," all that really remains, of course, are our memories and our summations of what, if anything, was the significance of it all. And in helping us make sense of this, no one is more suited than Kenith Trodd: the man who produced not only *Karaoke* and *Cold Lazarus* but many of Dennis Potter's most famous TV works, including *Pennies from Heaven* and *The Singing Detective*. Trodd is uniquely placed to comment. As he himself points out in his piece, he knew Potter way before he started as a TV playwright; he was there from the beginning and he was there at the end; indeed with the final posthumously produced plays, beyond the end. But what did it all mean? And as Trodd not unreasonably asks at the close of a collection such as this: "Whose Dennis is it anyway?" In a piece both personal and witty, Trodd reviews his history with Potter, regarding both of them with hindsight as "paranoid guerillas" battling for survival and advantage at the very heart of the British media. It is an appropriate and in a sense poignant way to end a "media" section such as this, not to mention the entire essay collection itself. But, as Trodd asks at the close—what survives of Potter for posterity? It is a question in relation to which this volume, by its very existence, has hopefully at least tried to offer some positive encouragement, if not necessarily too many final answers.

NOTES

1. Philip Purser's essay was "Dennis Potter," in *British Television Drama*, ed. George W. Brandt (Cambridge: Cambridge University Press, 1981), pp.168–193. Purser has subsequently written about the critical interest in Potter that his essay helped spawn, in his memoirs of being a TV critic, *Done Viewing* (London: Quartet Books, 1992). This also includes a chapter on Potter.
2. This quotation is actually taken from Purser's earlier 1981 essay (p.191), but it illustrates the point of his present piece well.
3. Dennis Potter, "Paradise, Perhaps," interview by John Wyver, *Time Out*, 3–9 March 1978, p.13.
4. In interview with John Cook in 1990, Potter labeled psychoanalysis as "one of the beautiful myths but it *is* a myth. There's very little empirical evidence that it has any value for a patient and even so, it is an extraordinarily uneconomic way of dealing with these outbreaks of mental illness we have." Dennis Potter, personal interview by John R. Cook, London, 10 May 1990. See the extracts from the interview reproduced at the end of this volume.

CHAPTER 11

DENNIS'S OTHER HAT

Philip Purser

DENNIS POTTER WAS A PROFESSIONAL TELEVISION REVIEWER, on and off, for 16 years: a period covering all his early strivings as a television dramatist and not finally over until some two years after *Pennies from Heaven* had made him popular and courted. It is only natural to wonder to what extent this critical function informed his creative process and vice versa. How many of the familiar obsessions of the plays can be first discerned in the reviews? Does he draw on his experience of writing for television to write *about* television? Did he, like Shaw as a theatre critic in the 1880s, use his platform to prepare an audience for the kind of play he proposed to offer? As I embarked on a study of Potter as critic, it was soon clear that I would pick up constant echoes of Potter in his other capacities, whether as author or as the public figure he eventually became. The vehemence and intemperance and splutters of adjectives he deployed on page five of the *Sun,* for example, could have come/could yet come from a character in a script of his, or even the camera directions to it. More sustained correspondences would perhaps be harder to find. But first, the context.

At Oxford, Potter had flung himself into student dramatics, politics and journalism, as well as writing a polemic on class, culture and Oxford itself that would eventually be published as *The Glittering Coffin* (1960). After two years as a general trainee in the BBC, which institution he found too cautious and (politically) impartial, he left in 1961 for the more partisan possibilities of journalism. He was taken on by the *Daily Herald,* then unique among British newspapers in that it was part-owned by a political organization, the Trades Union Congress, and formally supported the Labour Party. The notion of employing bright young graduates was still rather suspect in Fleet Street: Potter wrote features, covered one or two political occasions and chafed at lesser tasks he was handed. Then illness struck. On his return to duties, he was made television reviewer: a post he wryly defined as the refuge of the sick and crippled. In fact, television was by this time being taken very seriously by most newspapers, though of the dailies, only the *Daily Mail* gave its critics a regular site and a fixed allotment of words. Potter's space would vary wildly—from as little as 150 words to maybe 450—according to the needs (or claims) of the theatre and music and ballet critics, and the general news of the day, against which they collectively had to compete.

Television in Britain, then, was still mostly live, or recorded to be broadcast "as live." Previews were rare. The critic watched at home and telephoned in his copy by, say, 10:45 P.M. Often the most interesting program would barely have finished; inevitably, the review would be more of a frontline report than a measured judgment, but from September 1962, Potter also had a Saturday column in which he could mull more reflectively over some aspect of TV that had caught his attention. With periodic absences back in hospital, he wrote about TV for the *Herald* over a period of 27 months.

In the cuttings, his voice is already distinctive. He takes swipes at class snobbery, Conservatism and the military. He is vehemently opposed to censorship. He champions sturdy old features of British life, especially working class British life—for example, brass bands. He writes often about sport and comedians and regularly reviews the topical public affairs programs, *Panorama, This Week* and *World in Action*. He resents the party political broadcasts that both TV channels, BBC and ITV (or with the advent of a second BBC TV channel in April 1964, all three) were obliged to transmit, particularly during election-tide. Less expectedly, he is unimpressed by the Beatles, or indeed the whole Mersey-beat phenomenon that was then at its peak, preferring Tommy Steele or the American rock singer Little Richard.

It is in the song and dance department that we can start to pick up the preoccupations that were to color Potter's drama. He likes, needless to say, the popular music he grew up with; the singers who sang it and the singers who are still singing it. Vera Lynn, Sarah Vaughan and the Tommy Dorsey Band, with Frank Sinatra Jr., all come in for praise. "Popular songs," he says, "have an uncanny, mind-jangling knack of capturing and concentrating the passing fads and fancies of the day."[1] But inconsistency shows up when he ventures further into nostalgia. Two popular programs of the day sought to reproduce the conviviality of (a) the old music hall and (b) the pub entertainers who still worked a few taverns in London. Potter rightly enthuses over *Stars and Garters* (b), although its "pub" was a studio set and not every performer had actually trodden the spit and sawdust, while scorning *The Good Old Days* (a), which came from a real working theatre in Leeds, the City Varieties, before an audience who used to turn up, voluntarily, in Edwardian clothes. "A backward-looking hotch-potch,"[2] he calls it, evidently irritated by this ultimate complicity. I've noticed several times that those whose business it is to create illusion are the first to be worried if the customers start pretending as well.

In a rather similar reaction to a more serious matter, Potter is uneasy about the readiness of people, just becoming noticeable in the mid sixties, to confess on television things they would never reveal in ordinary life. To the dramatist, disclosure is a precious art. If everything is going to be blurted out, he is in trouble. But what of drama? Potter admires the northern soap opera *Coronation Street* (first tx. 1960) and the innovative police series *Z Cars* (1962–78), though he decides that both have been going on too long for their own good. He brings a sour expertise to medical and hospital series. The single play, then regarded as the queen piece of television drama, he chooses not to review as often as might have been expected and when he does, sometimes fails to give the author's name. But there are enough clues to the way he wants the form to go.

He is bored by the everyday naturalism, which since the fifties has been regarded as the style that makes the most of the intimacy of television watching and also conforms with the matter-of-fact traffic occupying the TV screen the rest of the time. In September 1963, he greets a tough crime story from the Liverpool-Welsh writer Alun Owen as a "welcome change from the anaemic grunts and mumbles of recent TV drama."[3] A week later he is full of praise for a period piece, *The Road*, by the author of the legendary *Quatermass* science fiction serial and adapter of George Orwell's *1984* for television, Nigel Kneale:

> Like all good science fiction, *The Road* was thus able to build, debate and construct ideas as well as grip us with the conventions of fear and the unknown. Our ancestors were haunted by obscure terrors. An occasional shiver down the spine reminds us of their irrationality.[4]

In fact, *The Road* eventually discloses a striking rationale for its particular terrors. Its eighteenth century characters are picking up panic and fear from the future, as the highway that will one day pass by their country house is jammed by desperate motorists trying to flee an imminent nuclear attack. But irrationality was what Potter craved. Another week goes by and he lights on Giles Cooper, a dramatist who liked to take the bricks and mortar of conventional naturalism and invest them with bizarre goings-on. "Giles Cooper," Potter says approvingly when the next Cooper script comes up in March 1964, "can be guaranteed to find something rotting and horrible beneath even the most placid surface."[5]

Later that year, Troy Kennedy Martin and John McGrath, who (as writer and director) had been instrumental in setting up *Z Cars*, mounted a full-scale onslaught on naturalism, with a manifesto in the theatrical quarterly *Encore* to pave the way for what was to be their decisive breakthrough: a BBC 2 serial called *Diary of a Young Man*. Potter joined in, devoting his Saturday column to them. We all did. Alas, *Diary* proved to be just an ordinary lads-together story whose only novelty lay in the use of still pictures and an overlaid, *faux-naif* commentary. The real revolution Martin and McGrath had wrought was going ahead, unperceived, in the elliptic storytelling of *Z Cars*. And the revolution Dennis Potter really sought had been invoiced in a review that I bravely quote in full, mixed metaphor and all. John Bowen was—is—a versatile novelist and screenwriter still active in both disciplines:

> Four keen executives up for promotion—but only one will get the job. So to help decide, the company hire a psychiatrist and pack the candidates off to a house party.
>
> John Bowen's *A Case of Character* on ITV last night was a modish but efficient study of men deliberately placed under social and mental stress.
>
> Plays that prowl around inside the head can be even more exciting than those that deal only with external actions and physical dangers. This one cut a few corners to pile on the tensions, quickly dragging out the cowardice of one of the candidates when a teenage officer at Dunkirk. The favourite for the job, skilfully played by Michael Craig, was turned down, much to the consternation of the orthodox, pin-striped and very British chairman.
>
> From then, the play gathered momentum like a racing toboggan, with fragments of gossip and splinters of argument flying by in a scurry of melodrama. Well made, well acted and reasonably intriguing, *A Case of Character* was the kind of play you forget easily but dare not switch off at the time.
>
> And that puts it well clear of the great muddy heap of most TV drama.[6]

So: again a lunge at the generality of TV drama; again some surrender to action, or anyway to activity; and for the first time, a profession of faith in the interior drama ("plays that prowl round inside the head") that Potter was to make so much his own. It could even be argued that he is thinking ahead to his own first play, *The Confidence Course*, which must have been hatching by now. It was provoked by an assignment he was given when still a reporter, to attend a free sample session of just such a course offered, in London, by the Dale Carnegie Institute; its plot shares with *A Case of Character* a scorn of psychiatrists and other "experts" presuming to evaluate or instruct the rest of us.

Potter was given leave of absence by the *Herald* in September 1964 to stand for Parliament in the October British General Election. He lost, and after another attack of his illness, decided not to go back to a staff job but concentrate on his plays. *The Confidence Course* went out in February 1965, followed by *Alice* and the *Nigel Barton* pair: *Stand Up, Nigel Barton* and *Vote, Vote, Vote for Nigel Barton*. Except for some book reviews for *The Times* and a preliminary spell with the *New Statesman*, he did not return to journalism until 1968, by which time he had had seven TV plays on the air and the *Daily Herald* had changed hands and been renamed *The Sun*.[7] Potter stood in as television critic while the regular incumbent, Nancy Banks-Smith, was on maternity leave, then wrote a general column. On TV this time, he was given regular space, and more of it—some 650 words every day. He devotes the whole lot one day to *The Virginian,* lamenting the suburbanization (as he sees it) of a once-rugged TV Western. He sighs over the umpteenth production of an old West End stage farce. Only a few times does he deal at length with original drama and in one of the instances, his eloquence is lavished chiefly (and why not?) on the charms of a young actress. The most useful piece, in our context, develops his predilection for interior drama, but now he's concerned with the practical means of imparting this on television. The occasion is the BBC production of Jean Anouilh's first TV play, *Monsieur Barnett,* in which the eponymous hero expires in a barber's shop:

> He died because his own past welled up and choked him. A past, unfortunately, which had dwindled to voices heard in his head—and this, as so often, became merely voices from the other side of the studio. Memory is always a great problem for the dramatist. We carry it around with us as a raw, insistent, perpetually challenging burden. But to translate it into dramatic terms on the television screen, one needs more than an off-screen voice, a dissonant chord of music or a dip in the lighting.[8]

Potter's own solution to the problem was to be demonstrated in his next burst of TV plays, most boldly in *Moonlight on the Highway* (1969), which was also the first to make use of the potency of popular music. He did away with all devices to invoice a "flashback," as it used to be called and simply cut from the now to the then, from the moment of remembering to what was remembered. If the drive of the story was strong enough, the audience would make the connection, though I must confess to being left somewhat in the dark, on a first viewing of *Moonlight,* by the glimpse of a childhood encounter in a dim alley. We didn't know then of the traumatic episode in Potter's own childhood that went on to invade more and more of his work. Dennis Potter, I ought to add, was not alone in breaking the old narrative conventions. Many other writers were experimenting along the same lines, and not only in writing for the screen.

Potter signed off from this stint as a television reviewer in characteristic fashion: "Time to put down the little hard balls and climb back among the coconuts. Critics? Ah, what do they know?"[9] The general column he wrote instead appeared every Monday, ranged over topics from cricket to hymn-singing and immigration to hospital treatment (especially his own), and still bore occasional reference to television (likewise his own). On 13 May 1968, the headline is "I Really Must Tell You I'm So Very Happy, says Dennis Potter." One reason is that his health has taken an unexpected turn for the better, another that he has three new commissions: to write a movie, a play for the National Theatre and a Life of Christ for the BBC.[10] But most immediately, he is looking forward to the transmission this very evening of his unfortunate ITV play *The Bonegrinder*. A week later, on 20 May, it's a very different story. The critics have savaged *The Bonegrinder*. He starts off in rage and despair, reaches for a dash of self-pity and then, in the midst of it all, produces the personal affirmation that was to be so poignantly realised when he died. He says he has long since accepted the "terrible proposition" that he is going to be either a laughable nut as a writer or a good (meaning great?) one—nothing in between. He can only write by using himself, indeed by using himself up:

> So when I die I want to be completely emptied and completely exhausted. Which means, of course, that I am still rejoicing. Only a happy human being can write a sentence like that.[11]

One more column is relevant and historically of interest, too. In the heady summer of the Paris *evenements* and with student riots everywhere, the French revolutionary Daniel Cohn-Bendit was invited to London to meet his British counterparts. Potter attended the party and while admiring of Cohn-Bendit himself, was deeply disillusioned by the locals:

> There they all were. A boiling, bubbling collection of the British militant Left, draping themselves on the expensive furniture, the light of battle glinting through their fringes. . . .
>
> Public school voices talked about the need to give arms to your actual workers and other such horsehair. The discussion soon degenerated into utter farce, with competing vanities, meaningless jargon, ideological confusion, grandiose threats and boutique chatter filling the air. . . . A classic and bitterly comic demonstration of why the Left in this country is more impotent at this moment than it has ever been. Even the booze ran out a couple of hours too soon.[12]

Potter, as he had revealed in his " . . . I Am So Happy" column, had already been commissioned to write the play about Christ that materialized the following year as *Son of Man* (1969). But it was this sudden disillusionment with the Left, he told me, that had driven him to shape the script to what he saw as Jesus's simple, *truly* revolutionary message of love.[13] What he didn't accord his hero, despite all those yearnings for the supernatural and the irrational, and to the reproaches of churchmen, was divinity. Years later, he admits in the course of a lengthy dissertation on "The Celluloid Messiahs," that the rough, tough Jesus, played by Colin Blakely, was the Jesus of the agnostics. He hadn't yet dared face up to the Christ figure who haunted him now.[14]

Dennis Potter was still a socialist, of course, whatever distaste for its parlor zealots he felt. He had supplied the television review for the respectable socialist weekly *The New Statesman* for six weeks in 1967. In June 1972 he took

it on again for a limited spell, or so he thought. In October, he reviews *The Reporters,* a wry comedy of newspaper life by Arthur Hopcraft. Potter's own
newspaper play, *Paper Roses* (1971), had gone out 16 months earlier. Potter
praises the Hopcraft play and the performance of Robert Urquhart as a
gnarled old journalist at the end of his career (he had fielded a similar character, played by Bill Maynard) but his only reference to *Paper Roses* is elusive,
almost a private joke. For that play he had invented an apt little narrative trick:
the voice of the paper's TV critic providing a kind of counterpoint to the story
as he dictated his nightly review to a copytaker. Potter closes his review of *The
Reporters* with the same device—"Quote, Enough to give any critic the jitters,
end quote, full period. Thank God I'm not doing this for very long."[15] In the
event, he stayed away throughout 1973, but then went back until he was head-
hunted by the *Sunday Times* in 1976.

Obviously, these weekly essays of up to 1200 words are more considered
than any overnight squibs, but the voice and the sensibilities are mostly familiar. He is still against confessionals and against documentarists muscling into
the province of the dramatist. He mocks *Sunley's Daughter,* a "real-life" love
story filmed on a Yorkshire farm, complete, as he points out, with "a bloody
great orchestra hidden in the cornfield, a narrator with an unctuous voice, a
girl who did not want to talk and a boy-friend who, in contrast, was prepared
to tell all, as well as act through various reconstructions of previous incidents."[16] And though William Cobbett was a hero of Potter's (he quotes the
master's advice on writing that, all too evidently, he has always followed: "Put
down the first thing that occurs to you. Do not alter!"[17]) he is irritated, in a
program about the radical countryman, *Cobbett's Rural Rides,* by the
galumphing devices of having an actor dressed as Cobbett clatter his horse
through present-day landscapes to add "relevance" to his strictures on city life.
It is a literalism akin to the naturalism that irritates him in drama.

Only the next week, he is being stifled by *War and Peace,* the BBC's vast
(20 x 45 mins.) serialization of Tolstoy with elaborate sets, the Jugoslav army
hired for the battle scenes and the band of the Welsh Guards to furnish the title
music: "Everyone moves under a great glass dome of stuffed museum detail.
The tyranny of things, the bluster of objects, the rhetoric of design make sure
it is pretty and dead . . ." He harks back to Granada Television's 1963 production of the abbreviated Piscator-Neumann-Prufer version, "dispensing with
the suffocating naturalism so beloved of BBC classic serials and yet cutting
cleanly through to the bigger bones of the original." He also recalls *Country
Matters,* a then-recent anthology series derived from stories by A. E. Coppard
and H. E. Bates and still, arguably, the finest literary conversion ever:

[These] were, of course, adaptions of short stories, without anything like the
same problems of scale or the same debilitating awe. But they established their

own kind of truths, and their own distinctive claims, often movingly, always creatively. Original drama, in fact. And it is now only in . . . the so-called one-shot play not written to a series format that we can still pick up the no doubt irritating cadences of the individual voice.[18]

Ah! the individual voice. This is a new and two-headed hobby-horse, in one sense no more than a predilection for words and voices rather than images—when he's done with the dressing-up in *Cobbett's Rural Rides,* Potter turns to the content and wishes that the views of contemporary townsfolk might have been sought. "In documentaries about places," he complains, "we look at buildings and rarely listen to people."[19] Another time, he dwells on a son of the soil who presented gardening programs: "Listen to the way he talks, the measured cadences of a man for whom speech is still directly shaped by the tasks and objects in front of him. He *grows* his words . . ."[20] But Potter is also using the idea of the individual voice, of course, as a metaphor for the self-contained, original television play written by one person. Having not taken much notice of it in *Daily Herald* days, he is now its champion, to the extent of resenting slot titles such as *Against the Crowd* and *Love Story* and even the non-committal *Play for Today,* lest they impose or imply a house style. He also continues to distinguish between the plodding and more imaginative varieties of the genus:

> I prefer to see plays in which the "ideas" are not exposed on the surface like basking sharks (or, in some cases, stranded cod) but arise with the insistence of discovery out of the fumbling yearnings, uncertain liaisons and perilous stratagems we usually make out of life. . . . People even react to those things in each other which are beyond the reach of reason.[21]

Thus Potter on *All Good Men,* Trevor Griffiths's play about a Labour politician of the old school that he might be expected to approve of, and in all other respects does approve of. He carries this thought further in the course of some unqualified enthusiasm for a linked pair of plays by Simon Gray, *Plaintiffs & Defendants* and *Two Sundays.* These went out on consecutive weeks in the *Play for Today* slot. After duly noting how each began with some tranquil wordless scene-setting at odds with the "irritating stridency" of the regular signature tune and titles, Potter welcomes Gray's dialogue because it, too, refuses to conform to the "expected mode by which dramatists on television subside into the habitual charms of 'relevance'":

> In both these plays, the words were holding back some cold and distant horror, and one which is endemic to the human condition, rather than letting it all (what is the old, old phrase?) hang out. . . . Both were peculiarly haunting

in a manner that acknowledged how nearly the muscular spasm which produces a smile is the same as that needed to carry a wince.[22]

The perilous proximity of pleasure to pain he detects here may well have touched a nerve with Potter, whose jostling of accepted ideas of good and evil in *Brimstone and Treacle* (1976) was soon to run that play into trouble. Its banning by the BBC's Director of Television, Alasdair Milne, six months later was the occasion for one of Potter's last and most famous *New Statesman* diatribes: "A Note from Mr Milne."[23] But his most revealing variation on this theme of uniqueness in drama comes at the end of his review of *Bedtime Stories*, a series in which traditional fairy stories were goosed into present-day contexts by various hands—the two he is considering are *Goldilocks* by Alan Plater and *The Water Maiden* by Andrew Davies. He is full of praise for both but still uneasy about the curly bracket enclosing them:

> Imagine both these plays as single productions free of the *Bedtime Story* imprimatur. The potency of their source would surely have been buried much deeper and yielded the richness more slowly, more satisfyingly.[24]

To sum up: what Potter is saying over the run of these *New Statesman* pieces is (1) he doesn't much like adaptations, (2) nor series and serials, (3) even when they are made up of single plays or (4) are the work of a single writer. (5) He prizes the unalloyed, unregimented single play above all else, (6) especially when it is not bogged down in naturalism. Yet by now he had written one series (*Casanova* 1971), contributed to another along with other writers (*Wessex Tales* 1973) and in the same commission adapted the work of another man (Thomas Hardy). Dramatizations, or rather serializations of Angus Wilson, Hardy again, F. Scott Fitzgerald and Christabel Bielenberg would henceforth be the bread of his bread and butter. We have to put Potter into the professional circumstances he was reluctantly acknowledging himself. Series and serials were more popular and easier to schedule. The single play was an endangered species. Potter would write and fight for it in its purest (or most wayward) form, but he would also write six-parters, or whatever, and take on dramatizations, though not without brooding on the ethics of the craft. Here, he is prompted by Simon Raven's dramatization of Iris Murdoch's *An Unofficial Rose:*

> When a novel is drained of the opaque fluid of its prose and exposed in the world of speech and gesture which drama claims for its own, then something extremely dangerous to both forms is bound to happen.[25]

As he moves in October 1976 to his last and loftiest critical platform, he will extend such misgivings to the use television makes of every kind of source—history, events and real lives as well as books. The *Sunday Times,* owned at this time by the Canadian Roy Thomson, was still widely regarded as the foremost "quality" newspaper. It had also been the first (in 1970) to introduce a regular critical guide to the coming week's television. There was someone else to deal methodically with the schedules. Potter was free to expound on anything he chose, which is not the statement of the obvious it might seem. As their deadlines moved steadily forward, daily paper reviewers became dependent on previews, i.e., on a limited range of programs that were available ahead of transmission. Only the Sunday or weekly reviewer was still exposed to the haphazard flux of news and sports and live and canned TV that came off the air; only he (or she) could make the little connections, spot the synchronicities, which from time to time would have the most disparate programs striking sparks off each other.

Potter loved to exercise his serendipity thus. He skips from Mickey Mouse (in a documentary about Walt Disney) to a party political broadcast by the leader of the Liberal Party and back to Mickey Mouse. He writes sagely about William Blake as subject of an arts program and in the next breath about *Blake's Seven,* a science fiction serial that happens to have started the same week. Another week, he uses this same entertainment as the entry to a serious meditation on the reporting of terrorism and other threats to civilisation and thence on to David Edgar's play about the dangerous lure of fascism, *Destiny.*

By now he is well-known: indeed after *Pennies from Heaven,* a household name. He neglects no opportunity to attack censorship nor to take a dig at timorous program controllers. He drops references to his own work freely into his column and reports encounters he has had in his dual capacity as writer and critic. An unnamed BBC executive tells him that he runs the risk of schizophrenia; a left-wing playwright assails him for failing to appreciate other left-wing playwrights. Asked by a journalist writing an article on TV criticism if a critic needs to be entertaining (there was much heart-searching at this time over would-be humorists exercizing their wit at the expense of the medium), he tells him yes. "It's like writing rhyming couplets: finding the rhyme can actually sharpen the mind. Making the column lively and readable can quicken the critical response."[26]

With a formidable body of work transmitted, he has less cause to preach the kind of drama he wants to supply. An audience that has grown up with his plays accepts his narrative idiom without difficulty. New writers have adopted it, at least to some degree. It has become part of the language of the screen. The old enemy, naturalism, still has to be fought, of course, particularly when it means the domination of a production by elaborately "authentic" sets and props. Potter's dismay at this aspect of *Jesus of Nazareth* is a rerun of his onslaught on *War and Peace.* But there is now a complication—a complication so large that it will swallow the original naturalism versus antinaturalism issue: the switch from studio (or video) drama to filmed, which, in Britain, began in the sixties but only started to take over in the mid-seventies. Though Dennis Potter had several of his scripts done on film and his friend and producer Kenith Trodd was an ardent campaigner for going over to film, at the end of 1976, he still proclaims his loyalty to studio drama:

> Television drama has been needlessly throttling itself for too long in the narrow space left by its two progenitors, theatre and cinema. The studio play is still, I believe, the most fruitful way out of overt theatricality or shrunken celluloid, for it necessarily keeps the primacy of words which distinguishes the former without necessarily losing the potency of image which feeds the latter. And the physical limitations of purely electronic drama can, like all restrictions, be coiled back at the edges to attack the "naturalism" which so often gives us the muscle and bone of a face without much insight into the thoughts or emotions that live behind it.
>
> Thus, although it was miniaturised cinema that added the excess lushness to [an adaptation of Winifred Foley's *A Child of the Forest*], I kept wanting the music and the drooling camera pan to stop, for the cinema bits to be banished so that the conflict and slowly growing sympathy between the two main characters could take up the slack . . . [27]

Jump-cut to our next clip, less than two years later. The occasion is *Langrishe, Go Down,* an adaptation by Harold Pinter of Aidan Higgins's love story set in a slumbrous and conveniently unpopulated Irish country house. Can this really be Dennis Potter?

> Moods and feelings are often easier to convey in accumulated images or in the use of light and shadow than in the crippling, necessary obviousness of words tumbling from the mouth. Harold Pinter's spare and lyrical film script looked at times as though it needed no dialogue at all. . . . Judi Dench and Jeremy Irons nosed about in each other's minds and bodies in a manner which suggested that they, too, could dispense with words. . . . Bravura acting in an astonishing production.[28]

As well as upturning his former beliefs, this was surprising praise, I thought, for a curiously insulated piece. It seemed to me to be taking place in a bubble of time and place that existed only for it to take place in. Was the change of heart out of awe for Harold Pinter? No, awe did not come readily to Dennis. His knowing use of the term "film script" is the give-away. *Langrishe* was in fact an unfulfilled movie script rescued by the director David Jones and shot as a television film. All at once, Potter is interested in film and film aesthetics. It's not really surprising if we put him in his writer's shoes again. Of his early plays, one had gone out live and not been preserved for posterity, while the tapes of three others had been wiped.[29] Those that had been filmed (*A Beast with Two Backs* [1968], *Paper Roses* [1971], *Double Dare* [1976] and *Where Adam Stood* [1976]) were safe. Moreover, the first and the last of these wouldn't have been so effective done in the studio. Most persuasively of all, he has now written and had filmed, something that could not conceivably have been realized by any other means: his little masterpiece *Blue Remembered Hills* (1979). It will go out in three months time.

Meanwhile Potter's ethical preoccupation throughout the *Sunday Times* period has also come to a head. This, I hazarded, was the use any kind of television makes of its raw material, especially if the raw material is raw people. It's a renewal of his disquiet, back in *Daily Herald* days, at their willingness to bare their souls on camera, but now directed at those who organise the display. He is particularly suspicious of the cinema verite or fly-on-the-wall documentaries that have become fashionable, because (a) they ignore the effect on the subject of the presence of the camera and (b) he believes them to be conducted *de haut en bas,* the privileged examining the underprivileged: "We will not see fly-on-the-wall studies of the home life of our own dear bank manager or his cousin the television producer or his uncle the stockbroker . . . such people know how to protect themselves, know how to edit their responses, and would eke out their "revelations" with a tight fist and a canny eye."[30]

He is disgusted by a program called *Marriage Guidance* because it filmed an actual attempt to reconcile a doomed couple—"the exposed intestines," he fumes, "of a husband and wife gutting each other in the misery of a sacrament gone sour."[31] He is outraged by a studio debate held to gather a phone-in verdict on a cause célèbre still with us: should the convicted child-tormentor and killer Myra Hindley ever be released from prison? "Crime and punishment are, of course, the staple fare of the television schedule but this is the first (and, I hope, the last) time that real murder and an actual prisoner have been turned into a grisly variant of a studio panel game."[32]

He is driven to expand on his attitude, indeed devote a whole column to it, by a chance concatenation of events in the one month of November 1977. He is reluctantly following a trio of observational documentaries by the respected producer, Michael Whyte, on the subject of delinquent youngsters. He has also reviewed a play about a victimized boy. He has watched and hated a sombre dramatization of the case of a deaf girl charged with manslaughter after killing her attacker. The last straw is an invitation from an unnamed BBC producer to write a play from another awful story in the news: the murder of one child by another (the Mary Bell case). It's all too much. Though Potter has only lately—when reviewing the marriage guidance program—reiterated his belief that it's acceptable for drama to tackle the most painful story, because it distances emotions and experiences that would otherwise be unendurable, he now seems equally distressed by fact and fiction. His indignation grows fiercer and fiercer until, with touching candor (if not much contrition), he surrenders and owns up. It is, as far as I know, the first time he alludes openly in print to the sexual abuse hinted at in *Moonlight on the Highway:*

> The nearly unbearable distress I felt when watching this programme [the last of the Whyte trilogy] and what I now see to be my consistent yet often excessive opposition to the whole new range of documentaries that it typifies, has roots which are tangled like nerves in the half-suppressed memory of my own experience of life. I cannot specify—except in fictional or dramatic form—the kind of assault which I endured in the summer between VE Day and VJ Day, when I was 10 years old. But—
>
> No. To hell with it. I should not review such programmes. I simply ask whether the questions I have put do not have some relevance. Cannot we be a little more careful when zooming in to map the shape of real life, real pain and real indignity? Especially with those who are bereft of genuine protection.
>
> "Not only will I not write a Mary Bell play," I said to the producer, "but I will make damn sure that I review it if anyone else does!"
>
> The remark has clearly dishonourable intentions, and it led both to an icy rebuke and to the content of this column. In which, of course, I have said too much and too little. But I believe that a critic who is not prepared to respond with his full emotions and failings, who does not occasionally expose the darker workings of his own mind, is little more than an impertinent oik [*sic*].[33]

In November 1978, during a conflict with the trade unions, the *Sunday Times* was closed down for what eventually proved to be a whole year. Potter delivered his angry resignation in the text of his last column. What he felt about the function he was leaving had been most neatly summed up in a book review he wrote during the year he wasn't a TV critic: 1973. Milton Shulman, former television executive and now a commentator on the loftier issues of the medium, had published a study of British television grudgingly called *The Least Worst Television in the World.* Torn between his passionate belief in the people's medium and reluctant agreement with Shulman's litany of its deficiencies, Potter finally zooms in on his proposal, couched in abstractions, for a Broadcasting Council. Its "prime duty would be to ensure that the most powerful medium of our time conscientiously reflected the true values, the cultural heritage and the life style of the nation." "Words that roll about on the page," says Potter rudely, "not prescriptions for good programmes." He prefers to rely on those whose job it is to deal with specifics: "Let the critics concentrate on identifying what they think is worthwhile and be mercilessly contemptuous of what they think is bad, dishonest and untruthful. Their role is far more crucial than even they dare to acknowledge."[34]

NOTES

1. Dennis Potter, *Daily Herald*, 2 August 1963. Cf. lines in *Pennies from Heaven* fifteen years later: "Songs. They're like the pictures, and that ... they just drop into your head and help you to look at things" (Dennis Potter, *Pennies from Heaven* (published scripts) London: Faber and Faber, 1996, p.226).

2. Potter, *Daily Herald*, 11 April 1964.

3. Potter, *Daily Herald*, 23 September 1963.

4. Potter, *Daily Herald*, 30 September 1964.

5. Potter, *Daily Herald*, 9 March 1964.

6. Potter, *Daily Herald*, 3 March 1964.

7. In 1969, the *Sun* was taken over by Rupert Murdoch (later to become Potter's own bête noire) whence it began its gradual transformation into a famously aggressive, right-wing tabloid daily. Potter, however, only ever wrote for the pre-Murdoch *Sun,* in the days when it still regarded itself as a left-wing paper—though clearly, there is irony in the fact that under Murdoch, *The Sun* would become one of Potter's most ferocious enemies in the 1980s and 90s.

8. Dennis Potter, *The Sun*, 25 January 1968.

9. Potter, *The Sun*, 23 February 1968.

10. Only the Life of Christ would finally make it into production—as the TV play *Son of Man* tx. BBC-1, 16 April 1969.

11. Potter, *The Sun*, 20 May 1968.

12. Potter, *The Sun*, 17 June 1968.

13. Dennis Potter, interview by Philip Purser, *Daily Telegraph Magazine*, 2 April 1969: "I suppose the play represents a retreat from political positions I previously held ... I listened and felt very lonely and out of it. The same old hates, the same old dogma, the same belief that if only the systems of the world could be changed, everyone would be happy. No concern for the sick and the bereft and the lonely and the suffering. Jesus was *their* man. He was their man the instant he asked himself the terrible question: 'Am I He? Am I the Messiah?'"

14. Dennis Potter, "The Celluloid Messiahs," *Sunday Times*, 10 April 1977. The occasion was the British TV transmission of Franco Zeffirelli's *Jesus of Nazareth.*

15. Dennis Potter, *New Statesman*, 20 October 1972.

16. Potter, *New Statesman*, 24 May 1974.

17. Potter, *New Statesman*, 6 October 1972.

18. Potter, *New Statesman*, 13 October 1972.

19. Potter, *New Statesman*, 6 October 1972.

20. Potter, *New Statesman*, 18 October 1974. The TV gardener was Percy Thrower.

21. Potter, *New Statesman*, 8 February 1975.

22. Potter, *New Statesman*, 24 October 1975.

23. Published *New Statesman*, 23 April 1976.

24. Potter, *New Statesman*, 15 March 1974.

25. Potter, *New Statesman*, 10 January 1975.

26. Dennis Potter, interview by Jeremy Bugler, *The Listener*, 2 December 1976.

27. Potter, *Sunday Times*, 28 November 1976.

28. Potter, *Sunday Times,* 24 September 1978.
29. A half hour Potter TV play, *Emergency-Ward 9,* had been broadcast live in BBC-2's *Thirty-Minute Theatre* slot on 11 April 1966. Like three other full-length Potter plays, *The Confidence Course* (1965) [his first TV play], *Message for Posterity* (1967) and *Shaggy Dog* (1968), the transmission tapes had not survived to be archived for posterity. The reason was the high cost of videotape at this time, which necessitated a policy of old tapes frequently being wiped over to record new programs. Now regarded as a tragedy by historians and archivists, this was simply a reflection of a wider managerial sensibility of the period (very different from today's) that as an "ephemeral medium," most of TV's programs could not possibly be of any long-term interest or value.
30. Potter, *Sunday Times,* 4 December 1978. In fact, the British TV viewing public has gone on to enjoy fly-on-the-wall exercises featuring such groups as commodity brokers, aspirant submarine captains, public (ie., private) schoolboys, members of a Cambridge college, the directorate of the Royal Opera House and in the run-up to the 1997 British General Election, a dinner party table of country conservatives conspicuously failing either to edit or eke out any of their indiscretions.
31. Potter, *Sunday Times,* 22 May 1977.
32. Potter, *Sunday Times,* 10 July 1977. Myra Hindley, together with her partner Ian Brady, were the notorious "Moors Murderers," responsible for a series of horrific tortures and murders of children in the 1960s, until they were caught and sentenced to indefinite terms of life imprisonment. Since the seventies, Hindley and her supporters have been campaigning for her parole.
33. Potter, *Sunday Times,* 4 December 1977. Michael Whyte's documentary is *Aycliffe,* concluding a trilogy which began with *Billy—Violence in the Family.* The two plays were *Nipper* by Barrie Keeffe and *Dummy* by Hugh Whitemore. The [*sic*] is Potter's.
34. Dennis Potter, *The Times,* 15 March 1973.

CHAPTER 12

PENNIES FROM HEAVEN, THE SINGING DETECTIVE AND LIPSTICK ON YOUR COLLAR

Redefining the Genre of Musical Film

Samuel G. Marinov

INTRODUCTION

DRAMATIC WORKS OF THE LATE BRITISH SCREENWRITER Dennis Potter already occupy a special place in the history of writing for television and film. A number of film scholars such as John R. Cook,[1] W. Stephen Gilbert,[2] Peter Stead,[3] Glen Creeber,[4] and others have covered many aspects of Potter's work. However, so far there has been no detailed investigation of Potter's contributions to musical TV/film, which in part can be explained by the lack of agreement of how to define the genre. While some like Stanley Green use primarily quantitative criteria such as number of songs and musical selections as well as length of their presentations,[5] others like Rick Altman[6] rely more on qualitative criteria tied to the contribution musical numbers make to the film's narrative. Because musical numbers in Potter's films are closely linked with the film's narrative, Altman's diegetic approach—rather than simply counting the number of songs and dances—appears to be more suitable for analyzing Potter's work.

EARLY MUSICALS

Before examining Potter's contributions, it would be helpful to look at the established Hollywood tradition of musical films, which have been standard-bearers throughout the history of this genre. In his analysis of Hollywood musicals, Rick Altman defines the genre as " . . . a film with music that emanates from . . . the fictional world created by the film (as opposed to . . . typical background music which come instead out of nowhere)."[7] His taxonomy of the genre takes place on two levels: semantic and syntactic. On the semantic level, Hollywood musicals, according to Altman, are marked by the linear narrative that presupposes the existence of a causal link between formation of a romantic couple and progression of a plot. Syntactically, they typically employ alternation and confrontation, as well as parallelism between male and female, with each sex identified by a specific set of cultural values; music/plot interact as music and dance numbers to express personal and communal joy, typically serving as a signifier of romantic triumph over all limitations; and reversal of the typical image/sound hierarchy (dominance of image over sound, especially at climactic moments).[8] In general, a Hollywood musical, in addition to realist and even naturalist style of acting, is marked by a mixture of diegetic music and dialogue, as well as rhythmic movement in dance parts where song and dance are used, in the words of Robert Stam, "to lubricate the spectator's psyche and oil the wheels of narrative continuity."[9]

Perhaps the best way to demonstrate the degree of change Potter's TV/films brought to the genre of musical film is to juxtapose them with the early musical film classics, such as the 1936 *Swing Time* with Fred Astaire and Ginger Rogers, and *Singin' in the Rain* with Gene Kelly and Debbie Reynolds. *Swing Time,* directed by George Stevens and choreographed by Hermes Pan, with music by Jerome Kern and Dorothy Fields, is largely considered one of the best musicals ever. The Astaire-Rogers dancing and singing team were at their peak, and director Stevens brought a sentimental quality to the light romantic story line that, along with the musical numbers, became the trademark of the musical film genre. Semantically, *Swing Time* employs a linear narrative with a straightforward causal link between events that shape both plot and subplots. The visual and aural elements also contribute to the smooth, unobstructed flow of the narrative. Syntactically, music/plot interaction expresses various protagonists' emotional states culminating in a romantic triumph over all limitations; the acting style is defined by a mixture of diegetic music and dialogue. For example, the musical number "Never Gonna' Dance" begins with the lyrical song sung by the protagonist to his love interest (in this case, Fred Astaire sings a song to a beautiful dancer played by Ginger Rogers); at the end, the song is smoothly integrated into a dance that complements and embellishes it. The music and lyrics of the song, as well as the scenery and costumes, are selected in such a way as to reinforce the romantic mood of the scene.

A very similar pattern can be found in another Hollywood classic: the 1952 *Singin' In the Rain,* starring Gene Kelly and Debbie Reynolds. Directed by Stanley Donen and choreographed by Gene Kelly, *Singin' In the Rain,* like its predecessor, tells a sentimental story of two beautiful young people who have to overcome seemingly "insurmountable" obstacles to their happiness, which they of course eventually do. Semantically, the film again employs a linear narrative with a few subplots that are completely subordinate to the main story. Syntactically, the music and the lyrics of the songs, as well as the dance, are aimed to create a sentimental mood in the audience and evoke sympathy for the heroes. Once again, the main purpose of musical numbers in *Singin' In the Rain* is to embellish the film's simple and straightforward narrative. For example, in the number called "You're Meant For Me," the character played by Gene Kelly sings a lyrical song addressed to his love interest played by Debbie Reynolds, while both symbolically stand on the ladder in the empty Hollywood studio (!). As in the case of Astaire-Rogers, Kelly's song at the end is transformed into the dance clearly meant to symbolize the ultimate unification of two loving souls. The impression of ultimate happiness is created not only aurally but also visually, through the selection of colors in both the scenery and costumes (the setting of this scene inside the Hollywood studio allows the recreation of a beautiful sunset, perhaps too beautiful to be real, which ironically becomes a symbol of the artificiality of this Hollywood genre).

POTTER'S WORKS

For those who are familiar with film history, the radical change in the genre of musical film coming from someone like Dennis Potter is unusual. Although technically only a screenwriter and occasionally also a producer, Potter nevertheless was a true "auteur" of practically all his major works. Using Andre Bazin's terminology, he was "responsible for choosing in the artistic creation the personal factor as a criterion of reference, and then postulating its permanence and progress from one work to the next."[10] In practical terms, Potter was actively involved in every aspect of the production of his work, from the conceptualization to the selection of imagery and sound.

The idea of using popular period songs as an essential ingredient in the dramatic story first surfaced in *Moonlight on the Highway* (1969) where the protagonist, played by Ian Holm, is an emotionally disturbed young man who is obsessed with Al Bowlly songs. For him, the loving and happy world of Bowlly' songs is an alternative to the painful reality of his everyday life, where he has to deal with the daunting memories of childhood rape. Although technically in this piece the character does not perform the songs, their essential role in the film's narrative clearly sets the stage for Potter to explore period music in his later dramatic works.

The next opportunity to use period songs as an integral part of film narrative came in 1978, with the television series called *Pennies from Heaven*.

Musical numbers were employed to uncover a hidden, even sinister side in his characters. *Pennies from Heaven* tells a dark, complicated and tragic story of a small-time sheet music salesman named Arthur Parker, played by Bob Hoskins, who was wrongly accused and eventually executed for a murder he had not committed. Both Arthur and Elaine, his love interest, a schoolteacher-turned-hooker and later murderer, played by Sheryl Campbell, are far more complex characters than their Hollywood counterparts. Neither Arthur nor Elaine are what might be called attractive, positive heroes. And yet, despite their moral flaws, they come across as quite likable characters for whom the audience clearly feels a certain degree of sympathy. In addition to the unusual protagonists, Potter introduces other characters not typically found in a musical film: Arthur's frigid, hypocritical wife Joan; her petty bourgeois friends; Arthur's colleagues, traveling salesmen, bitter and angry men; an epileptic tramp whose crime was mistakenly attributed to Arthur; policemen, detectives and other incidental characters. It is interesting to note that many of them have their own so called "musical voices," a series of musical numbers whose purpose is to explore otherwise hidden parts of their personalities.

Furthermore, unlike *Moonlight on the Highway*, the characters in *Pennies* actually sing and dance themselves, rather than just listening to the songs performed by someone else. However, their method of singing is not typical of the genre: instead of giving voice themselves, the actors in *Pennies* perform a synchronized lip singing that occasionally includes a gender discrepancy between the real singer and the actor who lip-synchs the song. As in the other films that use synchronized lip singing, such as Peter Medak's *The Ruling Class* (1973), this seemingly insignificant change actually leads to a substantially different perception of the scene, giving it an invariably ironic or even mocking overtone by highlighting the artificiality of the screen action and the characters involved. As a device, lip-synch makes it virtually impossible to maintain the romantic realism of a traditional musical, with its mimetic structure and linear narrative. The lip-synch singing is frequently accompanied by a stylized dance, creating an even larger emotional distance between the audience and the characters. The distancing effect is further strengthened by the occasional use of such nonrealist acting devices as exaggerated voice, gesture, body language, and facial expressions, which aim to remove any remaining vestiges of familiarity with or empathy for the characters involved.

Along with the various syntactic devices that include lip-synch, stylized dance and nonrealist acting style, the musical numbers in *Pennies* offer the semantic richness and diversity not typically found in the traditional musicals. While some musical numbers fulfill the familiar function of helping to create romantic links between the characters—as for example, the musical number in the scene between Arthur and Elaine on the lake (although the lip-synch performance of the songs still slightly jolts audiences from fully accepting the romantic underpinning of this scene), most musical numbers in *Pennies* produce the opposite effect. They destroy any possibility of romantic or realistic perception of the scenes. Perhaps the best example is the scene between Arthur's wife Joan and the detective who interviews her on the disappearance of her husband. In this scene, Joan, played by Gemma Crevens, does a lip-synch of the song "Anything Goes," actually being sung by Radio Trio. A short pantomime leads into a highly stylized sexually suggestive dance that Joan performs with the detective, played by Dave King. Their style of singing and dancing clearly contradicts the previously established images of these characters: Joan, as a sexually repressed housewife of the 1930s; and the detective, as a stuffy buffoon. Both Crevens and especially King employ slightly exaggerated, what might be called the Meyerholdian style of acting, which ultimately destroys any possibility of a mimetic perception of the scene. As a result, these two characters are perceived not as real-life individuals but as archetypes, representatives of certain categories of people, stylistically similar to those found in the theatre of Vsevolod Meyerhold and Bertold Brecht.

Furthermore, the musical numbers in *Pennies*, especially those that are used in "hallucinatory scenes," fulfill another, perhaps even more important and unique function. They reach into the deepest level of the characters' subconsciouses and, in the process, unmask their most intimate dreams and desires. Perhaps the best example of this type of musical number is the scene where the Tramp/Accordion Man played by Kenneth Colley, in a hallucinatory dream recreates the murder of the blind girl. Haunted by his guilty conscience, he hallucinates the scene where his fellow tramps rise up and begin to imitate an ensemble of accordion players lip-synching "Serenade in the Night" (actually performed by Bixio, Cheryubin, and Kennedy with vocals by Ronnie Hill). This musical number is highly effective in allowing the audience to see deep inside the Tramp's subconscious. In fact, it is precisely this kind of musical number that later becomes a "trademark" of Potter's works and makes the most substantial impact on the genre.

Musical numbers play an equally important and complex role in Potter's other masterpiece, *The Singing Detective* (1986), where they are organically interwoven into the fabric of the TV film and help create a multiplicity of narrative layers. The protagonist, a mystery writer named Philip Marlow, is connected to popular music through the memories of his childhood and also through his novel's fictional protagonist, the Singing Detective. As part of this "play-within-play" dual reality, musical numbers become a device to create layers of repeatedly colliding and convoluting narratives. As in *Pennies,* songs are used in a variety of ways: some of them are semantically similar to the traditional musicals, such as those that reflect Marlow's nostalgic memories of his childhood and evoke in the audience an empathy for the characters involved. Others achieve exactly the opposite goal, namely they destroy any emotional bond that may have been built between the audience and the characters. Again, similarly to *Pennies,* this effect is achieved by using the same devices: lip-synch singing, stylized dance and nonrealist acting style. The musical numbers in *The Singing Detective* are particularly effective in the "hallucinatory" scenes where they allow interaction between different layers of narrative: Marlow's experience in the hospital, where uncomfortable dreams about his childhood mesh with the ominous story of his own protagonist, the Singing Detective. The complex function of the musical numbers in *The Singing Detective* becomes particularly evident in the scene where Philip Marlow, at the worst stage of his illness, is visited by a group of physicians. Frustrated by his physical condition and exacerbated by the condescension of the medical personnel, feverish Marlow hallucinates that the doctors and nurses, all of a sudden, begin performing a comical and slightly eerie version of "Dry Bones." Like those in *Pennies,* this mocking hallucinatory musical number, which also includes such elements as lip-synch singing and a highly stylized dance, is clearly aimed to jolt the audience out of any mimetic perception of the scene and, at the same time, provide a venue for stinging criticism of the public health care system in England.

This purely Brechtian device to "estrange" the audience from the characters and the action while making a social commentary becomes even more evident in the 1993 TV series, *Lipstick On Your Collar.* As in the previous cases, the musical numbers in *Lipstick* are used in a variety of ways, most effectively when they convey Potter's sarcastic view of 1950s England, which at that time was going through a small cultural war between the older generation desperately trying to hold on to vestiges of the crumbling British Empire, and the younger generation ready to embrace "decadent" American culture. The satirical use of song and dance in this series is brilliantly demonstrated in such musical numbers as "Blueberry Hill," "I See the Moon" and "Sh 'Boom: Life Could Be a Dream." In the "Blueberry Hill" number, the song and dance are built around such a decisively unromantic topic as used toilet papers that presumably contain intelligence information about the Russian army. Similarly, the song and dance in "I See the Moon" contains rather unappealing bodily functions and exaggerated drag costumes clearly aimed to satirize the bigotry and hypocrisy of British military officers, their turpitude and hidden predatory sexual inclinations. The "Sh 'Boom: Life Could Be a Dream" number delves into another seemingly unsuitable category: funerals, the solemnity of which is broken by a rather frivolous, even prurient rendition of this number. The "Sh 'Boom: Life Could Be a Dream" number broke yet another taboo by introducing topics considered inappropriate to the musical genre.

ANALYSIS

The above examples demonstrate that there is a certain pattern in the application of musical numbers in Potter's films. Depending on their uses, they can be divided into the following categories:

1. traditional use of musical numbers to illustrate or strengthen links between the romantically involved characters;
2. use of musical numbers to distance the audience from any kind of empathy or association with the characters;
3. use of musical numbers by characters in a hallucinatory state of mind.

The musical numbers in these three categories redefine the genre of musical film on both syntactic and semantic levels. On the syntactic level, most musical numbers in Potter films employ post-synchronized popular songs, sung not by the film actors but by well-known singers. Combined with stylized dance and the elements of nonrealist acting they produce, using Peter Wollen's terms, a *narrative intransitivity* aimed to ridicule the type of relationships typically present in the musical genre.

On the semantic level, Potter's musical numbers help create the layers of nonlinear narratives that break superficial causal links in the plot and resort to alternation, confrontation, and parallelism between the characters. A romantic couple or a romantic triangle, an almost obligatory attribute of a classical Hollywood musical, is replaced in Potter's films with a set of far more sophisticated, frequently "flawed" individuals who form a web of complex interpersonal relationships. Causal links between romantic characters, the reactions and behavior normally expected in a musical film, disappear; they are replaced with incidental interactions that do not contribute to the linear progression of the plot. The musical numbers in Potter's works do not become expressions of what Altman calls "personal and communal joy . . . or signify a romantic triumph over all limitations . . ."[11]; on the contrary, they highlight the personal misery of the individuals trapped in the fictional world of their impossible dreams and unfulfilled desires.

By calling attention to the gaps and seams in the narrative, which create a sense of omnipresent discontinuity, Potter undermines the illusionist (realist) art striving for an impression of spatio-temporal coherence. The discontinuity becomes programmatic and assertive; the interruption preempts spectacle; it becomes the spectacle. Musical numbers in Potter's works create what Gerald Gennette calls their own "metatext,"[12] which intersects with and relativizes the film's main narrative. This metatext is always created by shifting the point of view to a character's mind or, using Shlomith Rimmon-Kenan's terms, to the "psychological and ideological facets of internal focalization," where the camera becomes an eye into the "mind" of a character, revealing that character's "cognitive, emotive, and ideological orientation."[13] The intersection and collision of diverse textual surfaces create a dialogical discourse that becomes open to a variety of interpretations (Bakhtin). The "relativism" and "dialogism" of Potter's films run contrary to the "monologism" and "singular truth" concept implied in "traditional" musical films, where the musical numbers simply serve to complement the film's narrative.

A typical musical number in Potter's films becomes an instrument for an authorial intrusion, a digression that creates a stylistic incongruity largely inconsistent with the canon of the musical genre. By doing that, Potter destroys the key element of realist drama, that is a perception of the characters acting as real people in real time, space and circumstances. Potter's use of musical numbers to undermine an otherwise realistic flow of action draws a clear parallel with the postmodern theatre, in particular that of Brecht. Brecht too used song and dance extensively to achieve what he called *Verfremdung* or "alienation" effects, a process of making events, actions, and characters "strange" by sufficiently distancing spectators from the action so that they can watch it critically. Similarly to the Brechtian theatre, the narrative in Potter's films is advanced by interruptions and juxtaposition of the scenes rather than development of causal narrative sequences. Music and lyrics in songs as well as dance style are customarily used to mutually discredit emotional realism rather than complement it. The use of such anti-illusionist devices is particularly refreshing today, as it sharply contrasts the "superficial modernity and technological razzle-dazzle" of mainstream cinema, which remains a bastion of realism and naturalism aesthetically linked to the tradition of the nineteenth-century mimetic European novel.[14]

While telling the story, Potter, like Brecht, creates not a single but a multiple diegesis that he typically leaves open, instead of narratively tying up loose ends. In the process, he is not afraid to step out of the narrative and question it. The resulting interruptions typically produce a comic effect, not just for evoking laughter but also for helping highlight the critical awareness of the artificiality of the action. It is hardly a coincidence that in Potter's films those interruptions typically occur in the form of dreams. As Robert Stam points out, dreams not only contain a potential for alienation, they are a "sanctuary for desire, an imitation of possible transcendence of stale dichotomies, and a source of a kind of knowledge denied cerebral rationality."[15] Potter's desire to reach beyond cerebral rationality necessitates the use of such nonrealist devices as an exaggerated, nonrealist acting style, which forces the audience to perceive his characters more as archetypes than real-life individuals. However, all these measures to build a wall between the audience and the screen action do not mean that Potter wants his audience completely detached emotionally from his characters, nor does he deny his audiences entertainment. Potter uses

Verfremdung as an aesthetic device—first involving the spectators emotionally and then jarring them out of their empathic responses—to force the audience to contemplate and judge the action. Consequently, the spectators experience a perpetual shifting, dynamic relationship between empathy and alienation. While their ratio may vary, reflexivity and realism in Potter's films almost never become mutually excluded; they find not only a peaceful coexistence but a harmonious relationship in his filmic texts. As Potter himself puts it, "The songs are genuine artifacts I'm picking up but it's not serendipity. You're picking them up in order to use them, so it's part of the drama, as though you'd written the tune yourself. You reclaim it in order to remake it so it takes on the reverberation of all that's around it and then those lyrics start having added ironies."[16] In the words of Kenith Trodd, long-time producer and friend of Potter, " . . . the essence of Dennis's way with the songs was to dislocate us from the entranced naturalism of television drama."[17] For Potter, the songs are not the way to illustrate the azure, to show the sunny side of the world, but a device to contradict what Trodd calls "the cheap reality of life."[18] As the above examples demonstrate, while Potter intentionally subverts such terms as "good sense" and "reason" and foregrounds such elements as chance, incongruity, and shock, he does not reject the whole genre of musical film, but rather expands its familiar boundaries.

CONCLUSION

Today, almost five years after Potter's death, his influence continues to be felt in more than one way. The growing interest in Potter's work throughout the world is manifested, among other ways, by proliferation of Potter sites on the Internet, as well as by his impact on other filmmakers. For example, renowned French filmmaker Alain Resnais, in the opening credits to his new film *The Same Old Song (On Connait la Chanson)*, acknowledges Dennis Potter's influence on his direction of this movie. The 75-year-old director of such iconoclastic movies as *Hiroshima, Mon Amour* and *Last Year in Marienbad,* has actors lip-synch in a manner that instantly recalls Potter's work. Another indication of Potter's mark on television and film is the use of the Potter-style musical numbers in America's CBS television serial *Chicago Hope*. On this TV show, broadcast in the Fall of 1997, several characters perform hallucinatory musical numbers with lip-synch singing and stylized dance, instantly recognizable as influenced by Potter.[19] In the recently released *Dark City,* directed by Alex Proyas, the influence of Potter is openly admitted in the closing credits, which carry the line: "In memory of Dennis Potter with gratitude and admiration." These examples demonstrate that the influence of Potter's work on the genre of musical film continues to grow and expand far beyond his native land.

NOTES

1. John R. Cook, *Dennis Potter: A Life on Screen* (Manchester and New York: Manchester University Press, 1996).
2. W. Stephen Gilbert, *Fight & Kick & Bite: The Life and Work of Dennis Potter* (London: Holder and Stoughton, 1995).
3. Peter Stead, *Dennis Potter* (Oxford: Seren Books, 1993).
4. Glen Creeber, *Dennis Potter: Between Two Worlds* (London: Macmillan Press Ltd, 1998).
5. Stanley Green, in the preface to *Encyclopedia of the Musical Film* (Oxford and New York: Oxford University Press, 1981).
6. Rick Altman, *The American Film Musical* (Bloomington: Indiana University Press, 1987), 2–15.
7. Altman, p.12.
8. Altman, p.17.
9. Robert Stam, *Reflexivity in Film and Literature: From Don Quixote to Jean-Luc Godard* (Ann Arbor: University of Michigan Press, 1985), p.263.
10. Andre Bazin, *What is Cinema?* (Berkeley: University of California Press, 1967), p.137.
11. Altman, p.29.
12. Gerald Gennette, *Narrative Discourse: An Essay on Method* (Ithaca: Cornell University Press, 1980).
13. Shlomith Rimmon-Kenan, *Narrative Fiction: Contemporary Poetics* (London: Methuen Press, 1983), p.71.
14. Stam, p.270.
15. Stam, p.271.
16. Kenith Trodd, introduction to *Pennies from Heaven* (London: Faber and Faber, 1996), p.x.
17. Trodd, p.xi.
18. Trodd, p.xiv.
19. The creators of this series didn't even bother to give Potter a proper credit. Well, what can we say? American commercial television at its "best."

CHAPTER 13

"YESTERDAY ONCE MORE"

Thoughts on the Relationship Between Popular Music, Audience and Authorial Intention in Dennis Potter's *Pennies from Heaven, The Singing Detective* and *Lipstick on Your Collar*

Steve Brie

THE AIM OF THIS ESSAY IS TO PRESENT A NUMBER OF hypotheses concerning some of the ways in which popular music may function in Dennis Potter's *Pennies from Heaven* (1978), *The Singing Detective* (1986) and *Lipstick on Your Collar* (1993). The following discussion is based on the results of a pilot study into British audience reception of *Lipstick on Your Collar*.[1]

British viewers have come to expect, although not necessarily to accept, the utilization of popular music in Potter's work. It might even be argued that in the later part of his career, his trademark "lip-synch" technique, rather like Pinter's silences, was overworked and often came dangerously close to the self-parodic.[2] Potter is usually seen as a promoter of popular culture, with his mixing of mass-market music and "quality" drama, but in truth, he vehemently disliked most of the music he used in his work.

Potter's views on the nature and value of post–World War II popular music often echoed those of modernist critics such as Adorno, Hoggart and Leavis.[3] In 1962, for example, in his "condition of England" polemic, *The Changing Forest*, Potter attacked the "new" music that, he claimed, had brought moral degeneration to his beloved Forest of Dean; the jukebox, he lamented, had become "lord and master";[4] the new generation of popular entertainers were dismissed as "neon-dressed pop singer[s], jerking over the echo-chambered microphone[s] as if in orgasm";[5] and contemporary lyrics were only concerned with "sex, sex, sex."[6]

Potter's vilification of popular music as cheap "drivel" that reduces everything "to the utmost simplification" was based on his belief that it is easily produced by often anonymous teams of "hack" writers for commercial gain, and that its main characteristic is standardization: by such reasoning, the popular song should not be considered "art."[7] Like Adorno,[8] Potter saw the popular music "product" as a form of "catharsis for the masses,"[9] seducing listeners into ideological passivity.[10] Such a perspective can be criticized for applying what Tagg has termed "haut-bourgeois norms of aesthetic reference" to popular music, and for paying scant regard to "the social, economic or cultural situations of the popular majority."[11] Also problematic is Potter's reluctance, or inability, to differentiate between popular music genres: essentially, he indiscriminately bracketed all post-1940s music as "pop." In addition, as Frith argues, transcendence is "as much a part of the popular as of the serious music aesthetic,"[12] and we cannot, as Novitz highlights, unproblematically distinguish "high" and "low" culture in terms of formal differences (complex vs. simple), effective difference (challenging vs. confirming), or creative difference (individual vs. collective production).[13] Potter would, for example, struggle convincingly to describe Elmore James's blues lyrics as "sugary"[14] or the Sex Pistols' punk rock aesthetic as promoting conservative ideology.

Again echoing Adorno and the Frankfurt School, Potter consistently railed against the commercialization of the culture industries. In his final TV interview, for example, he claimed that "commercialization . . . means . . . you're putting a commercial value upon everything. . . . We're not citizens, we're consumers."[15] In contrast to the commercialized present, Potter consistently valorized his vision of an organic (possibly mythic, possibly apocryphal[16]) past in which music was played and enjoyed as a socially-binding activity uncontaminated by commerce. In 1962, for example, when Britain was about to enter the first throes of Beatlemania, Potter, at the age of 27, produced a nostalgic lamentation for the decline of his village brass band whose live, spontaneous, organic music had been superseded by what he saw as commercialized, recorded pop:

> The band used to be in constant demand and the men who belonged to it . . . thought themselves possessors of a massive and enviable privilege. . . . Then, there were regular concerts, local contests, marching for the chapel behind the tassled admonitory banner . . . [now] it is as if you could feel the life changing under your feet like a mild but sustained tremor . . . [17]

As Colley and Davies have argued in relation to *Pennies from Heaven,* Potter exhibits a "classic Leavis/Thompson pessimism" about the way in which a voraciously commercial music industry sets out to colonize "the emotional life of the petit-bourgeoisie"[18] with its "cheap songs." Potter's defense against the sweeping tide of commercialism was to seek solace in an idealized, pre-rock 'n' roll past—a past typified in his depiction of the cozy working class rural community singalongs led by his real father in *Between Two Rivers* (1960)[19] and by Mr. Marlow in *The Singing Detective.*

In spite of his prejudices, Potter did understand the dramatic potential inherent in the popular tune. It is this understanding that lies behind his pragmatic annexation of the music industry's "products." In the words of his character, Nigel Barton, Potter was rather like "an atheist who is fond of hymn tunes,"[20] being simultaneously fearful of and fascinated by the inherent power of the popular song. Alongside what he termed its "cheapness," he also, perhaps reluctantly, acknowledged that there was "something of the Psalms of David"[21] about popular music; that certain tunes could "tinkle tinkle their simple sweetness and yet somehow complicated accusations out of the most personally demeaning residues of what had seemed to be lost and gone forever."[22]

He was not immune, either, to the seductive properties of a well crooned tune. In 1968, for example, he wrote:

> Whenever the cold winds blow too bleakly through my mind, I like to listen to some elderly and rather scratchy recordings of Al Bowlly . . . the big crooning swoon on the wireless round about the time I was cutting my first milk teeth. . . . For me . . . [his] throatily-velvety version of "You May Not Be An Angel" has the lingering flavors of chewy rusks, cod-liver oil and National Dried Milk.[23]

By the mid-seventies, however, such lapses seem to have been airbrushed from Potter's consciousness. Nostalgia, he wrote " . . . runs free in the broken gutters, overflows the cracked drains and gurgles up in a choking swirl as high as the open mouth."[24] By the late eighties, he was vehemently dissociating himself and his work from any nostalgic sensibility—"I don't know 'nostalgia' . . . Nostalgia is a second-order emotion . . . I'm not dealing in nostalgia"[25]—and by the nineties, he was arguing that any memory corrupted by nostalgia was little more than " . . . a twee, Technicolor version of the so-called past."[26]

Potter's categorization of nostalgia as a form of cultural philistinism is rather ironic. The empirical evidence suggests that the concept of nostalgia that crucially motivates many of his characters (Arthur Parker, Philip Marlow, Daniel Feeld in *Karaoke* and *Cold Lazarus* [1996, posthumous]), may also fundamentally influence the ways in which some and perhaps even the majority of viewers negotiate his musically infused texts. For example, for my pilot study viewers old enough to have memories of the fifties, the period itself became the dominant aspect of *Lipstick on Your Collar.* They remembered much more about period details within the mise-en-scène than they did about the profiles and narrative functions of the characters. This ability to recall period detail from the narrative was sometimes linked to their own individual memories of the era in question. One respondent remembered the familiar pattern of a stained-glass panel in the front door in minute detail, yet after six hours of viewing, could name only three of the characters in the serial. Another was able independently to recall and accurately describe some drinking glasses fleetingly seen in one episode because they had reminded her of the type she remembered using herself as a young child. The same respondent struggled to retell the basic story line.

My findings suggest that Potter and many critics may have taken too much for granted in relation to text-audience dynamics. For example, Hunningher's claim that the songs in *The Singing Detective* "connect and underline different narrative strands"[27] and Corrigan's argument that its narrative allows viewers to "think clues through the songs"[28] are essentially "preferred readings" based on the interaction between the text and an ideal or implied viewer. In a medium where continuous and concentrated audience attention cannot be taken for granted, authorial intention must invariably lose some of its relevance. Responses made by some pilot study viewers, for example, suggest that the songs in *Lipstick on Your Collar* induced or stimulated certain pleasures that, in many cases, appear to have been extradiegetic. In other words, many of the songs were decontextualized and enjoyed as discrete pieces of often nostalgia-inducing entertainment.

Sometimes, a particular piece of music, deemed by viewers to be inappropriately or seemingly arbitrarily inserted into the narrative, would produce a "distancing" effect, as in the following pair of responses:

> I couldn't understand half the time what some of the songs were in relation to the story.
> . . . Half the time they sang the songs, I just couldn't see what it was and that was obviously a bit of the story I didn't pick up on.

In such cases, the songs seemed neither to connect nor underline the narrative. Indeed, for these respondents, they had the opposite effect. They fragmented it.

Some respondents struggled to accept the idea of a "musical play." Potter's fusion of popular music with "serious" drama caused a degree of irritation on the part of certain viewers who, in contrast to the "postmodernist audience,"[29] tended to favor formalistic conservatism:

> When I go to a musical, I know I'm going to a musical. I wasn't going to see a musical. I was going to see a drama.

I like the music, or a play. But I'm not really stuck on them when they're mixed.

Other respondents criticized the choice of music and offered suggestions for achieving a greater degree of historical accuracy:

There's not a single song . . . that I would have associated with [the Suez campaign]. Not like . . ."Pack Up Your Troubles in Your Old Kit-Bag," or "Goodbye Piccadilly, Hello Leicester Square."
Two-Way Family Favorites . . . or . . . Billy Cotton, that would be the thing that would depict Britain in the fifties.

While highlighting the music as a source of pleasure, some respondents argued that its utilization allowed weaknesses in Potter's writing to be glossed over:

His writing isn't good enough to portray what he wants to portray, so he uses the songs.
I think [the songs] let him get away with a lot.
Take away the music and you've got a shallow piece.

Such expressions of viewer cynicism, which were not confined to the musical content of the serial, provide an interesting populist counterpoint to the views of critics such as Creeber, who sees Potter as one of the most "important of all contemporary British writers";[30] to Fuller, who positions Potter as "the most important creative figure in the history of British television";[31] and to Stead, who describes him as "the most gifted and influential playwright in television history."[32]

Perhaps the most interesting aspect of the pilot study results concerns the difficulty respondents found in recalling the songs and tunes used in the serial. From a possible maximum recollection figure of 369 (calculated on the basis of 9 respondents and 41 pieces of music), only 10 instances were recorded at what I termed the "unmotivated stage" of the interviews.

Why did respondents, some of whom had earlier described the music as the most enjoyable part of the serial, struggle to recollect individual songs and their positions within the narrative? It is difficult to lay the blame for this phenomenon on a basic lack of familiarity with the songs. With only one or two exceptions, the songs in *Lipstick on Your Collar* are rather predictable fifties standards. At the "motivated" stage of their interviews, when audio extracts of the songs were played, respondents consistently claimed familiarity with the songs that they subsequently failed to locate within the narrative; some even claimed to have no recollection whatsoever of their ever having been used in the serial.

It appears that in *Lipstick on Your Collar* and perhaps in *Pennies from Heaven* and *The Singing Detective,* the musical mediation of zeitgeist helps to create a situation in which period becomes the dominant character. These "character decades" can in turn facilitate "memory excursions": pleasurable, often nostalgic interludes that Potter might dismissively term "lapses of concentration." These periods of subjective analepsis can produce readings that diverge significantly from the producers' preferred reading.[33]

For some viewers, the music seemed to operate like a catalyst, inducing fictional or semifictional memory vignettes. Some respondents described how they would find themselves "drifting off" into musically-induced fabricated imaginings, or into memory narratives underpinned by personal history. As Colley and Davies have previously argued in relation to *Pennies from Heaven,*[34] many of the songs may metonymize a happier, more carefree world than the one in which the viewer is immediately situated. When such a situation occurs, the viewer may, consciously or unconsciously, temporarily reject the present for a musically signified, nostalgia-based, idealized version of the past:

> I sort of drifted off into the song for my own personal reasons. I think I stopped taking in what was going on as they were singing.

It seems, then, that the musical sequences can operate as extremely powerful "distancing" devices, but perhaps not always in the pedagogical way Potter appears to have imagined they would.[35]

Whether we term *The Singing Detective* a detective story with music, or a musical detective story, this "drift-off" effect can be seen as highly problematic for a genre so dependent upon the maintenance of audience attention. If Potter's clues, so carefully infused into the musical sequences, are often partially "erased," or even completely "edited" from viewers' memories in favor of alternative memory narratives, the detective genre's desire to produce a narrative that leads its viewers toward a conclusive resolution may be undermined.

The televisual text of *The Singing Detective* utilizes 35 identifiable pieces of music and over 40 generic "noirish" underscore samples.[36] As period signifiers, the songs form a reasonably accurate representation of the types of music particularly popular in middle class England during the late thirties and early forties. Songs such as "The Teddy Bears' Picnic," "Cruising Down The River" and "We'll Meet Again" are particularly efficient vehicles for signifying an often nostalgically distorted concept of "Englishness." The big band sound, at its peak in the early forties, is well represented, as are popular crooners of the period such as Al Bowlly, Bing Crosby and Sam Browne. In terms of representing the swing era in general, however, it could be argued that the choice of music reflects Potter's musical conservatism. Apart from the anarchic novelty song, "Dry Bones," the only real stylistic deviation comes in the form of the proto "doo-wop," urban American harmonies of The Inkspots' "Do I Worry?"

Unlike Hollywood musical set-pieces, where time stands still as characters transcend their interpersonal conflicts through song and dance, the musical sequences in *The Singing Detective* are unmistakably diegetic: they exist within their own fictional space, in a hallucinogenically defamiliarized now. In contrast to both *Pennies from Heaven* and *Lipstick on Your Collar,* where liberational music is deliberately evoked and orchestrated by the protagonists, Potter casts Marlow as a victim of intrusive, often emotionally debilitating melodies. In *Pennies,* argues Potter: "Arthur Parker, believing in the songs in his simpleminded kind of way, had licence, as it were, to inject those songs everywhere and in any way and make them seem real." But in *The Singing Detective:* "Marlow . . . was resisting them, didn't believe in them . . . they were hard little stones being thrown at [him]."[37]

Using one of these "hard little stones" as an example, I will argue that Potter's explanation of how the songs work in relation to Marlow ironically mirrors the way in which they appear to work for some viewers.

My chosen example is the ballad "The Very Thought of You," performed by Al Bowlly and the Ray Noble Orchestra, in a sequence that occurs approximately halfway through the final episode. The sequence begins with the still-hospitalized adult Marlow telling Nurse Mills of how, as a child, he often heard "those songs" creeping up the stairs "when you [were] supposed to be asleep."[38]

As the curtain is drawn around the bed, the tinkling piano intro to "The Very Thought of You" begins. A memory-signifying slow dissolve transports us into Marlow's representation of 1940s London. After an establishing right-to-left pan along a row of terraced houses, we are offered a close-up of a period gramophone playing a '78 recording of the Al Bowlly number, "the needle biting and hissing along the deeply etched groove."[39] The music is thus confirmed as being diegetic within the memory narrative. In the center of the tiny, dimly lit room is Marlow's grandfather, a generic figure dressed in black, drinking a glass of stout. Next, we see young Philip lying on his bed upstairs reading a *Hotspur* comic. As the smooth, brass-led orchestration gives way to Bowlly's vocal, the adult Philip's memory-self is seen in close-up, listening to the melody that, with the passing of time, will come to exhibit the poignant connotations that induced this memory. The next shot returns us to Philip's grandfather in the parlor. Now, we are able to see a highly polished coffin along the window wall. Inside the coffin is the body of Philip's mother, who committed suicide by jumping from Hammersmith Bridge. Philip comes down the stairs and gives his grandfather a fright. A cut then takes us and a distressed Philip into the carriage of a steam train. As the train pulls into a station, smoke threatening to engulf the shot, we see a forlorn Mr. Marlow waiting for Philip on the platform.

The sequence is drenched in period signifiers. The mise-en-scène is suitably starved of color; even the flowers on the coffin and the trees around the railway station are conventionally dechromatized. The collective memories of Potter and his production team offer a highly stylized, highly sepia-ized impression of the forties. In common with the pasts depicted in both *Pennies from Heaven* and *Lipstick on Your Collar*,[40] the sequence takes its visual points of reference not from "official history" but from popular memory and from other media representations of the period.[41] Those viewers without memories of the forties may therefore accept the representation as faithful because its stylized "thenness" provides a cross-reference to other filmic or televisual versions of the period.[42] Some of those viewers who do remember the period may, to varying degrees, be prone to the same tendency toward nostalgic essentialism that underpins Potter's re-presentation and may thus accept it as "realistic."

Both visually and aurally, the sequence foregrounds technological "periodness."[43] The camera lingers over the naïve gramophone, baring its device, celebrating its crudity. The original mono recording is retained, its crackling white noise conventionally suggesting period fidelity. Although Potter specified in the published script that the volume of the music should be "diminished . . . a little"[44] as we move upstairs, so as to take account of the physical distance between the parlor and the bedroom, no such change is discernible in the transmitted version. This unrealistic consistency in volume across space tends to reinforce the impressionistic, often selective, often inaccurate nature of memory.

Written in 1934, "The Very Thought of You" may connote, for those with memories of the original version, what might arguably be termed a mythical, prewar, innocent "golden age."[45] As is typical of many songs of the period, Ray Noble's ballad is essentially metaphysical in its approach to love and romance.[46] It is the idea rather than the physicality of love that is celebrated. The longing for an absent, idealized female is typical of what Horton has classified as the "wishing and dreaming" subgenre of the popular song.[47] The innocence of "golden age" popular music is also embodied in what Barthes might term the "grain" in the voice of Al Bowlly.[48] The crooner's elegant, "whispering" style and his romance-based, sanitized repertoire present a sharp contrast to what Potter saw as "sexually explicit," postwar music. As one of Potter's characters argues in *Moonlight on the Highway* (1969), Bowlly "makes sex sound lovely. Not a bit like sex at all, in fact. . . . All [his] songs are about love, never about making love. Never about copulation."[49] This innate lyrical innocence may act as a powerful nostalgia-prompt, inducing memories of, or longings for, a vanished mythical past in viewers of a certain age, suffering from what might be termed "the ache of postmodernism."

"The Very Thought of You" is just one example of a piece of music that, when coupled with overtly stylized period visuals, does its job too well.[50] Rather than reading the visual and aural "periodness" in terms of Marlow's narrative, some viewers may appropriate it for their own nostalgic pleasure.[51]

In conclusion, even accounting for all its associated methodological and representational problems, I would argue that my initial pilot study raises a series of pertinent questions relating to audience interpretations, not only of Potter's work but also of other visible fictions that utilize popular music within their narratives.

NOTES

1. The basic methodology employed for the study was as follows. Nine respondents were selected using the "snowball" method of recruitment: for detailed explanation of this process, see, for example, M. J. Heide, *Television Culture and Women's Lives* (Philadelphia: University of Pennsylvania Press, 1995), p.10. I was not specifically interested in a class-based analysis but I was keen to investigate the way in which age and gender might influence responses to Potter's work. I therefore chose nine "middle-class" respondents, varying in age between 32 and 64: six female and three male. I have since completed studies on *Pennies from Heaven* and *The Singing Detective* (gender distribution equals out over the three studies). Each respondent was invited to view the six episodes of *Lipstick on Your Collar* in their own homes. After watching the tapes, they completed an informal interview that lasted approximately 90 minutes. Respondents were not informed that I was focusing upon the popular music aspect of the texts. Respondents were initially asked to name any songs they recalled being used in the serial. They were then asked to listen to aural extracts from the 28 most prominently featured songs and to attempt to recall "what was happening on the screen" when they were used. "Most prominently featured" refers to examples that were either diegetic or that underscored the narrative for a duration of time that might realistically allow a possibility of recognition. These recollections, which I termed "Motivated Recollections" (as opposed to the previous "Unmotivated Recollections") were then divided into four categories: "Accurate Placements"; "Partial Placements"; "Inaccurate Placements" and "No Recollection." "Accurate Placements" were those responses that correctly placed the song in terms of each of the following: a) position within the narrative order; b) narrative function; c) characters involved in the scene; d) source of music and e) setting. "Partial Placements" correctly identified at least one of the above. "Inaccurate Placements" failed correctly to identify any of the above. "No Recollection" meant no recollection of the music having been used in the serial. The data from this study will appear in my forthcoming Ph.D. thesis on this topic.

2. In Britain, Potter's "lip-synch" device has been overtly parodied in a series of television commercials produced throughout the 1990s for insurance company

Allied Dunbar. A number of these commercials were based around the Irving Berlin number "Let's Face the Music and Dance."

3. See, for example, Richard Hoggart, *The Uses of Literacy* (Manchester: Manchester University Press, 1957). Potter first read Hoggart's book during his student days at Oxford University. Both Cook and Gilbert discuss Hoggart's influence on Potter: see John R. Cook, *Dennis Potter: A Life on Screen*, (Manchester: Manchester University Press, 1995; rev. second edition, 1998); and W. Stephen Gilbert, *Fight and Kick and Bite: The Life and Work of Dennis Potter* (London: Hodder and Stoughton, 1995). F. R. Leavis believed that popular culture was substandard culture which had little intrinsic value: see F. R. Leavis, *Culture and Environment* (London: Chatto and Windus, 1993).

4. Dennis Potter, *The Changing Forest: Life in the Forest of Dean Today* (London: Secker and Warburg, 1962; repr. London: Minerva Press, 1996), p.18.

5. Potter, p.78.

6. Potter, p.18. Such condemnation can also be found in many of Potter's fictions—for example, in *Moonlight on the Highway* (1969) in which the central protagonist, David Peters, lambasts the popular singers of the 1960s who "whine and howl through their long hair like a lot of bloody apes."

7. In *Pennies from Heaven* (1978), one of Arthur Parker's fellow traveling salesmen claims that most of the songs are "dreamed up in a back office by a couple of Jew-boys with green eyeshades" (Dennis Potter, *Pennies from Heaven* [published scripts] London: Faber and Faber, 1996, p.70).

8. See, for example, Theodor Adorno, "On Popular Music," in *Studies in Philosophy and Science*, vol. 9, 1941, pp.17–48. Adorno tended to bracket all nonclassical music as "jazz" and all "jazz" as commercialized ephemera. In "Perennial Fashion—Jazz," he wrote: "Anyone who allows the growing respectability of mass culture to seduce him into equating popular song with modern art because of a few false notes squeaked on a clarinet . . . has already capitulated to barbarism" (Theodor Adorno, "Perennial Fashion—Jazz," *Prisms* [Cambridge, Massachusetts: MIT Press, 1982], p.127). For Adorno, only the Modernist music of Schoenberg and his followers presented an autonomous "analogue of the pain and alienation" of the human condition: see A. Blake, *The Land Without Music* (Manchester: Manchester University Press, 1997), p.129.

9. Adorno in *Cultural Theory and Popular Culture: A Reader*, ed. John Storey (London: Harvester and Wheatsheaf, 1994), p.213.

10. Potter focuses on the repetitive nature of popular music in *Karaoke* (1996, posthumous).

11. P. Tagg, "The Goteborg Connection: Lessons in the History and Politics of Popular Music Education and Research," in *Popular Music*, vol.17, bk.2, 1998, p.228.

12. Simon Frith, *Music for Pleasure* (Cambridge: Polity Press, 1988), p.275.

13. See D. Novitz, "Ways of Artmaking: The High and the Popular in Art," *British Journal of Aesthetics*, vol.29, bk.1, 1989; and Frith, p.282.

14. Levine argues that in the blues, "love seldom resembled the ethereal, ideal relationship so often pictured in popular songs." See L. W. Levine, *Black Culture*

and Black Consciousness (New York: Oxford University Press, 1977), pp.274–283. For discussions of the ideology of punk, see Greil Marcus, *In the Fascist Bathroom: Writings on Punk 1977–1992* (London: Viking, 1993) and Jon Savage, *England's Dreaming: Sex Pistols and Punk Rock* (London: Faber and Faber, 1991).

15. Dennis Potter, interview by Melvyn Bragg, 1st tx. Channel Four, 5 April 1994. Published in Dennis Potter, *Seeing the Blossom: Two Interviews and a Lecture* (London: Faber and Faber, 1994), pp14–15. Potter's distaste for commercialization was by no means limited to the field of popular music. Some of his most passionate anticonsumerist diatribes were aimed at the television commercial, as in his 1972 TV play, *Follow the Yellow Brick Road*. Such beliefs did not prevent Potter from offering his work to commercial television, where his dramas were interrupted by advertisements.

16. Raymond Williams claimed that "if there is one thing about 'the organic community,' it is that it has always gone." Raymond Williams, *Culture and Society 1780–1950* (Harmondsworth: Penguin, 1958), p.252.

17. Potter, *The Changing Forest*, pp.106–8.

18. Ian Colley and Gill Davies, "*Pennies from Heaven*: Music, Image, Text," *Screen Education* 25 (Summer 1980), p.65.

19. In Potter's early TV documentary about his beloved Forest of Dean, *Between Two Rivers* (1960), his father is seen leading the villagers in a rendition of "Painting the Clouds with Sunshine." Potter would later use the song to close Episode 5 of the TV *Pennies from Heaven*.

20. Dennis Potter, *The Nigel Barton Plays*, published scripts (London: Harmondsworth: Penguin, 1967), p.61. This is how Nigel Barton describes himself at one point in *Stand Up, Nigel Barton* (1965).

21. Potter, *Seeing the Blossom*, p.19. Potter took the religious metaphor even further in an interview with Ray Connolly, describing the songs in *Pennies from Heaven* as "diminished versions of the oldest myths of all in the Garden of Eden" (see Dennis Potter, "When The Penny Dropped," interview by Ray Connolly, *London Evening Standard*, 21 March 1978, p.8). The link is graphically illustrated when in Episode 2, Potter makes his character Eileen segue from singing Psalm 35 into "You've Got Me Crying Again."

22. Potter, *Seeing the Blossom*, p.43.

23. Dennis Potter, "It May Be That Twiggy Has The Right Idea After All," *The Sun*, 18 March 1968. The wistful references to primitive technology suggest that for Potter, connotations of "scratchiness" were as influential as the particular tune in inducing nostalgic memories of his childhood.

24. Dennis Potter, "Paper Thin," *The New Statesman*, 17 October 1975.

25. Potter, *Seeing the Blossom*, p.67.

26. Dennis Potter, interview by Graham Fuller, *Potter on Potter*, ed. Graham Fuller (London: Faber and Faber, 1993), p.22.

27. Joost Hunningher, "*The Singing Detective* (Dennis Potter): Who Done It?" in *British Television Drama in the 1980s*, ed. George W. Brandt (Cambridge: Cambridge University Press, 1993), p.248.

28. Timothy Corrigan, "Music from Heaven, Bodies in Hell: *The Singing Detective*," in *A Cinema without Walls: Movies and Culture after Vietnam* (London: Routledge, 1991), p.186.

29. For discussions of the "postmodernist audience," see Nicholas Abercrombie, *Television and Society* (London: Polity Press, 1996); and Robin Nelson, *TV Drama in Transition: Forms, Values and Cultural Change* (London: Macmillan, 1997).

30. Glen Creeber, *Dennis Potter: Between Two Worlds—A Critical Reassessment* (London: Macmillan, 1998), p.2.

31. Graham Fuller, "Introduction," *Potter on Potter*, p.xiv.

32. Dust jacket notes, Peter Stead, *Dennis Potter* (Bridgend: Seren Books, 1993).

33. Television is an ensemble medium and by "producer," I mean all the decision-makers, from writer to editor.

34. Colley and Davies, p.74.

35. See Colley and Davies (p.69) for discussion of distancing effects in *Pennies from Heaven*. Cook (p.293) and Gilbert (p.193) also discuss distancing in Potter's work.

36. The title music, "Peg O' My Heart" and the generic underscore samples were chosen by director Jon Amiel. See Hunningher, pp.248–49.

37. Potter, *Potter on Potter*, p.87.

38. Dennis Potter, *The Singing Detective* (published scripts) (London: Faber and Faber, 1986), p.220.

39. Potter, *The Singing Detective* (published scripts), p.220.

40. My pilot study viewer-respondents born too late to have actual memories of the fifties, read *Lipstick on Your Collar*'s highly stylized, "pop-art" depiction of the period as "truthful" because the fantasy scenes reflected a zeitgeist popularized and therefore legitimized by films such as *American Graffiti* (dir.: George Lucas, 1973) and television programs such as *Happy Days* (Paramount, 1974–84). Although the representation of the fifties in *Lipstick on Your Collar* is stylistically very different to *The Singing Detective*'s forties mise-en-scène, the presence of actual memories of the period in question may, similarly, crucially influence the ways in which viewers read "The Very Thought of You" sequence.

41. Frederic Jameson discusses connotations of "pastness" in which the history of aesthetic styles displaces "real" history in Jameson, "Postmodernism, or the Cultural Logic of Late Capitalism" in *Postmodernism: A Reader*, ed. T. Docherty (London: Harvester/Wheatsheaf, 1991), p.76.

42. In terms of British television, see, for example, *Family at War* (Granada television, 1970–2), *Sam* (Granada, 1973–5) and *No Bananas* (BBC TV, 1996).

43. Corrigan discusses the foregrounding of the technology of performance in relation to other songs in the serial in his chapter on *The Singing Detective* in Corrigan, *A Cinema Without Walls*, pp.179–193.

44. Potter, *The Singing Detective* (published scripts), p.221.

45. Some viewers may know the Doris Day version from the 1950 film, *Young Man with a Horn* (dir.: Michael Curtiz) and may therefore make different associations that may exclude the prewar "golden age" concept. An instrumental version of the song had already been utilized in the TV version of *Pennies from Heaven*.

46. Samuel argues that the metaphysical preoccupations of prewar song lyrics are similar to those expounded in some areas of Elizabethan love poetry: see R. Samuel, *Theatres of Memory: Past and Present in Contemporary Culture* (London: Verso, 1994), p.90. Frith, however, argues that such lyrics are in fact time-specific and represent the "sentimental ideology of capitalist society": see Frith, pp.106–115.

47. See D. Horton, "The Dialogue of Courtship in Popular Songs," *American Journal of Sociology* 62 (1957): 569–578.

48. Roland Barthes, *Image Music Text* (London: Fontana Press, 1977).

49. Potter chose Bowlly's versions of "You Couldn't Be Cuter" and "Edie Was A Lady" as part of the "top ten" records he would like to have with him if stranded on a mythical desert island in the popular and long-running BBC Radio program, *Desert Island Discs* (tx. BBC Radio Four, 17 December 1977).

50. A song's melody can, of course, also act as a memory prompt. Trumpeter Nat Gonella's silkily tactile minor-key anaphones, for example, may cause what Adorno might term "the emotional listener" to project sentimental emotions and memories onto the music: see Theodor Adorno, *Introduction to the Sociology of Music*, trans. E. B. Ashton (New York: Seabury, 1976).

51. Jameson talks of a "Nostalgia Mode," which he describes as "the desperate attempt to appropriate a missing past" in Jameson, p.75.

CHAPTER 14

THE FINAL DAYS,
THE FINAL PLAYS,
THE FINAL PLOYS

Irving B. Harrison

I'm out of here in the morning.
I can afford to offend whomsoever I choose.

—Daniel Feeld, in *Karaoke*

IN APRIL 1994, DENNIS POTTER LEARNED THAT HE HAD cancer of the pancreas, and that it had already spread to his liver. He had but a few months to live. The only medical treatment was the prescription of powerful painkillers, which Potter complemented with his usual indulgence in alcohol and cigarettes. Almost at once he determined that he would live out his remaining days immersed in a writing project, accommodating his daily working hours to the intervals between sleep and narcotic-induced stupefaction. He had already begun *Karaoke,* but decided to rewrite it and add another play. *Karaoke* and *Cold Lazarus* was the result, with four parts each, intended for interlocking posthumous presentation. At the end, he expressed dismay: had he but known that he could continue a bit longer, he quipped, he would have written six-part plays. As it was, and as the quotation above suggests, Potter found sufficient time to express all he intended.

Gilbert[1] noted Potter's preoccupation with himself as a victim, and offered the word "prisoner." BBC producer Kenith Trodd agreed. Both were responding to the physical horror that Potter expressed by way of Marlow: "A prisoner in my own skin and bones." My own focus is, rather, on Potter held prisoner by the repressed, unconscious part of his mind.

KARAOKE

Karaoke, in characteristic Potter fashion, mixes multiple levels of narrative and is constructed with a strong sense of character doubling. As is the case in other works, such as *The Singing Detective,* the writing ensures that the jumps from one scenario to the other are unexpected and sometimes jarring and confusing, problematizing the distinctions between fiction and "reality" and ultimately culminating in a dramatic synthesis and resolution.

The protagonist of *Karaoke,* Daniel Feeld, is a heavy-drinking, chain-smoking, and very sick writer. His teleplay, *Karaoke,* is in production, and Feeld is being his typically difficult and irascible self on the set. Also typical for Potter, Feeld is a partial double for the author, and is in turn related to other characters within the play in complex layers of doubling and opposition.

As the play begins, two contrasting scenes rapidly succeed each other. One is set in a karaoke bar, replete with a screen, music, and Japanese businessmen on stage to participate in the fun. In the other, at the next moment, Feeld is seen about to undergo a barium enema to determine the cause of his pain. The physician is comically fearful that Daniel will defecate, a typical Potter gag. A voice is heard that seems to come from the nurse, but is obviously not hers: "He can do what he likes, can't he." The words are from the dialogue Feeld has written. They can be read as a direct confirmation of Feeld's opportunity to embarrass the diagnostician but, typically, have multiple layers of other interpretations. In the karaoke club scene, a bar girl named Sandra had made that bored, flat and indifferent remark to her client about "Pig" Mailion, the owner of the club. Her sour acknowledgment that Mailion could do as he pleased was Feeld's hallucinated association to the diagnostic procedure, which he likened to anal rape.

As the story progresses, Feeld becomes obsessed with the feeling that people he encounters are speaking the lines of his play. The eerie experience of seeing and hearing strangers living out in public what he has written is profoundly upsetting to him. Dining with his producer (who harangues him about his health, lifestyle and battles with the film's director), Feeld believes that he overhears a couple engaging in a dialogue that occurs between characters named Sandra and Peter from his play. The woman is in fact Sandra, the bar girl from the opening sequence. According to Feeld's plot, the character Sandra is destined to be fatally strangled by the character Peter during an episode of rough sex. Terrified, and determined to "save" "Sandra," Feeld follows the girl to the karaoke bar where she works, ultimately collapsing. He is, subsequently, taken to the hospital. The lines between "reality" and writing become blurred in this story, as both Feeld and Potter struggle to wrest control of their stories and to create a closure for themselves. In the climatic scene, facing his imminent death, Feeld shoots the exploitative club owner, "Pig" Malion, to protect Sandra from the consequences of her killing him in revenge.

Potter worked further elements into *Karaoke* as it neared its finale: when Ben explains the nature of the dying Feeld's financial bequest to Sandra, he reveals that Feeld has no living family members. Feeld had once been close to marrying, but a tragedy had occurred, about which he had never spoken. A twin brother named Chris, an expert in cryogenics, had committed suicide several years before. Ben surmises that Feeld was leaving a major share of his estate to a cryogenics organization in the twin's memory. Feeld had also become intrigued with cyberspace and virtual reality, and with accounts of "out of body" experiences,[2] and decided to have his head frozen cryogenically, with the expectation that future technology might restore him to health. With that discovery, all of the complexities of *Karaoke* seem to fall into place, or almost all. The dying man's last agonized words are: "No biography!" Potter has set the stage for *Cold Lazarus*.

COLD LAZARUS

Cold Lazarus, the companion piece to *Karaoke*, is concerned with the posthumous life of the writer Daniel Feeld. Prior to his death, Feeld decided to have his head frozen cryogenically, and *Cold Lazarus*, set in the year 2368, concerns the awakening of Feeld's consciousness and the struggle that ensues over the control of this mind from the past. In a society in which all experience is mediated and virtual reality is the norm, scientist, political figures and entertainment moguls are all captivated by the power of a man who remembers "authentic" experiences. But, as the story unfolds, the relationship between experience and fantasy is questioned, much as the line between narrative and reality in *Karaoke*.

The plot of *Cold Lazarus* traces the work of a scientific team who are investigating the memories in Feeld's newly reawakend mind.

One problem with which the play is concerned is a possible outcome of man's current scientific efforts to master and duplicate—or simulate—the mechanisms and physicochemical processes of life and mind. As such, it is expressed through Potter's dramatization of the horror of a mind that has lost its freedom and of that mind's yearning for release to God's benevolent embrace. It epitomizes his passion, with the many significations of the word, such as suffering, Christian belief, and passivity.

Potter deftly interweaves the first tale, of the struggle over Daniel's Feeld's head, with flashes of the second, namely, Daniel Feeld's childhood and adolescence as observed on the screen—which of course soon disappears as the action completely fills the field. A host of Feeld's twentieth-century experiences are dramatized.[3] The most consequential: Daniel, actively thinking and feeling as a child and portrayed as such on the screen, is consumed with guilt.

He confuses himself in his mind with his twin, Chris.[4] Chris points his finger at Daniel, who is skipping a Chapel service. Daniel, sinning, goes off into the Forest with his dog. Worse, he compounds his delinquency by pulling a forbidden cigarette from his pocket and taking a puff. Shortly after that, his dog is killed and he is seized by a tramp and brutally raped. He drags his defiled, pain-wracked body and soul to the Chapel, where his father embraces him. Later scenes portray him, healthy and happy at Oxford. A lovely young woman, Beth, is seen shyly removing her bra; the next scene portrays Daniel, coattails flying in the wind as he exuberantly bikes—and falls. That apparently irrelevant fall proves to be a clue.

Chris had been institutionalized after running a woman down. After his release, he ran down and killed the girl with whom Daniel was in love. Finally one can understand why Daniel falls in love with Sandra. Although the full (speculative) answer is given in the "Commentary" section of this essay, the combination of the fall and the destruction, by Daniel's other self, Chris, indicates that it was Beth who became a fallen woman. There is here a typical Potter double reversal, and the evil of the protagonist is doubly displaced. Evil resides elsewhere, in the fallen woman and in the other man. Sandra has become Beth's embodiment. Her less-than-virtuous past, and her present readiness to offer Daniel a "hand job" facilitate the displacement.

It begins to dawn on the scientists that the head is not merely a neuromechanical ledger. Daniel, they come to realize, is somehow aware that his most private and precious memories and his most agonizing experiences are up for grabs. In a re-articulation of the living Daniel Feeld's plea, "No biography," his residual self is able, finally, to communicate: "Let me go!" This is so profoundly unsettling to the scientific team that they realize the torture must cease. One of the scientists, Fyodor, a leader of the underground political movement Reality or Nothing, has been able to imagine a less repressive and more humane society. When he becomes aware that Feeld has feelings, his cause becomes almost sacred; at the cost of his own life, he destroys laboratory and with it, the tank This liberates Daniel's soul, enabling it to ascend through a swirling tunnel of heavenly light to a young girl's call to him, and then, finally, to an angel's embrace. At long, long last, Daniel can rest.

Did Potter really believe in such a Heaven? No one will ever know.[5] Perhaps he could not know himself. It would have depended on which Dennis Potter held his attention.

COMMENTARY

Potter wrote *Karaoke* and *Cold Lazarus* about himself as well as about his view of current affairs. At the outset, Potter's brief quote of Feeld conveyed his only slightly disguised intention to say whatever he pleased. Gilbert[6] quotes actor Roy Hudd (Ben): "It really is Dennis getting [sic] the boot to everyone finally and completely." An amusing if trivial example is a poke at those who express antipathy to cigarette smoking: cigarettes are forbidden in the nightmare society of A.D. 2368. This disgustingly outrageous interference with individual liberties, Potter implies in *Cold Lazarus,* is just what one could expect in that insane society—and what he has experienced in the present one.

These plays are, however, far more substantial than mere vehicles to serve for Potter's emotional catharsis. He obviously intended a posthumous message: Feeld's name suggests an expression of Potter's wish for personal obliteration: Potter's Feeld. By attributing to Feeld a grasping at immortality by cryogenesis, Potter differentiates himself from his created stand-in. It is on this sort of distinction that Potter rested his repeated insistence that what he wrote was not autobiographical. Why did he proclaim that to the very end? Why did he seem to beg, via Feeld's last words, "No biography," for obliteration? Potter was decidedly ambivalent about his own biography, at once exhibitionistic and reticent. His message is, as one should anticipate, complex and obscure: "All clues, no solutions."[7]

There is, of course, a psychodynamic solution. Discovering it necessitates comprehension and appreciation of the fact that Potter had to grapple with intense intrapsychic conflict and that he often approached this, in his creative writing, by using doubles of himself. The role of Nick, the director obsessed with his leading lady, in *Karaoke* is an example: the situation in the play can readily be regarded as a redramatization of the creation of *Blackeyes.*[8] Potter had insisted on directing it himself, and broken with Trodd, the producer of many of his best plays. As director of *Blackeyes,* Potter provided a tastelessly excessive display of Gina Bellman's physical charms. He later acknowledged in an interview that he had fallen in love with her,[9] and he smarted at the contempt many critics had voiced about that play. In *Karaoke* we have a confession and an apology, however disguised and trivialized. Potter's whipping boy, director Nick Balmer, gets thrashed, and admits he got sucked in by his lust. Insofar as Linda, the object of Nick's affection who embroils him in a sexual blackmail, represents Gina Bellman, Potter again gets himself off a hook by passing the buck, characterizing her as "tacky and tarty."[10] Most intriguing to the Potter fan, however, is Potter's subtle bow to Trodd: Nick acknowledges that his associate had been wiser than he about how the play should be filmed.[11]

Potter could not, as did Oscar Wilde, with Dorian Gray, acknowledge the single identity which has been split by the introduction of the double. Potter seemed compelled to deny his own culpability. The denial rests on a reversal: "Pig" Mailion created nothing, and his outlandish greed and sadism rendered him almost unrecognizable as a split-off part of Potter.[12] Potter wove many other strands into *Cold Lazarus,* not all fully successful but nonetheless indispensable for a full exploration of the meaning of these works to Potter, and for a deeper insight into Potter himself. Feeld's male twin, Chris, with whom Feeld would have shared a childhood intimacy was gifted, but became murderously psychotic. In every respect, Chris is the classic literary double for Feeld, and hence for Dennis. Potter has also remembered, or created, a first love, represented in the play by Beth. And, because it was Potter himself who was gravely damaged in childhood, his dramatization of Daniel's fall after his first sexual intimacy with Beth may have been a clue to his own. I suggest a hidden source of guilt as the explanation for Potter having Daniel fall from his bicycle.

The scenes of Daniel's getting raped, commingled with his guilt, are among indications that Potter did not intend to defy every effort to resolve the clues he planted. The most far reaching of these efforts depend upon a selection taken both from his personal admissions and from certain striking details in *The Singing Detective,* suggesting for my Freudian conjecture that Potter's creativity was enhanced and perhaps inspired by the sexual abuse inflicted on him. I speculate that this arose due to his own role in what his biographers have seen only as abuse. It is a tragic and common outcome of the sexual abuse of a child that the child becomes sexually aroused and desirous. The repudiation of that desire can lead to extreme emotional distress.

The salient facts:

1. He tacitly admitted, in "Some Sort of Preface" a degree of complicity in the sexual abuse he suffered, adding that "with a kind of cunning shame I grew for long into someone too wary, too cut off, too introspective, too reclusive, and finally as though out of the blue—or black—too ill to function properly."[13]

2. He did not complain about the abuse he suffered, he said, because he did not want to create family friction, a weak and unconvincing explanation, as was his aside, "It didn't happen all that often," and "It was the drink, you know,"—this in an interview with journalist Ginny Dougary (1992). The admission of repeated sexual encounters is at strong variance with the dreadful scenes of rape which Potter wrote into this and other plays.

3. In *The Singing Detective,* shortly after the boy Phillip returns to his father after having accused his mother of sexual impropriety (and thus driven her to her death), and in a setting almost identical with the sexual tryst between his mother and her lover which he had witnessed, Philip cautions his father to be quiet, mimicking the conversation between the adulterous couple, and slides his

hand into his father's. By way of that brilliant dramatic gesture, the hint of sexual seductiveness—of a shamanistic act designed magically to bring about a desired result of becoming a wife to his father—is entirely obscured and rationalized as a simple expression of a son's love.

Somewhat concealed in the twenty-fourth century drama is an impressive exposition of the role of memory as a continual vital component of every moment of life. Potter expressed closely related concepts a decade previous in an interview with Yentob, which I cited[14] as extraordinarily similar to the views of Freudians:

The past and the present are not in your head in chronological sequence. Neither are they, in terms of the way you discover things about yourself, where an event twenty years ago can follow yesterday instead of precede it . . . If you don't have an alert awareness of the immediate past, then you're being complicit with your seductive present totally . . . I use the immediate past to intrude on the present . . . so that it isn't a thing over there—the past—which is done with. It is actually running around inside us now; and its misconceptions and its values and its correct conception can be seen just that degree more clearly.

Potter also wrote:

The past isn't safely tucked away. Psychoanalysis or your own memory will tell you that what made you in the wider sense—your own culture, your own language, your own communality which you shared with your forebears—is actually shaping the future, too.[15]

Early in this essay, I drew attention to Potter's wish for stars in his crown. His performance during the Bragg interview moved the hearts and minds of a nation, and of many far beyond; it opened the coffers of two tight-fisted capitalistic concerns. The BBC and Channel 4 cooperated—itself a major news story—to provide an astonishing outpouring of money.[16] As important to many viewers as his courage was Potter's apparent religiosity. Some may have been persuaded of Potter's conventional religious beliefs. His pious query, "Will there be stars in my crown . . ." seems to me, however, an artifice, the ad hoc pretense of a man who had repeatedly—and not only in his dramas—belittled the Chapel and its hymns.[17] At the completion of the interview, Potter exulted that he had been "flying." But, BUT!: one cannot withhold respect for a man who, under sentence of imminent death, manages such a spectacle and carries it out with panache. He could not have believed fully the childlike hopes which he voiced; this adds to appreciation of his fearlessness, and has other implications. His allusion to those hopes draws attention to the nature of his passions.

The first remarkable clue to these lies is in the words: "No biography." Potter put them in Feeld's mouth, but Feeld had, at that moment, no evident reason for any such concern. (His twin's finger-pointing when Daniel skipped Chapel illustrates the most innocent of transgressions, as does his forbidden cigarette.) The clue to a resolution comes in the following episode, with indications that Feeld might have felt such consuming guilt as to need to die with his sins undiscovered. But what sins? A well hidden, clever psychological device points toward the answer. Specifically, Daniel's otherwise apparently irrelevant fall from his bicycle, after the implied sexual intimacy, is, as a symbol, momentous: both relevant and reverent. Dennis Potter, closing the books on his life, did not lightly introduce a fall. Fundamentally a profoundly religious man, he achieved everything he set out to do, providing his fortunate audience not with answers but again with cryptic clues set in a dramatic work. Among the marvelous psychological devices Potter contrived, this one is a stunning bit of legerdemain, a dramatist's version of the "gypsy switch." Daniel himself did not suffer a significant Fall from Grace. Beth did. And Potter suggests, dramatically, both that sin and then, by having Daniel's twin, his self-evident alter ego, bang into her, knock her down, and kill her, its classic mortal and moral punishment.

The passions that energize man's noblest acts—as well as, to be sure, man's most vicious—do not arise as an end result of perfusion of love through the heart and soul of a child free of conflict and pain. Potter's passion was inextricably linked—fused, rather—with his early conflicts. But what concerns us primarily with Dennis Potter and his passion is the principal form in which he expressed it, his plays. Whence came his inspiration? It is appropriate to speculate that, as is so often true of great writers, Dennis's creativity was psychologically inspired by the sexual abuse he suffered at ten and the tormenting complex of feelings to which it gave rise.

Why did the dying Potter create a writer who is deeply divided, ambivalent, desperate to leave no biography, yet who perpetuates himself through cryogenesis? This clue corresponds directly to the ambivalence underlying Potter's repeated demand that no one read autobiography into his works, works that are drenched in self-revelation. Often, while attacking and belittling those who thought they recognized the "real" Potter, he seemed in need to substantiate some assumptions by way of admissions about sexual conflict.[18] Nowhere, however, aside from the evidence I cited, did he indicate even obliquely that he recognized any guilt over his participation in his early sexual victimization.

Full resolution depends on a further consideration of clues which he seemed compelled to advance. For example, in *Moonlight on the Highway*,[19] the song, "Lover Come Back to Me," during the protagonist's recounting of the rape, implied the protagonist's wish for passive sexual gratification. Potter injects a far more direct, astonishing confession in *Karaoke*. Lying on the X-ray table as he awaits anal penetration for an enteroscopy, Feeld hallucinates "He can do what he wants, can't he." At that moment, Feeld unwittingly vocalizes (from the song "A Teenager in Love,") the words: "loving you." Asked by the enteroscopist what he had said, Feeld replies: " . . . I was thinking about something else. At least, I *hope* I was thinking about thinking about something else." A more direct implication of an ambivalently desired sodomy would be difficult to create.

That thinly disguised disclosure supports my view that Potter confused such gratification with creative inspiration through God-the-Father's loving gifts. This confusion added power to his creative urge, but impeded and hindered him in its expression. Spin-offs of related expressions in Potter's creative output are frequent. The most direct earlier example is that of Jack Black, in *Follow the Yellow Brick Road*. Agonized, Black tells a physician that he had asked God for a manifestation; what he got was a mouthful of semen and feces. Why? A plausible speculation is that Black was relating a memory or fantasy of having performed fellatio on the sodomizer who has been confused with God.

When, in *The Singing Detective*, Philip Marlow admitted that his heart's desire would have been " to praise the loving God and all his loving creation," instead of writing trash, Potter was baring his deepest longing. When in *Blackeyes*, author Kingsley realized, in agony, that he was a fraud and a failure because he had not fulfilled that same calling (a religious term), Potter again expressed that heart's desire. Potter yearned to go to Heaven and to God, even if he did not himself take literally the words of his hymn. But that childlike aspect of his religiousness, insofar as it actually existed, was not what imbued his passion with pervasive significance. What he finally achieved was to articulate, dramatically, a profoundly disturbing question: the provenance of the (human) mind, the impossibility of reducing it to bundles of neurons and their activities, and the implications of its distinction, if any, from that of the soul. His consuming passion lay in his need to liberate the soul, starting with his own. His exploration of this concern as he approached death constitutes an inmost personal soul-searching, as well as his idiosyncratic approach to the drama of life.

For many, a religious explanation is conjured up by the word "soul," and yet Freud, who used the word (*Seele*), was devoid of religious thinking. Scientists have not succeeded in creating a soul, and most rigorous logicians have persuaded themselves and others that it does not exist, or exists like beauty, only in the eye of the beholder. Perhaps it is fitting to close with the words of a song from another Potter play: " . . . it will have to do, until the real thing comes along."

NOTES

1. Gilbert, W., *Fight & Kick & Bite: The Life and Work of Dennis Potter* (London: Hodder and Stoughton, 1995), pp. 294, 295

2. For example, persons who seemed to be at the brink of dying later allege to have traveled, en route, through a tunnel with light at the end. These beliefs support the notion of an immortal soul and of life after death.

3. However much dramatic license he allowed himself in this, the last of his allegedly nonautobiographical self-dramatizations, it is the clearest expression of Potter's own childhood and youth.

4. Christopher is the second of the series of names with which Dennis was christened.

5. Although Potter does not close in on this issue, the horrors and evils he confronts in the production he has created provide a counterpoint to the one posed in *Clockwork Orange* (Anthony Burgess, *A Clockwork Orange*. New York: Norton, 1987). Burgess recognized that the human soul must be free to do evil in order that man be a moral creature; Potter sought freedom from externally imposed evil, but one can recognize throughout his writings, speeches, and interviews that he sought relief from inner evil.

6. Gilbert, p. 294

7. As he had Marlow express that intent, in *The Singing Detective* (London: Faber and Faber, 1988), p. 140

8. Dennis Potter, *Blackeyes*. BBC-2, 4 episodes, Nov. - Dec. 1989 based on Potter's 1987 novel *Blackeyes* (London: Faber & Faber).

9. When he confessed his infatuation to his wife, she cured him, he claimed, with astringent words: "And you know what my wife said? She said, 'Dennis, don't be such a silly old bugger'—and she was right, that's what I am." Gilbert (p.170) quoted this from a 1993 Potter interview with Leslie White, published in *The Sunday Times,* 12 June 1994.

10. Miss Bellman later revealed that Potter inflicted humiliating and belittling insults, apparently as he began to sense his own failure as director.

11. After several years estrangement, Potter turned to Trodd to produce *Karaoke* and *Cold Lazarus*. Students of the psychology of Dennis Potter will be engrossed by the means with which he then went about clipping Trodd's wings, at no matter what cost to his last two plays. The controversy was aired in many British papers.

12. The same may be surmised with respect to Fyodor. In fact, it was Potter himself who at last set himself free. But he had, unquestionably, an abundance of deeply repressed rage—which he once wrote into the thoughts of Marlow. Fyodor, apart from accidentally leading his colleagues into a near slaughter, shot several before blowing up the tank.

13. Dennis Potter, *Waiting for the Boat* (London: Faber and Faber, 1984), p.33

14. Irving Harrison, " Doubling Back on Dennis Potter's Doubles" (*Psychoanalytical Review* 83: 1, 1996).

15. Dennis Potter, *Potter on Potter* edited by Graham Fuller (London: Faber and Faber, 1993), p.22

16. Potter once explained about his enthusiasm for television that the attack ought to take place within the barracks as well as outside.

17. See, for example, the videotaped Potter-Yentob interview, and the words Potter wrote for Kingsley, in *Blackeyes* (1987).

18. It is impossible to prove or to disprove a psychosomatic etiology, but Potter's belief that his own behavior contributed to his problems, including his disease, must have added to his physical and emotional suffering.

19. Dennis Potter (1973b) Kestral Productions.

Albert Finney with Kenith Trodd on the set of *Karaoke*. Courtesy of Kenith Trodd.

CHAPTER 15

"WHOSE DENNIS IS IT ANYWAY?"

Kenith Trodd

"WHOSE DENNIS IS IT ANYWAY?" IS A FAIR AND WRY enough question to raise, not offensively, at the end of a collection, most of whose contributors cannot have met him nor been involved with his work firsthand. Was Potter his work or does his work amount to Potter?

Given that most of his output demanded a collaboratively industrial process for its realization, should you rely on text as evidence when the text only exists for the purposes of production? Is it that you can't trust the teller, or that in Potter's case the teller is so much part and pain of the tale that the artistic tension may almost be measured by how successfully integrated are the high-octane personal angst and the talent antennae within the particular piece? The material can be as close to Potter as *The Singing Detective* (1986), or as remote from him personally as *Brimstone and Treacle* (1976), but in writing both, he managed to listen out for his incoming audience's willingness to bridge the no-man's-land between their ordinariness and his bizarre territory. When that instinctive listening antenna failed him and he took a crass missionary stance about his material—*Blackeyes* (1989) is the saddest example— the writing hollowed out and the audience stopped welcoming him.

The size and, in a way, the narrowness of his personality made the personal and professional hard to separate. In biographical contexts, I tend to be designated "his friend, the producer" because as he said himself, he felt he knew me longer than anyone except his mother. Because I met him before we were even at Oxford together, he turned to me when he entered the television industry, characteristically preferring an old, difficult acquaintance to making new ones. So gradually, I came to be at the critical frontiers of his activity— life and writing alike.

Producing Potter in the seventies and eighties involved the crucial mutation of script into film or play—all the creative, logistical and financial interplay—

but there were two other areas of struggle that did not apply to the other developing writers I took on. With Dennis, the fight for health and survival shadowed every project. *Double Dare* (1976) is, for me, as much associated with breaking a writer's block through a piece of sexual misadventurism as it is with the emergence of a strange and seminal little film. *Pennies from Heaven* (1978) is a rich achievement, the first masterwork and underrated in the later shadow of the *Detective,* but the parallel drama of its gestation is of Dennis dicing with unproved and perilous medication in a Faustian deal that was to present its invoice with his death less than 20 years later. At the time, though, it provided him with an instant miracle-happiness, vigor and multiplied creativity. Oh, how we danced.

The other struggle was with the television institutions, mainly the BBC that, despite the relative liberalism of the time, repeatedly tried to mutilate or ban his work. *Vote, Vote, Vote for Nigel Barton* (1965) and *Brimstone* were the principal victims, but the harassment hovered all the time and Potter and I became paranoid guerillas fighting . . . what? A golden era of unprecedented expansion and permissiveness. We were, I suppose, always one limb further out than even the prevailing liberality, but this aspect of that time is still, for me, bewilderingly focused, especially if you remember how conventional, frightened and unrelaxed much of Dennis was. However, we certainly played the system well—that duopolistic idyll of British public service broadcasting that lasted almost into the nineties.[1] Sometimes Dennis and I, not always together and well aware that the BBC would not last forever, went off and raided other money—LWT;[2] MGM; Channel Four;[3] Hollywood, both major and dodgy. Not much love was lost amongst all this flirting. They had their passing need of us and we of them. Money was never the point on our side, though Dennis earned plenty. Doing good work was the drive and the bond but we were looking for different satisfactions. By the time of *The Singing Detective* and *Christabel* (1988), our rows and separations were legendary entertainment among colleagues. I think he either wanted me disappeared or exclusively at his disposal, but had no strategy for either aim. For me, he was certainly the most awesome bit of the professional field I liked to play, but giving up the rest wasn't an option, even for love of Dennis.

In 1989, *Blackeyes* (TV: four episodes) became the sad watershed—the moment of wrong turn for Dennis and of bleak rethink about him for the industry, the public and for me. When both Nicolas Roeg[4] and Jon Amiel[5] turned the script down, Dennis decided to direct it himself and an uneasy, ambitious enterprise became grand hubristic folly for him and the BBC alike. I felt well out of it, though relieved rather than proud to have jumped a ship that turned out to be his SS *Titanic.* His true nadir with the BBC didn't come until 1993 when its ailing drama department encouraged him to put more than half a million pounds of his own money into making *Midnight Movie* and

Albert Finney in *Karaoke*. Courtesy of Kenith Trodd.

bankrolled a project that elementary in-house savvy should have seen as un-workable either critically or commercially, even with Dennis's fearsome pressure behind it. It didn't work and he lost every penny.

Quite some time before his final illness, I think Dennis was becoming confused by the spell of his own eminence. His fame and wealth had nowhere to go in Britain except maybe upward to hit the roof. When he was seriously honored internationally in New York in 1992, he scorned the retrospective of his past work and gave most of his limited energy and pain-free time to hyping *Secret Friends,* which some local, myopic enthusiasts were trying to launch as a movie. Yet even then, his dross would give way to shafts of something like the old gold. Though he was at icy odds with me, he let me persuade him to write a piece for the event, "Downloading,"[6] which includes the most gripping description of the physical writing process he ever gave; and at one of the seminars, he admitted—grudgingly but without vanity—to being completely overwhelmed by the emotional punch of a *Singing Detective* clip I had programmed rather casually, with an eye to its technical interest more than its depth. For its creator, publicly confronted by a charged sliver of his best work after some years, this was a moment of endearing authenticity in an otherwise arid and ungracious week.

From then until the onset of his last illness, we had little contact. He had asked me to produce *Lipstick on Your Collar* (1993), but his fury at not being allowed to direct it himself complicated and confused the edgy and insecure basis of our professional reunion. It didn't last and he eventually allocated me the credit of, I think, "creative consultant"—the generous and ironic backhand ever in good play. In early 1994, when I was starting production of the movie *Circle of Friends* (1995)[7], he tried again—this time to ask me to be part of his final plans. Three months to live, two last hefty pieces of work to start and finish and a master plan to ensure they were made posthumously to his characteristic and imperious agenda. At our first meeting, me catatonic and migrained, he relaxed and on vintage form (hey, who's sick here?), the irony and barbed affection worked just short of overtime: "I only have one real fear of death. It's that you might get asked to speak at my memorial service!"

Stoked by ever rising doses of morphine and his 30 year learned skills at dealing with pain, he determined to marshal all his talents for the last crusade. His public campaign majored on the Bragg interview,[8] in which he defined to the key mandarins of British television the offer they could not refuse him—ideal production and broadcast conditions for the scripts he was going to bequeath. He also achieved a superb redefinition of himself for the viewing public, erasing the memory of "Dirty Den," his Murdoch press sobriquet since *Blackeyes*[9] and bringing in the stricken sage—eloquent, insightful and probably touching more hearts than at the peak of his popularity as a dramatist.

He and I ended pretty well personally. A final face-to-face goodbye when he had terrifically the right words and I didn't, then for the last two weeks, an almost daily phone call: me working in Ireland, he still wanting to work, on the edge of his beloved Forest. Friendly and mutually comforting, but again, he was better at it and his game stayed keen. Once, late on, I dared to raise an ongoing contentious professional issue. Instant and unanswerable response: "If you go on bringing that up, I won't be able to die happy."

I believe the prospect of death brought out much of his best in both behavior and writing. *Karaoke* and *Cold Lazarus* (1996, posthumous), if he had merely turned them out as his next deliveries, were certainly going to be fairly dire. Written as last testaments, they are firstly spectacular physical achievements, triumphs of driven mind over failing matter but making no allowances for the rushed feat of stamina, they are still far classier pieces of writing for television than anyone else, including Potter, had managed for years. The sheer scale, cheek and originality of *Lazarus* entitle it to credit beyond any reservations about the production or the fact that there could be no considered debate with Dennis about revisions.

Karaoke is a miniature revisiting and embellishment of his major themes and obsessions, with a finale that rediscovers the title song from *Pennies from Heaven* in a context witty and elegiac, a celebration of his artistic landscape. *Karaoke,* in fact, can be taken as a study in creative dilemma of the Potter kind. The main character, a writer of course, finds or puts himself in a world where passersby speak his lines, women from his scripts are re-embodied in restaurants and he is bedevilled by visions, some authentic and some just neurotic. He is possessed and confused by his own creations and is in a race with death, but he plots his own escape route, heading to his final artistic delivery. It will be a piece intended to immortalize him and he will still be its hero—as a disembodied head.

The wrought connectedness of *Karaoke* makes it typical Potter, the emotional validation makes it very good Potter. And yet both final pieces were undervalued almost to derision by British reviewers and audiences. There was clearly a critical agenda set by one or two individuals in advance of transmission, which enabled people to feel they needn't pay serious attention, that there was a get-out, an excuse for saying "We've had too much Potter; he's been indulged too much and postmodern is surely, legitimately, post-Dennis." His own absence from the launch climate—sounding the keynote, insisting on the importance, working the media—made this detracting tactic easier to operate. By 1996, his core audience good-willing his next appearance had much diminished and the structures that, for all their periodic resistance, had fostered him for decades were themselves under question and on the wane. A few years further on and although the BBC can still afford—just—to whistle in the light, all the public service providers have their share, their vividness, their credibility, their self-belief steadily on the public slide. Regular scandals about both upmarket documentaries and crappy daytime chat shows—both extremes now desperate hostage to ratings hysteria—are not just gleeful fodder for Murdoch's tabloids to destabilize his rivals.[10] The slippage is real, the land has receded and whether Potter would still manage a foothold is mercifully pointless guesswork.

So what is around of him? Leanish pickings. Internet sites slowly multiplying; an "official" biography, not terribly well received. Other books fueling some kind of appetite for him, college courses presumably ditto. A literary estate, not particularly user-friendly, administered by a still-grieving daughter, an agent/confidante and a long-serving accountant. Maybe some texts findable in print but in the form it matters, production, most of his huge output is inaccessible. *The Singing Detective* you might find on video, but *Pennies from Heaven* only in book form without even the lyrics of the songs and such published texts are suspect—based, usually, on unrevised first script drafts. The BBC, which owns much of the material, shows little interest and that little is casual and misplaced. In the autumn of 1998, it tried to show *Brimstone and Treacle* but broadcast an embarrassingly incomplete edit. So there is a current samizdat fostered by indifference and contractual paralysis. Without the black prince himself around to talk it up, can he live again beyond the cognoscenti to nourish us as widely as he wished? He flourished in a cocoon of mass media now anachronistic. That oxygen is used up. So I wonder—how much of his work can survive in some new element? Is there anyone for Dennis?

NOTES

1. "Duopolistic idyll": until the advent and challenge of satellite television in the late 1980s, spearheaded by Rupert Murdoch, British television was dominated, on the one hand, by the British Broadcasting Corporation, and on the other, ITV (Independent Television), which, though commercial and funded by advertising, was nevertheless heavily regulated and subject to much the same public service criteria as applied at the BBC. Such a postwar television settlement has frequently been labeled a "duopoly."
2. "LWT": London Weekend Television—an ITV company that first began broadcasting in 1968. In the mid-1990s, it became the victim of a takeover by another ITV company, Granada.
3. "Channel Four": Britain's fourth terrestrial TV network launched in November 1982—funded by commercial advertising but subject to a clear public service remit to cater for "minority" tastes and interests.
4. Nicolas Roeg: eminent British film director of such seventies "art house" hits as *Don't Look Now* (1973) and *The Man Who Fell to Earth* (1976). In 1987, he collaborated with Potter on the feature film, *Track 29*.

5. Jon Amiel: director of *The Singing Detective* who subsequently graduated to making Hollywood feature films such as *Sommersby* (1992), *Copycat* (1995) and *Entrapment* (1999).

6. Dennis Potter, "Downloading," published in The Official Programme Guide to Complete Retrospective Season, *The Television of Dennis Potter*, The Museum of Television and Radio, New York, 23 January - 31 May 1992, pp.55–58.

7. *Circle of Friends*, dir.: Pat O'Connor; scr.: Andrew Davies (ad. from Maeve Binchy novel); co-produced by Kenith Trodd for Savoy Pictures, 1995. Amongst the cast of this film were Saffron Burrows (Nan) and Ciaran Hinds (Prof. Flynn), who would both later be cast in the posthumous productions of *Karaoke* and *Cold Lazarus* as, respectively, Sandra Sollars and Fyodor Glazunov.

8. "The Bragg interview": reference to Dennis Potter's famous final TV interview, conducted by broadcaster Melvyn Bragg and first transmitted on British television (Channel Four) on 5 April 1994.

9. "Dirty Den" was the nickname of a fictional character, Den Watts, who featured in the popular BBC TV soap opera, *Eastenders* (1985 -) during the 1980s. After the critical bloodbath Potter received in Britain for *Blackeyes* in 1989, it came to be applied to the dramatist by journalists of the British tabloid press, particularly those working for *The Sun* and the *News of the World*: both of which are owned by Potter's *bete noire*, Rupert Murdoch.

10. "upmarket documentaries and crappy daytime chat shows": in late 1998 - early 1999, scandal erupted around the alleged faking of factual programs on British television eg., *The Connection* (Carlton TV, 1997), a documentary about drug smuggling that was exposed in the press as having been largely faked, plus tabloid stories about the use of actors as fake guests on British daytime talk shows. Such scandals not only served as "pennies from heaven" for British newspapers embroiled in a desperate circulation war, but seemed to be an index of declining standards in British TV as well.

DENNIS POTTER

A Personal Interview (10 May 1990)

EDITORS' INTRODUCTION BY JOHN COOK

As KENITH TRODD ASKS IN THE FINAL ESSAY OVERLEAF, without "the black prince" himself around to "sound the keynote"; "to insist on the importance" and "to talk things up," can he live again? Well, in one small but significant respect, he can. In May 1990, after some months of chasing, I finally managed to persuade Dennis Potter to agree to an interview with me. I was then knee-deep into researching my Ph.D. thesis on him (it would eventually become the book *Dennis Potter: A Life on Screen,* published in 1995, a year after Potter's death) and I had managed to interview nearly all the principal colleagues who had worked with him over the years: producers such as Ken Trodd and Rick McCallum, directors such as Jon Amiel (*The Singing Detective*) and Piers Haggard (*Pennies from Heaven*) and so on. It was when I managed to get some material from Lord Mayhew (who as plain old Christopher had interviewed Potter, then a young student, for a TV program on class in 1958) that the normally reclusive playwright finally had to concede defeat: "Christ, this little so-and-so is digging here, there and everywhere. I better see him" was how Potter recalled for me when we met (I think, only half jokingly) the reasons why he finally agreed to an interview.

On 10 May 1990 (a week before the writer's 55th birthday), I nervously showed up at the London office of Judy Daish, his literary agent, at the appointed hour. Potter, of course, was late. When he did arrive, he immediately ordered some champagne to be brought down from the floor upstairs. He began by confessing that he wasn't feeling very well that day and that he was in the middle of writing: a screenplay draft of the D. M. Thomas novel, *The White Hotel* (then intended for director David Lynch[1]), the complexities of adapting which for the screen he was really struggling with. He got the champagne and began to pour out a glass to drink. Suddenly, he looked up: "Oh—I suppose you'll be wanting some of this too." He then proceeded to pour out a glass for me; his arthritically bent and twisted hands, I noticed, cupping the bottle awkwardly.

With that, it was down to the business of the interview. I switched on the tape recorder, and for the next approximately two and a half hours, I got drunk listening to Dennis Potter: in both senses, of course. *He* talked, drank and chain-smoked; *I* listened, sipping my champagne and occasionally interjecting some questions. Any semblance of an order or structure to the interview quickly went out of the window—there was no way Potter would be pinned down too closely to *that* kind of an agenda. So, at times, I was aware of how I was going to have to play devil's advocate with him in order to tease out what I wanted: flushing out, in a sense, what his work *was* by allowing him to say what it was *not*. Something of that, hopefully, comes over in these extracts. But on the whole, he was very benign and cooperative, in contrast to his apparently usual overcompensating aggressiveness with strangers. I think this may have been because I was young (then 24), someone from outside the media world, and because through my research, I had proven to him I was enthusiastic and knew a little bit about his work. Who knows—the whole interview may have been as some kind of reward for having temporarily managed to penetrate the normal veil of seclusion and secrecy. Whatever the case, it turned out to be a very friendly, only gently sparring affair.

On that day, neither of us could have known that he was only four years away from death or that in retrospect, the interview would take on a greater significance in that it would turn out to be the only time in his life, really, that Potter ever spoke to an independent researcher about his writing; independent, that is, of the normal platforms he would use to manage the publicity of his own work: interviews with journalists, public events, TV and so on. By contrast, this was a much more private and to that extent "unmanaged" occasion; I suppose, fraught with risk for a protective writer like Potter, in the sense that I could have been anyone and in theory, could have asked anything.

Looking back on my interview in hindsight, I see now that this was probably a more unusual request for Potter to accede to than I fully appreciated at the time. And I think, too, this is what makes it particularly interesting, for here is not the "public" Potter in front of the TV studio lights. Not that I am claiming this is the "real" private man, with all his defenses down, but I do think that in this, you see a slightly different side of Potter to the creature of the TV screen, precisely because he is not having to perform—at least, not quite in the same way. Also, a lot of the things he has to say in this interview are, to my knowledge, not replicated elsewhere in any of the other literature.

For many years, the interview lay untranscribed. I used short extracts of it to illustrate my arguments in *Dennis Potter: A Life on Screen* and in 1995, bits of it were also published in *The Observer* newspaper in Britain.[2] But substantial extracts have never been published verbatim in book form—until now. And the reason that I should decide that it appear here, now, at the end of a collection devoted to others' views of his writing, should be abundantly clear to anyone who has made it this far through the book: Potter himself would always have wanted to have the last word on his work. So we are going to give it to him. . . . Let the "black prince" ride again!

I began our interview by asking Potter why he always chose to fictionalize so many aspects of his own life in his writing? Was biography (as everyone apparently seemed to think) the key to understanding the writer and his work?

DENNIS POTTER: Uh, I don't know whether there is a key—that sort of reductionist criticism is, well, it's one tenable one way of looking . . . but I think there are a series of links, not keys.

JOHN COOK: You fictionalize in order to seek, really?

DP: You fictionalize what?

JC: Elements of your life—I'm not going to go down the road of saying a work like *The Singing Detective* (1986) is all straightforward autobiography . . .

DP: Thank you very much. . . . No, *The Singing Detective* played with the autobiographical genre. It pretended to be autobiographical because that's a very powerful way of writing. One thinks "Oh, this must be truth." And of course, it isn't . . . Autobiographies are a complicated series of lies. H. G. Wells said, "Who would write novels if they could write autobiography flat out ?" Nabokov oddly said the same order of things. He said, "Of course it's not me but if what I was writing was not in some sense *true* other than my own imagination, it wouldn't come across as true." And some people boast, "Oh, it's all out of my head," etc. etc. but of course, everything they've experienced and lived through and some of the closest emotional things they've experienced will sooner or later outcrop in a poem or a novel or a play, if they're writers. It's inevitable. But to deliberately choose to use what *appears* to be like one is in the same order as choosing to use, say, "the musical" genre or "the detective story" genre in that genres in themselves—i.e., audience expectations of a certain ritual form of behavior about "the narrative"—are very powerful, very potent weapons in the writer's hands. So I'm alert to what you mean when you say "key" but it's just simply not the case. It's choice of method. I choose the autobiographical genre to appear to be more self-exposing than it actually is because in fact, I'm a reclusive character and I don't expose myself. I appear to.

I actually despise biographies: they're hidden novels . . . And I do think that biographical criticism is such an easy way of assuming you get, well in effect what you've said, the key to a body of work. And I just know that that is not the case.

JC: It's obviously not the case that such and such is straightforward autobiography when it comes into the work. You argued this in almost every interview you did at the time of *The Singing Detective*. You said you got very irritated by it.

DP: I did and do because it's to diminish what one has achieved or not achieved, whatever the case may be. But also what it does show, what it does prove is that the quote "autobiographical" unquote convention is an extraordinarily powerful one—perhaps the most powerful one that is left in the hands of a writer. You know, because of the way writing now is and because of the styles of realism, so-called naturalism, the documentary style which has invaded everything: the plethora of television programs that say "this is the truth," all that. That's reflected into novels and plays and so on, so that people want to know "Is this *true?*" which is a very curious question to ask in that sense about a play or a novel. It should be true in another sense, of course: I mean "art" and "truth" (I apologize for using the word "art" but as a shorthand term—easiest way for me to talk). You can tell a writer who is a liar, not by the events but by the style. It is style that is truth.

JC: Style is truth?

DP: Yes, because if you get a piece of overwrite or flatulent writing, you know that it is *emotionally* untrue and it is the style which tells you that, while the event itself may well be factual. I mean, somebody could sit down and write their life, for example, and be absolutely factually accurate and the style would be a lie if it was pompous, or if it was fickle, or if it played with the truth in that way. That is the truth to me: it's a far more important area of truth-telling than saying, "Well, did X actually happen and was that followed by Y or did Y actually precede it?" It's the truth of the content, the truth emotionally, the truth socially, the truth in any useful sense as a manipulable, handleable thing . . .

JC: Let's move on, then, to the emotional truths of your life, as opposed to the mere facts. You've mentioned in other interviews how the topography of your childhood was biblical.

DP: Or the other way round—that my view of the Bible became the Forest of Dean.

JC: So it was a complete world in other words—the Forest of Dean?

DP: Yes, but I believe, I suspect, that any child anywhere sees that world as "the world." It just so happens that the Forest of Dean was green and hilly and gray and reared up between two rivers and the dialect was "thee" and "thou," just like in the King James Bible. It was perfectly natural to speak "thee," "thou," and the more tenderly you felt, the more certainly you would use it. My father would always say "Is't thou alright, old butty?" if it was a kindly question: "Are you alright?" But the vividness, in particular the New Testament, I suppose, allowed the landscape around me to be *that* landscape. It did not seem to be very different from any illustrations one saw. There was a big pond outside the pit, for example: Cannop Pond which went into a string of ponds which, to me, was Galilee, even though they were a bit small. But as a child, of course, they seemed enormous then. They seem small now. And the lanes and the trees and the sloping and rather, sometimes, strange rocks in fields and sheep wandering about the roads. All that, to a six-, seven-year-old, would certainly be the landscape of the Holy Land.

JC: I get the sense that childhood to you is a sort of lost land and this comes out in your writing.

DP: I think childhood is to everyone a lost land . . .

JC: . . . a lost land which can't be reclaimed because as you grow up, everything gets smaller, like Alice.

DP: There's that but also not only does it get smaller, it's drained of some wonder. The loss of Eden is personally experienced by each and every one of us as we leave the wonder and magic and also the pains and terrors of childhood into—well, it's the same reason why children can write poetry and then stop when they reach, unless they're poets, they stop when they reach puberty. And when the temptations and torrents of the world in a more adult sense come to them, their behavior becomes more restrained; social conventions become more important: everything, discipline, self-discipline, all those things become of greater relevance. Whereas the discipline is imposed by an adult, when children are amongst themselves, it's all continual fidget and movement, exploration, speculation, wonder, which, in a sense, to lose that is to lose Eden, is to be expelled from the Garden. And I only use that metaphor as a continuous one because I believe that if when Jesus said "Be as little children," that is what is meant. In other words, be as open and be as innocent, if you like, although in post-Freudian times, "innocence" is in quotes. But the knowledge that we have about what it is to be human that we have as a child is something that we necessarily *must* lose but we don't have to lose it totally, if we can remember. We remember an Eden even though it wasn't perfect but it was an Eden in terms of its possibilities and potentialities.

JC: You touched on innocence in post-Freudian times. There is a sense which comes out in several of your plays of the nature of "original sin." You talk about the innocence of childhood in one breath but there's also, for example, I'm thinking of the scene in *Blue Remembered Hills* (1979) where the kids kill the squirrel . . .

DP: Oh, children are very cruel, yes. So I'm using "innocence" in that older sense, not innocence as we would define it now in terms of Freudian or any subsequent way of analyzing human behavior but in that openness of both the love and the cruelty, the joy and the despair, naiveté in a sense. Yes, of course, children are extraordinarily cruel little creatures.

JC: But yet they don't know it . . .

DP: They don't know it. But I believe that is basically what it is to be human. I mean even as we talk at this very minute, somebody is being tortured and there are hideous, almost unspeakable cruelties being committed every second of the day which, if we were really angels, we couldn't bear to walk out on to the street knowing that this was going on.

JC: So hence the device of adult actors as children in a sense. We are still children in a way because we do not know.

DP: We can be, we can be. But the point is we do know as adults or should know more. We do know more but we don't know enough and people can be very unthinkingly callous. But the trouble is, you see and what tempers this, is that people can be thinkingly callous and deliberately cruel.

JC: Which you would define as "evil."

DP: Evil, yes. Evil. And I would even go so far as to say that "Evil" can sometimes be a noun and not just an adjective.

JC: There's a sense of integration (now that we've moved on to a religious discussion, really) in a lot of your work between God and the world. As a child, God, the world and the self are all integrated and it's something that we lose.

DP: It's something that we lose that some religious people are able to hold on to.

JC: Is that the spiritual yearning—to try and reclaim that integration; that God is within you as well as—?

DP: Within and without. I—I just sometimes very occasionally am conscious of what I would call "grace" but it's corroded by intellectual reservation, by the sheer improbabilities of thinking in that mode. And yet it remains within me—I wouldn't call it yearning. Yearning? Yes—I suppose that's a lazy way of putting it but somehow, the sense continually threatening to be present and occasionally flickering into life of the world behind the world which, of course, is what all metaphors and in a sense, all art (again to use that word), all of that is about the world behind the world. By definition. It is nonutilitarian and has no meaning. Or *appears* to have no meaning and the strangest thing that human speech and human writing can do is create a metaphor. Not just a simile: not just Rabbie Burns saying "My love is *like* a red, red rose," but in a sense, it *is* a red rose. That is an amazing leap, is it not?

JC: Some would argue it's just language, just words.

DP: It *is* "just words" but what is "just words"? What is this distinguishing thing that the human animal has? Where does it come—how is it borne up? What depths does it hint at that we cannot get to and yet feel conscious of?

JC: You talk about the "shimmer on the materiality of the brute" . . .

DP: Do I? I say "shimmer," do I? My God, I must have had a lazy day, that day.

(laughter)

JC: . . . beyond brute reality . . .

DP: The world *is* material, obviously. By definition.

JC: And brutish?

DP: And brutish in the sense of animal.

JC: Bestial?

DP: Well, except we use that as pejorative terms. Material when it is thing and brute when it's life is what it basically is. And on top of that there is grace or intelligence or human culture which is a very fragile and sometimes almost unsustainable thing, layer: not thing, nonthing but a substance that creates language, metaphors, love—I mean, if you can divorce love, say biologically, from sexual desire and so on. Maybe you can't but humans believe they can or they sentimentalize their sexual yearnings into quote "love" unquote. In that act, they half-recognize something which, for want of a better world, we call "spiritual." But it's almost impossible to wrestle with these concepts—you can only do it by metaphor . . .

. . . JC: The village school which is a prominent motif throughout the work . . .

DP: Well, it's in a couple of pieces out of what—50?

JC: A couple of very prominent pieces out of 50.

DP: Alright, yeh.

JC: The schoolteacher: the eagle-eyed God almost, programming retribution . . .

DP: Yes. I didn't really know any such person as that but just one's feeling about the authority and awe of—all teachers were disciplinarians in those days. They wouldn't hesitate to hit. But there was no venom—I mean, the character in the plays is more like the witch in *The Wizard of Oz* (1939). And again you know, using caricature sometimes is deliberate. I sometimes snigger to myself when a critic says about a character: "this was tending towards caricature." Well, I think "what the fuck!": it was caricature to start with, you know!

JC: It's a cartoon world in a sense . . .

DP: In a way and by manipulating very bright colors, sometimes you can get, you can release—the same way you use a cheap song—you can suddenly release a real feeling by juxtaposing the cheap song with the real, with something which is opposite, counter to the song and the combination of the two can produce that other layer. So cartoon(-ish) characters can do this. Also, you can make people accept a caricature (that's why they *are* caricatures, they readily do) and then tip that character over into something else, so that suddenly the caricature is talking of real pain, real feeling. You've taken people there because they accept the caricature or the cliché and suddenly you can play with the fact that they've gone along with it and you can release something else.

JC: There's a scene—out of your 50 works—which recurs . . . the betrayal of one child by another in the classroom . . .

DP: Oh, the double scene—again, deliberate use of what was in *Stand Up, Nigel Barton* (1965) and *The Singing Detective?*

JC: That was a deliberate reworking, then, was it?

DP: Oh, absolutely, yes. That was why we then sought to cast the same teacher [played by Janet Henfrey in both productions] just to make sure, to emphasize. The impossibility of referring to something 20 years ago in television terms—nevertheless, I was arrogant enough to attempt to do that. You know to say, yes, there is, this medium *does,* after all, have some continuity and so does the work of any one person in it have some continuity.

JC: We could argue about that—I mean, how many people, apart from people who have followed your work closely, would cop that?

DP: Quite a few did judging by my letters. People remember odd things, you see and usually, they remember things connected with children. People remember *Blue Remembered Hills,* for example and astonishingly, lots of people remember that as being played by children, rather than adult actors. Lots of people remember *Stand Up, Nigel Barton* and they see in their heads as they remember, they see children in that classroom.

JC: And perhaps even themselves as children.

DP: Maybe but they certainly see children and because the scene had a certain dynamic—it was about hunting down and blame and punishment—people remember it. So obviously, not someone who was six or seven at the time but quite a few hundred thousand people remember.

JC: That's interesting but going back—that scene, the *Nigel Barton/Singing Detective* one in which the main character, in betraying, becomes a writer, in a sense. A liar . . .

DP: Yes, well—writing and lying . . .

JC: . . . a storyteller. It seems to me—is it impertinent to ask if that comes from—?

DP: Why do you want to ask that? I mean does it give any more kick or relevance? Does it in any way address itself to the scene to know whether any such thing *actually* happened?

JC: I don't know. You can perhaps tell me . . .

DP: I can't tell you why. It's just ordinary, prurient curiosity and gossip. Yes, it's of interest but I can't see that it makes—in a way—say it were the case that something very much less dramatic but similar had happened, in a way that diminishes the piece . . . People are infinitely curious and the point is that curiosity is exactly what I'm trying to use and if I said, "Oh well, that was partly true; that was totally untrue," I would destroy the very machine that I'm building—the engine. I would be draining the fuel out of it.

. . . You see, biographical criticism—it doesn't really *discover* anything and by that, I don't mean the relationship between the so-called "writer" and the so-called autobiographical things. I'm slightly concerned—not in any defensive way but as a writer that . . . no one seems to *get* what it is I've been trying to do over all these years which is to build a body of work that *is* consistent with itself, that *does* send out tentacles and relationships and nudges and hints to other work within a sequence of work and will unashamedly repeat themes, motifs, because I believe that would be acceptable in a novel, it would be acceptable in the theater, it would be acceptable in any other . . . form. But because television is so unregarded and treated normally with such intellectual contempt, it became all the more imperative, having thought about it and thought about it and thought about it, that I tried to do what other television writers had not tried to do—because usually they then wanted to go on and write for something else.

JC: Well, the interest . . . if people are thinking it's elements from a life, the reason is because they can't believe that someone has actually, incredibly done this. And you're saying that you've actually . . .

DP: I'm claiming that but I'm acknowledging at the same time, I will use emotional truths and certain actual geographical facts, certain real things I will weave into that same tapestry, like every writer does, except I've done it much more explicitly because I'm using that genre as my deliberate method of making connections—connections, obviously, with my own life but connections I think with everyone's lives. And not even just British people's lives either . . .

It's very interesting. Several times, publishers have written to me saying, "Will you write your autobiography," and I say "no": I've had a very reclusive life. The most dramatic thing that's happened to me is illness. I have a 30-year-*long* marriage. I have three adult children. Sometimes, I get drunk and sometimes I'm a hell-raiser but I mean, I was over 40 before I even left England.

JC: On the other hand, you have had quite a remarkable life if you look at your career as opposed to your—

DP: If you look at the page, yes, and the page as sold on; but what was it—Oxford, a bit of. Yes—I manoeuvred my way along the class system, put it that way. And I was cursed by having a very high IQ which is not a blessing as a child. It's a blessing in what it leads to as an adult but it's not too clever to be clever as a kid, is it?

JC: To go on—it's very interesting what you've said about the links between all the works. You've really set up an area—it's interesting people should think the work is simple biography or autobiography. Why? Is it because you've used your . . . ?

DP: Because I use it with skill and I give it that present tense kind of immediacy which is—well, this is not easy for me to talk about, why they should . . . my answer to that is because I've done it skilfully, so it comes across as true. It comes across as characters you can't beat off. They're like somebody coming up to you and that's what I'm after. Obviously not all of them. I seldom pull it off in the way that I want to but that's my intention and that's why it feels like that.

JC: But in a sense, it's both success and both failure in your terms because people think—this man is just using . . . What was it one critic said? That he's "disembowelling his own . . ."

DP: " . . . his own psychological condition"[3] which is just, you know. I thought "Jesus Christ" and then at the time of *Blackeyes* (1989), the pain of which is still bumping within me, a previewer in *The Independent* newspaper [Stephen Pope] said "How does he get away with writing the same play over?"[4] And I thought "you philistine shitbag." Yes, you can easily put it that way if you're hostile . . .

JC: *Blackeyes* also brought complaints about the treatment of women in your work.

DP: People did get flustered. Misogyny is the common noun which, to me, is crap. The assumption that by describing what men do, I therefore approve or subscribe to that behavior. I think people have lost sight of what fiction is. I believe that men treat women badly. I know they do. I take it for granted that men exploit women as a fact to deal with and show. That doesn't mean that a) I do (because I don't believe I do as a person) or b) that I approve of it. I'm at a loss when given that as an attribute of my work.

JC: Also: the prostitute figures in your work. Prostitution recurs again and again.

DP: Well—it's the most vivid sexual exchange in its most basic and corrupted form. It's a very direct way of saying "what goes on." As George Bernard Shaw used to say, in what sense sometimes is marriage at root—could it be the same thing?

JC: In plays and films, such as *Schmoedipus* (1974) and *Track 29* (1987), you seem to regard sexuality as having its roots in terms of the relationship between a mother and son. And yet you have rejected Freudian psychoanalysis, with its idea of the Oedipus complex, as "one of the failed myths of our time"?

DP: It's also one of the most beautiful myths but it *is* a myth. There's very little empirical evidence that it has any value for a patient and even so, it is an extraordinarily uneconomic way of dealing with these outbreaks of mental illness we have.

JC: Have you yourself ever encountered such analysts?

DP: No, not Freudians. Just ordinary therapy. In 1962–63, when I was first in hospital and desperately ill beyond any measure I could possibly tell you, I asked to see such a guy who was attached to the hospital. And the dermatologist said, "Oh, you mean Freud and all that stuff"? I said "No—I just feel I need to talk to someone." I had three meetings with this guy at Charing Cross [London hospital] which I found both useful and threatening. What was useful about it was the very fact that I had the appointment enabled me to talk about some of the things that were troubling me—not to him but to others who were close to me. And that was like a turning point:

acknowledging I was in desperation was important. That was before I had written any of these plays and it may well have been that had I not acknowledged I was in extremis, I would never have written at all. That's the difference between psychoanalysis and therapy. Psychotherapy is a much more utilitarian and functional thing; an adjunct to a sick body. Analysis is a whole construct of myth, beautiful and creative in its own way, like the Oedipal myth, Thanatos and Eros. It's a very good way of looking at certain dramatic forces within us as people, but as a tool in medicine, it is extraordinarily limited and probably not effective empirically speaking. Yet as a piece of literary criticism . . . Freud's best writing is about Dostoevsky. It's a kind of displaced literary criticism.

JC: At one time, however, you believed your illness was psychosomatic.

DP: If you suddenly find yourself covered in lesions or scales or what have you, your normal tendency is to believe that there is something in you that is responsible. Especially if you are a Protestant. I mean, if you look at the prayers for the sick, it will say "cast out your sin." . . . The assumption is the sick person is a sinner. . . . And it's very easy to let that lodge if you're really desperately ill and everything seems to be collapsing: all your ambitions, your hopes and you don't know how you're going to earn your living, all that. The assumption is that the poison in your mind is on your skin. Everybody has poison in their mind. I know that for a fact. It's just that some people have got easier access to their emotions than others. I always remember Ann Scott, who was story editor on a number of my TV plays, saying to me, "You've got almost instant access to your emotions." And that's dangerous—dangerous for those who know you and very dangerous for yourself . . . I'm not going to say anything about my own personal struggles with my own nature except that at the end of the day, I have, through a long route and through my own Calvaries or whatever, remained, somehow or other against all the odds, a Christian. It's actually in the end what I believe in, even though intellectually, I am appalled by the very baldness of such a statement. I know that at root that is what I turn and respond to; that is what tortures and torments me. And whatever travails, mental or physical, social or sexual or whatever, that I go through, I end up, somehow or other, getting my life into order. And in the getting my life into order, my work improves or broadens or widens, the more surely I *tame* myself and put it all on the page.

This was why I was reclusive in that whatever struggles or mishaps, whatever happened to me as a child, whatever events—I mean, I was sexually assaulted when I was ten years of age. That is true. I was. A lot of things can be traced to that but [to] trace *everything* to that is absolute nonsense. People endure what they endure and they deal with it. It may corrupt them. It may lead them into all sorts of compensatory excesses in order to escape the nightmare and the memory of that but it is a footnote—or a sidenote, not a footnote. It's important but it's not *that* important. Because still, you're left with your basic human strivings and dignity and talent.

The odd thing about me which will explain some arrogances but will also explain some humilities is that I've been aware, I should say from about the age of six, that I had talent. And because I was brought up in a certain way, by decent people in an environment that implied certain standards, it was, whether through the chapel or through the home, the Parable of the Buried Talents which was always the one I first responded to. Just as I would expect somebody who was musical or somebody who played football or somebody who danced . . . not to get drunk on a Friday night and to train . . . similarly, there was an obligation on me—certainly, to use like an instrument, *some* of the details of my own life. Maybe, it was a delusion. It's one of the forms of sickness to have such a delusion *if* one didn't have the talent. And it would have been a tragedy, unbearably large in its dimensions, if I hadn't had the talent because it felt as if I had. I knew in the Forest of Dean, when I was looking at the banner in the chapel or whatever, I *knew* I had talent and I felt that imperative upon me. The early life was about how to express it—calling for political change and so on. Yet all the time, I never stopped writing. So maybe illness was a gift in the sense it rammed home to me that not only was there no choice, literally there was no choice: if you want to earn your bread, that's what you've got to do because you won't get any other kind of work. This maybe explains the *canon* of work [because] knowing that means you can make connections and that you are determined to make connections and that you want the *whole* work ultimately to be judged all together in the end. So some of those words, symbols and images from *that* childhood will continually be part and parcel of my personality. And that can lead to great misunderstanding—with people emphasizing this or that aspect of your life or that history, that stage; some people thinking I was very shy and withdrawn; some people thinking I was very arrogant, bullying and aggressive. They're looking, you see, at just one angle—at one piece of the self-same journey.

The fact I see it as a journey is obviously due to my childhood images but it's also the fact that I was given—*given*—talent. And if you're given it, it is your obligation to use it . . . [Hence] I *am* conscious of a body of work—and this may be pretentious and arrogant and all those sorts of things will come in, which is the other danger—but I am, for better or worse, conscious of a longer *purpose*. And sometimes I show it and sometimes I don't; sometimes I let other people see it and sometimes, I don't . . . I am weaving threads and connections. There is a sense in which I could abandon all my previous work as inadequate and incomplete versions of the work that one day, I will write. That is what I mean. Someday, somehow, all these threads will come together in one piece of work which will finally do what I'm at, maybe. And then I'll kill myself . . .

© John R. Cook, 1990.

NOTES

1. Lynch eventually passed on directing Potter's screenplay version of *The White Hotel* and current plans are that it will be directed by Yugoslavian director Emir Kusterica.
2. Short extracts from the interview were published in Richard Brooks, "A Matter of Life and Death," *The Observer: Review,* 4 June 1995, pp.2–3.
3. The article Potter clearly noticed too was: Lynne Truss, "Margins," *The Listener,* 15 March 1990, p.48. The accusation led Potter to write a stinging letter of reply, denying the accusation. It was published in "Letters," *The Listener,* 29 March 1990, p.22.
4. Stephen Pope, "Next Week's Television," preview of *Blackeyes, The Independent,* 25 November 1989, p.55.

SELECTED BIBLIOGRAPHY

WORKS BY DENNIS POTTER

Television drama

Note: Dates given are original transmission dates for British television.

24.2.65	*The Confidence Course*, BBC-1 *The Wednesday Play*.
13.10.65	*Alice*, BBC-1 *The Wednesday Play*.
8.12.65	*Stand Up, Nigel Barton*, BBC-1 *The Wednesday Play*.
15.12.65	*Vote, Vote, Vote for Nigel Barton*, BBC-1 *The Wednesday Play*.
11.4.66	*Emergency Ward 9*, BBC-2 *Thirty-Minute Theater*.
2.11.66	*Where the Buffalo Roam*, BBC-1 *The Wednesday Play*.
3.5.67	*Message for Posterity*, BBC-1 *The Wednesday Play*. Note: new production 29.10.94 BBC-2 *Performance*.
13.5.68	*The Bonegrinder*, Rediffusion *Playhouse*.
10.11.68	*Shaggy Dog*, LWT *Company of Five*.
20.11.68	*A Beast with Two Backs*, BBC-1 *The Wednesday Play*.
12.4.69	*Moonlight on the Highway*, Kestrel/LWT *Saturday Night Theater*.
16.4.69	*Son of Man*, BBC-1 *The Wednesday Play*.
23.5.70	*Lay Down Your Arms*, Kestrel/LWT *Saturday Night Theater*.
5.11.70	*Angels Are So Few*, BBC-1 *Play for Today*.
13.6.71	*Paper Roses*, Granada *Sunday Night Theater*.
14.10.71	*Traitor*, BBC-1 *Play for Today*.
16.11.71–21.12.71	*Casanova*, BBC-2, 6 episodes.
4.7.72	*Follow the Yellow Brick Road*, BBC-2 *The Sextet*.
12.2.73	*Only Make Believe*, BBC-1 *Play for Today*.
21.11.73	*A Tragedy of Two Ambitions*, BBC-2 *Wessex Tales* (adapted from the short story by Thomas Hardy).
14.2.74	*Joe's Ark*, BBC-1 *Play for Today*.
20.6.74	*Schmoedipus*, BBC-1 *Play for Today*.
1.3.75–22.3.75	*Late Call*, BBC-2, 4 episodes (adapted from the novel by Angus Wilson).

1976	(banned) *Brimstone and Treacle*, BBC-1 *Play for Today*. Original planned transmission date: 6.4.76. Unbanned:25.8.87 BBC-l Potter Retrospective Season.
6.4.76	*Double Dare*, BBC-1 Play for Today.
21.4.76	*Where Adam Stood*, BBC-2 *Playhouse* (based on *Father and Son* by Edmund Gosse).
22.1.78–5.3.78	*The Mayor of Casterbridge*, BBC-2, 7 episodes (adapted from the novel by Thomas Hardy).
7.3.78–11.4.78	*Pennies from Heaven*, BBC-1, 6 episodes.
30.1.79	*Blue Remembered Hills*, BBC-l *Play for Today*.
19.10.80	*Blade on the Feather*, PFH/LWT.
26.10.80	*Rain on the Roof*, PFH/LWT.
2.11.80	*Cream in My Coffee*, PFH/LWT.
23.9.85–28.10.85	*Tender Is the Night*, BBC-2, 6 episodes (adapted from the novel by F. Scott Fitzgerald).
16.11. 86 –21.12.86	*The Singing Detective*, BBC-1, 6 episodes.
22.2.87	*Visitors*, BBC-2 *Screen Two* (based on Potter's 1983 stage play, *Sufficient Carbohydrate*).
16.11.88–7.12.88	*Christabel*, BBC-2, 4 episodes (based on *The Past is Myself* by Christabel Bielenberg).
29.11.89–20.12.89	*Blackeyes*, BBC-2, 4 episodes (based on Potter's 1987 novel *Blackeyes*).
21.2.93 –28.3.93	*Lipstick on Your Collar*, Channel Four, 6 episodes.
26.12.94	*Midnight Movie* BBC-2 *Screen Two*.
28.4.96 - 20.5.96	*Karaoke* BBC-1 and Channel Four, 4 episodes.
26.5.9 –17.6.96	*Cold Lazarus* Channel Four and BBC-1, 4 episodes.

Feature films (in order of production)

1981	U.S.A.	*Pennies from Heaven*, dir. Herbert Ross.
1982	U.K.	*Brimstone and Treacle*, dir. Richard Loncraine.
1983	U.S.A.	*Gorky Park*, dir. Michael Apted.
1985	U.K.	*Dreamchild*, dir. Gavin Millar.
1987	U.K.	*Track 29*, dir. Nicolas Roeg.
1991	U.K.	*Secret Friends*, dir. Dennis Potter.
1993	U.K./Aus.	*Mesmer*, dir. Roger Spottiswoode. (Note: This film has never been released due to legal problems with the distributor relating to directorial deviations from the agreed shooting script.)

Published television scripts

Blue Remembered Hills in *Waiting for the Boat, On Television* (London: Faber and Faber, 1984).
Christabel (London: Faber and Faber, 1988).

Cream in My Coffee in *Waiting for the Boat, On Television* (London: Faber and Faber, 1984).

Follow the Yellow Brick Road in *The Television Dramatist*, ed. Robert Muller (London: Elek, 1973).

Joe's Ark in *Waiting for the Boat, On Television* (London: Faber and Faber, 1984).

Karaoke and *Cold Lazarus* (London: Faber and Faber, 1996).

Lipstick on Your Collar (London: Faber and Faber, 1993).

Pennies from Heaven (London: Faber and Faber, 1996).

The Singing Detective (London: Faber and Faber, 1986).

Stand Up, Nigel Barton in *The Nigel Barton Plays: Two Television Plays* (Harmondsworth: Penguin, 1967).

Vote, Vote, Vote for Nigel Barton in *The Nigel Barton Plays: Two Television Plays* (Harmondsworth: Penguin, 1967).

Published theater scripts

a. Original stage play

Sufficient Carbohydrate (London: Faber and Faber, 1983).

b. Stage plays adapted from original television material

Brimstone and Treacle (London: Eyre Methuen, 1978; repr. London: Samuel French, 1979).

Son of Man: A Play (London: Andre Deutsch/Samuel French, 1970).

Published fiction

a. Novels

Blackeyes (London: Faber and Faber, 1987; rev. edn., 1989).

Brimstone and Treacle (London: Quartet Books, 1982). (Note: novelization of Potter's 1981 screenplay, adapted by his daughter, Sarah Potter.)

Hide and Seek (London: Andre Deutsch/Quartet Books, 1973; repr. London: Faber and Faber, 1990).

Pennies from Heaven (London: Quartet Books, 1981). (Note: novelization by Potter of his own *Pennies* screenplay.)

Ticket to Ride (London: Faber and Faber, 1986).

b. Short stories

"Excalibur," Posthumous reading tx. BBC Radio 4, 8 June 1998.

"Last Pearls," Daily Telegraph, 4 June 1994, arts sec., p.2; also tx. BBC Radio 4, 9 June 1998.

Published nonfiction

a. Monographs

The Changing Forest: Life in the Forest of Dean Today, Britain Alive Series (London: Secker and Warburg, 1962; repr. London: Minerva, 1996).
The Glittering Coffin (London: Gollancz, 1960).

b. Collected interviews

Potter on Potter, ed. Graham Fuller (London: Faber and Faber, 1993).
Seeing the Blossom: Two Interviews and a Lecture (London: Faber and Faber, 1994); comprising transcripts of Potter's 1994 "Without Walls" interview; 1993 James MacTaggart Lecture; 1987 Arena interview.

CRITICISM ON POTTER

Ansorge, Peter, Sections on Potter in *From Liverpool to Los Angeles: Writing for Theatre, TV and Film* (London: Faber and Faber, 1996).

Barker, Adam, "What the Detective Saw or a Case of Mistaken Identity," BFI M*onthly Film Bulletin* 55:654, July 1988, pp.193–5.

Baxendale, J. and Pawling, C., *Narrating the Thirties—A Decade in the Making: 1930 to the Present* (Basingstoke: Macmillan, 1996).

Bondebjerg, Ib. "Intertextuality and Metafiction: Genre and Narration in the Television Fiction of Dennis Potter" in *Media Cultures: Reappraising Transnational Media,* ed. M. Skormand and K. C. Schroeder (London: Routledge, 1992), pp.161–79.

Colley, Ian, and Gill Davies, "Pennies from Heaven: Music, Image, Text," *Screen Education* 25 (Summer 1980), pp.63–78.

Cook, John, entries on "Dennis Potter," "Kenith Trodd" and "*The Wednesday Play*" in *International Encyclopedia of Television,* ed. Horace Newcomb (U.S.: Fitzroy Dearborn, 1997).

Cooper, Howard, "The Angel in Us," *The Month* (September-October 1995), pp.345-9.

Corrigan, Timothy, "Music from Heaven, Bodies in Hell: *The Singing Detective*" in *A Cinema Without Walls: Movies and Culture after Vietnam* (London: Routledge), pp.179–93.

Coward, Rosalind, "Dennis Potter and the Question of the Television Author," *Critical Quarterly* 29:4 (1987), pp.79–87.

Creeber, Glen, *Dennis Potter—Between Two Worlds: A Critical Reassessment* (Basingstoke: Macmillan, 1998).

Day-Lewis, Sean, "Switch on, Tune in and Grow" (on *Karaoke* and *Cold Lazarus*) in *Talk of Drama: Views of the Television Dramatist Now and Then* (Luton: University of Luton Press, 1998).

Delaney, Paul, "Potterland," *Dalhousie Review* 68: 4 (1988), pp.511–21.

Harrison, Irving, "Doubling Back on Dennis Potter's Double: The Invisible Man and the Invisible Woman," *Psychoanalytic Review,* 83:1 (1996), pp.67–96.

Hunningher, Joost, "*The Singing Detective* (Dennis Potter): Who Done It?" in *British Television Drama in the 1980s* (Cambridge: Cambridge University Press, 1993), pp.23–57.

Hunt, Albert, "'Plays Portentous' (on the three LWT Potter plays)," *New Society,* 6 Nov.1980, pp.1–19.

Lichtenstein, Therese, "Syncopated Thriller: Dennis Potter's The Singing Detective," *Artforum,* May 1990, pp.168–72.

Lippard, Chris, *The Auteurist Television Drama of Dennis Potter,* UMI Microform 9601015, 1994.

Purser, Philip, "Dennis Potter," in *British Television Drama,* ed. George W. Brandt (Cambridge: Cambridge University Press, 1981), pp.168–93.

Purser, Philip, chapter on Potter in *Done Viewing* (London: Quartet, 1992).

Stead, Peter, *Dennis Potter,* Borderlines Series (Bridgend: Seren Books, 1993).

Voight-Virchow, Eckart, *Maennerphantasien: Introspektion und gebrochene Wirklichkeitsillusion im Drama von Dennis Potter* (Trier:Wissenschaftlicher Verlag Trier, 1995).

Wu, Duncan, essay on Potter in *Six Contemporary Dramatists* (London: Macmillan, 1995).

BIOGRAPHY

Bose, Mihir, "'Coffee without Cream' (on Grade and the PFH deal)," in *Michael Grade: Screening the Image* (London: Virgin Books, 1992), pp.103–121.

Carpenter, Humphrey, *Dennis Potter: A Biography* (Faber and Faber, 1998).

Gilbert, W. Stephen, *Fight and Kick and Bite: The Life and Work of Dennis Potter* (London: Hodder and Stoughton, 1995).

Moline, Karen, "'Someplace Where the Song Is for Real' (on Hoskins and Pennies from Heaven)," in *Bob Hoskins: An Unlikely Hero* (London: Sidgwick and Jackson, 1986), pp.72–80.

Paton, Maureen, chapter on "The Making of Mesmer" in *Alan Rickman: The Unauthorized Biography* (London: Virgin Books, 1997).

SELECTED INTERNET SITES

Note: with the growth of the Internet, it is now possible to find Potter alive and well in cyberspace. Some significant Web site addresses are:

http://www.geocities.com./TelevisionCity/1956
http://www.oudenaarden.nl/potter
http://www.picpal.com/potter.html
http://www.ucrysj.ac.uk/potter/index.htm

CONTRIBUTORS

HEINZ ANTOR is Professor of English Literatures at Cologne University in Germany. His special interest is twentieth-century fiction in English. His books include *The Bloomsbury Group: Its Philosophy, Aesthetics, and Literary Achievement* (1986); *The Fictions of the Angry Young Men: Studies in the Reception of Group Stereotypes (Die Narrativik der Angry Young Men: Eine Studie zur literaturdidaktischen Bedeutung rezeptionslenkender Gruppenstereotypien),*(1989); *Text-Culture-Reception: Cross-Cultural Aspects of English Studies* (1992); *The English University Novel: Concepts of Culture and Education (Der englische Universitaetsroman: Bildungskonzepte und Erziehungsziele),*(1996); and *Intercultural Encounters: Studies in English Literatures* (1999), all published by Universitaetsverlag C. Winter, Heidelberg.

STEVE BRIE is a Lecturer in Literature and Screen Studies at Liverpool Hope University College, Liverpool, U.K., as well as a freelance television director. He is currently researching a doctoral thesis that investigates audience reactions to Dennis Potter's use of popular music in his dramas. The thesis is entitled "Authorial Intention, Audiences and Popular Music," and it is from this larger work that his current contribution to this volume derives.

GWENDOLYN CONNELLY pursues her graduate studies at George Mason University with the patient indulgence of her sons, Galen and Mason, and her husband, Michael. In addition to exploring Dennis Potter's work, she is interested in the films of Spike Lee, David Lynch, and Peter Greenaway, and the ever-expanding permutations and protestations of contemporary literary theory. She tutors student athletes at the university and is a voluntary English tutor for at-risk youth in association with the Fairfax County juvenile courts.

JOHN COOK is a Senior Lecturer in Media Studies at De Montfort University, Leicester, U.K. In 1994, he completed the first British Ph.D. thesis on the work of Dennis Potter, in the course of which he managed to negotiate access to a wealth of primary Potter sources—unpublished scripts; archive material; close colleagues—including, in May 1990, an interview with Potter himself. The thesis has since gone on to become two successful editions of a book, *Dennis Potter: A Life on Screen* (1995; 1998) which has found critical acclaim and sold all around the world. Cook also teaches courses on Potter and TV drama, and has had articles about him published in the British press.

GLEN CREEBER is a Research Fellow within the Department of Journalism, Media and Cultural Studies at the University of Cardiff, Wales. He is also the author of *Dennis Potter: Between Two Worlds—A Critical Reassessment,* which was based on his Ph.D. thesis and published in 1998. In addition, he has written journal articles and essays on Potter.

DAVE EVANS lectures in Cultural Studies at the College of Ripon and York St. John, Ripon, U.K. His own passion for Dennis Potter dates back to 1965 when he first saw *Stand Up, Nigel Barton* on TV. In 1994, he developed a course on Potter's work called "Clenched Fists: Potter, Politics, and Pop," which he teaches at the college. He is also the designer of probably the world's current most comprehensive Web site devoted to Potter and his work. This can be found at *http//:www.ucrysj.ac.uk/potter/*

VERNON GRAS is Professor of English and Cultural Studies at George Mason University in Virginia. He teaches and publishes in literary theory, mythology, and twentieth-century British literature. Most recently, he has become interested in film studies, from which this Potter book and a forthcoming anthology of Peter Greenaway interviews are direct results. He has taught both Potter and Greenaway since 1990.

IRVING B. HARRISON, M.D. is a former Faculty member, New York Psychoanalytic Institute, now retired. He has published numerous articles in leading psychoanalytic periodicals. This article, as well as "Doubling Back on Dennis Potter's Doubles," which appeared in *The Psychoanalytic Review* (February 1996), are part of a book in progress on Potter tentatively titled *Dennis Potter: The WHY of his Doubles and Devices.*

CHRIS LIPPARD teaches film and writing classes at the University of Utah. He is the editor of *By Angels Driven: The Films of Derek Jarman* and has published articles on the work of Potter and Jarman. He is currently working on a study of the ways in which writers and filmmakers attempt to construct their own memorials.

SAMUEL MARINOV taught drama and dramatic arts at the University of Kansas, Lawrence. He was then affiliated with the doctoral program of the College of Architecture at Georgia Institute of Technology, Atlanta. At present he is the director of Internet Educational Services for the Georgia State University system. He reads widely and has published on Russian literature. Besides Potter, his professional interests include film theory and film history, acting and directing.

PHILIP PURSER is retired television critic of the *Sunday Telegraph* and a well-known and respected British journalist. He is also the author of several novels, biographies and screenplays, as well as compiler (with Leslie Halliwell) of *Halliwell's Television Companion*. In terms of Potter, he was one of the playwright's earliest critical champions, watching and reviewing nearly all of his plays when they were first transmitted. He also knew Potter professionally as a TV critic and interviewed him several times. Purser wrote the first substantial critical essay on Potter's work (published in 1981), as well as a chapter on him for his own memoirs, *Done Viewing* (1992).

PETER STEAD is a prominent historian and Welsh broadcaster. His books include *Film and the Working Class* (1989, 1991) and *Richard Burton: So Much, So Little* (1991). In 1993, he interviewed Potter for a public event at the Hay-on-Wye literary festival and later that year, published *Dennis Potter*, a short critical monograph on his life and work. Of his encounter with Potter, he described it in his book as "perhaps the best England-Wales contest for several seasons." After that, it will come as no surprise for the reader to discover that Stead's most recent work has been on the history of Welsh rugby.

KENITH TRODD was the man responsible for producing nearly all of Potter's most celebrated work for television, and is also a semi-legendary figure within the British television and film industry in his own right. He met and befriended Potter when the two were in National Service together. He was at Oxford University with him and later became, first, his story editor, and then the producer of many of his plays, both for BBC and commercial television. In 1978, he produced Potter's *Pennies from Heaven,* and then set up one of the first independent drama production companies with him: Pennies from Heaven Limited. Subsequently, Trodd would go on to produce *The Singing Detective* (1986) and be entrusted with the production of the writer's final scripts, *Karaoke* and *Cold Lazarus* (1996, posthumous). Aside from Potter, Trodd has also produced for TV the work of such gifted writers as Simon Gray, Stephen Poliakoff and Colin Welland, as well as for cinema, films such as *A Month in the Country* (1986) and *Circle of Friends* (1995).

ECKART VOIGTS-VIRCHOW is Assistant Professor of English and American Literature at the University of Giessen, Germany. He was Fulbright scholar (New York University, 1994) and a Visiting Assistant Professor at the University of Wisconsin, Madison (1997). He has published numerous essays and reviews on contemporary British drama, cultural studies, film and media. His book on Dennis Potter was published in 1995: *Maennerphantasien—Intro-spektion und gebrochene Wirklichkeitsillusion im Drama von Dennis Potter* [Male fantasies—introspection and the broken illusion of reality in the drama of Dennis Potter]. At present he is researching a book on the interplay between technological culture, the industrial novel and early science fiction in the nineteenth century.

RICK WALLACH teaches literature at the University of Miami, Florida. He is editor of John Sepich's *Notes on Blood Meridian,* and coeditor with Wade Hall of *Sacred Violence: A Reader's Companion to Cormac McCarthy.* He has also written on critical theory, Patrick White, William Faulkner, Charles Brockden Brown, Ishmael Reed and Vassily Aksyonov. His articles have appeared in many leading periodicals, as well as several critical anthologies. His current projects include *Fictive Music,* a study of jazz influence on American fiction, and *Myth, Legend, Dust,* an anthology of criticism on Cormac McCarthy.

INDEX